# Praise for the Second Edition

Experience is not enough to make sense of our lives. We learn by reflecting on our experience. For years as a teacher, I have used *At Home in the Journey* as the primary text for those who are journeying through a process of re-entry and transition. I have not found another book like this, and I highly recommend it. I am very glad that this second edition makes it possible to keep this invaluable resource available. JoAnn McCaffrey has gifted us with a wonderful theological, spiritual, and personal reflection guide that continues to be relevant today for so many people. – Roger Schroeder, Interim Vice President and Academic Dean, Louis J. Luzbetak, SVD Chair of Mission and Culture, and Professor of Intercultural Studies and Ministry, Catholic Theological Union, Chicago.

*At Home in the Journey* is both a guide and a process that generates meaning and light for people who have had difficult journeys and transitions in life. Just as valuable, this book also brings understanding for those who love the person who struggles and wish to support them in their journey. JoAnn McCaffrey puts words to the "in-between void" I personally had been feeling within myself. Having the words helped me embrace the journey in trust and peace, until I found "home" once more. – Shirley Bell, PHJC, Returned Missioner

JoAnn McCaffrey breathes affirmation, truth, understanding, and wisdom into the transition process with *At Home in the Journey*. She gives words to feelings that resonate; leaves readers feeling seen and heard; and provides a tool to use for all of life's transitions. – Kelli Nelson, MNM, Executive Director of From Mission to Mission

I have been recommending *At Home in the Journey* for many years now as the single-best resource that exists for missioners dealing with re-entry. In this second edition, the author broadens her text to help all people struggling with feelings of isolation and being misunderstood or unappreciated for what they've experienced.... Through the author's stories and wisdom from her own transition, as well as from others she's met, readers will understand what is normal in transition and know they are not alone. – Julie Lupien, Director of From Mission to Mission (2002-2018)

Everyone who returns to his or her country of origin, has stories to tell, experiences to share, and sometimes trauma to integrate. Much adjusting is required. McCaffrey's *At Home in the Journey* blends her story as a returned missioner with the wisdom she has from her experiences and the knowledge she learned from her studies. It is a gift to all of us. – Sister Mary Tina Petrick, SND

At Home in the Journey is required reading for the Mission Integration course at CTU in Chicago. . . designed for those doing theological reflection over a recently completed cross-cultural experience. – CTU *Alumni Updates*, Winter 2020

**For the First Edition**

What JoAnn McCaffrey has succeeded in doing in this marvelous book is to take the process of "returning" seriously, to recognize the pain of women and men who struggle and suffer after years of service--in other lands and other cultures--and to devise a way of working through such pain and disorientation so that they can come to a new place.... Because the book ... shows us how to do this, it is not so much to be read as to be worked through. Instead of handing down "answers," it offers a way to wrestle with gnawing but ultimately life-giving questions. . . . The journey is not easy, but it is possible; and McCaffrey proves to be a wise, compassionate, and patient guide. – Stephen B. Bevans, SVD, Louis J. Luzbetak, SVD Professor of Mission and Culture, Catholic Theological Union

JoAnn McCaffrey lives *At Home in Journey* and transmits her wisdom as a missioner in this insightful work. She provides the spiritual tools to find meaning through the power of our own images. Her method for guiding us in this sensitive, on-going process allows us to unveil and name profound levels of insight for understanding our experience. Her work has become a primary source for integrating the tension of living the tragedy and joy of the mystery of faith in mission. – Dr. Alicia Marrill, Co-Founder of Amor en Accion, a lay missionary community of the Archdiocese of Miami, Retired Professor, Barry University, Miami.

I read *At Home in the Journey* when I experienced a huge transition from Maasai-land in Tanzania, to Formation Coordinator in Hyde Park, Chicago. JoAnn McCaffrey's very fine book helped uncover memories of experiences layered with emotion and meaning and gave me the language to share this with others. The author's personal stories and clear insights invite us all to ponder our lives, which can be of constant moving, instant change, and relentless transition. I recommend this book for everyone! – Sue Rech, MM

# At Home in the Journey

## Navigating the Transitions of Our Lives

JoAnn McCaffrey, DMin

*At Home in the Journey: Navigating the Transitions of Our Lives*
by JoAnn McCaffrey, DMin (second edition)

Copyright © 2021 by JoAnn McCaffrey

ISBN: 978-1-7366007-0-2 (paperback)
ISBN: 978-1-7366007-1-9 (e-book)

*At Home in the Journey* is sold and distributed through From Mission to Mission (missiontomission.org). It is a 2nd edition to *At Home in the Journey: Theological Reflection for Missioners in Transition* (2005).

DISCLAIMER: The intent of the author of this book is to relate her personal experience in the hope that it may help others in their quest for health and wellness. The author does not presume to offer therapy or advocate the use of any technique for the treatment of any specific mind, body, or spirit condition without the approval and guidance of a qualified healthcare practitioner. If you use any of the information here as a form of self-therapy, the author and publisher assume no responsibility for your actions. Do not listen to or practice any of the meditation or relaxation techniques while driving a car or engaging in any activity that requires your full attention.

NOTE: When quoting actual interviews, pseudonyms are used.

Cover design: Marguerite Patricia Gilner, Honeysuckle Hill Publishing

Cover photo: Labyrinth at Saint Fin Barre's Cathedral, Cork, Ireland

Interior design: MediaNeighbours.com

Poem, page 190, used with permission ©Vijali Hamilton (worldwheel.org)

### To Roma
### My Valiant Warrior

*Protecting me from harm*
*Squirrels, UPS trucks, strangers,*
*(and other such dangers)*

*Teaching me about life*
*Sniffing, snoozing, waiting, wagging*
*(and other such essentials)*

*Giving me so much, for so many years,*
*love and laughter, trials and tears*
*(and other such treasures)*

*b. March 4, 2004*

### With Deep Gratitude

*To my sister Angela, for her endless love and
support through all the years . . . the laughter and
the tears. . . .*

*And to Marty, for his loving her—and me too!*

*To Patricia, for being my faithful
"friend forged in fire."*

*And to Pablo, my best friend and soulmate
in the journey.*

FINALLY, TO ALL OF YOU WHO ARE COMMITTED TO "THE JOURNEY."
TOGETHER WE HAVE GIVEN BIRTH TO THIS BOOK.

# Contents

# Preface to the Second Edition by the Author

> *What we call the beginning is often the end*
> *And to make an end is to make a beginning.*
> *The end is where we start from . . .*
> *Not known, because not looked for*
> *But heard, half-heard, in the stillness*
> *Between two waves of the sea.*
> *Quick now, here, now, always—*
> *A condition of complete simplicity*
> *(Costing not less than everything)*
>
>               T. S. ELIOT, "LITTLE GIDDING"
>               (FOUR QUARTETS)

When I was approached by From Mission to Mission (FMTM) to consider a second edition to my book, *At Home in the Journey*, I was both honored and humbled. I am also extremely gratified that there is a genuine need for it, and a desire to republish it, to make it as accessible as possible. Based on my own and others' journeys across time and culture, it seems that this simple work has been helpful to many life travelers in search of meaning for their experience. Even fifteen years after its original publishing, there is still limited substantial literature available for those looking for understanding as they navigate significant cultural and societal transitions. I would feel a great sadness, for myself and others, if when looking back on our lives we "had the experience but missed the meaning"–another powerful line from T. S. Eliot's *Four Quartets*, this one found in "Dry Salvages."

If you are reading this now, perhaps it is because you are a companion sojourner, seeking a deeper meaning in some serious transition in your own life. Or perhaps you want to share this book with someone else in such a situation. *At Home in the Journey* was written primarily for "missionaries," those who have spent months, years, even decades, living and ministering in another cultural context, another language, another land. However, given my own experience and the feedback I've received from those who have read this book, it seems that in spite of the specific references to "mission" and "overseas ministry," the themes within these pages have spoken to those experiencing almost any kind of change, weathering the internal storms of many different kinds of transition. *So, while I often refer to "missioners," understand that I also mean sojourners–anyone on a journey (both within and without ourselves). And while I mention God, understand this in any way that you experience the Divine or a greater, unifying force. I will also sometimes refer to "the Divine," for this same reason. While often my references are to biblical scripture, I invite you to associate to any scriptures or stories you know, from books or from film or from oral traditions.* (I have included lists of books and films in the Appendix II.)

While it is still focused on cross-cultural mission, I have tried to "widen the net," so to speak, hoping that it might also address a broader audience. I've updated it by using more inclusive language and current examples. In this way, I hope that *At Home in the Journey* will be helpful to veterans and other service personnel, to journalists, healthcare workers, those returning from war zones or areas of chronic poverty or injustice. Many come "home" to try to continue their journey, covered in scars, walking with unhealed wounds, both inner and outer, often hidden deep within–especially from themselves.

Trauma is often a consequence of such journeys. There is a section in this edition on Post Traumatic Stress Disorder. At its original publication, PTSD was a little-known phenomenon. Today it is, unfortunately, a common household term–yet one still so often misunderstood. This syndrome is not so much a "disorder" but a new "normal" for those who must learn to live with it.

As you read through these reflections, I invite you to recall your own stories and reflect on your personal experiences. In the Appendices, you will find suggested exercises. Let these be the practical examples that guide you along your way. I encourage you to keep notes of your memories and feelings. *At Home in the Journey* is, in many ways, a snapshot in time. When I myself read these pages, it's like looking at old photos: sometimes I hardly recognize myself. But that was who I was then, where I was on my journey. Are not our life journeys made up of many snapshots, or small videos, capturing a moment, an emotion, covering an event: sometimes a dirge, and then again, perhaps a dance?

Finally, forgive the limitations of this work. *Ultimately, identifying and exploring the "heart of the matter" remains the primary quest and key to unlocking the deeper meaning of our life experiences.* No matter who we are, transformation often demands the willingness to sink into the darkness of loss and grief, in order to climb up the other side to new beginnings. If we can wade through the muddy waters and handle the crashing waves, we will find ourselves again and again on the wonders of a new shore. And, with cosmic grace and divine mercy, with each new beginning we will ". . . arrive where we started . . . and know the place for the first time" (T. S. Eliot, "Little Gidding").

*Author's Note*: The labyrinth is one of the world's oldest archetypal symbols. It represents life's paradoxical journey to the Center and also the return to begin anew. May this book, like the labyrinth, help guide us through the twists and turns of our lives, leading us home.

# Foreword to the Second Edition

*A t Home in the Journey* may have originally been written for those who had served in "mission" in another country. The gift of this book is the recognition that the root of re-entry *is* transition. So, not only is this a valuable resource for those returning from serving around the world, *but for anyone dealing with the transitions in their life*.

Transitions are challenging. The unique transition called "re-entry," which is the transition back to your home country after living and serving in another culture, comes with many challenges. In fact, for most returning missionaries and volunteers, re-entry is the hardest part of the experience. This is the reason our organization, From Mission to Mission, was created back in 1980. We have been offering re-entry workshops, retreats, and resources for returning missioners and volunteers. I had the privilege of facilitating the re-entry workshop JoAnn McCaffrey attended when she returned from Zaire (now the Democratic Republic of Congo). I am grateful that JoAnn created this valuable resource that flowed out of her own experience with re-entry and transition.

Transitions are hard for a number of reasons. One of the most important is a loss of identity: I don't know who I am now. One re-entry participant described her transition by saying, "My spirit has not caught up with me yet." Transition and grief go hand in hand. It can be an exhausting and overwhelming time.

Those returning from another culture often struggle with additional feelings and challenges. This includes feeling isolated because they don't feel understood, or that people don't seem to be interested in what they've done. They don't feel as needed here compared to where they were serving. They struggle with the wealth and abundance they see here, especially when returning from places of great poverty. And, unfortunately, many are dealing with the impact of violence and trauma.

John O'Donohue wrote in *Anam Cara*, "Where you are understood, you are at home." This is the purpose of *At Home in the Journey*. Through JoAnn's stories and wisdom from her own transition and others she's met, she helps the reader to understand what is normal in transition and to know they are not alone. What a relief it can be to know that not only do others in transition feel the same as you, but that it's normal to feel this way!

I have been recommending *At Home in the Journey* for many years now. It is the single, best resource that exists for those dealing with re-entry. It is also the perfect companion to our FMTM re-entry programs. I am grateful to JoAnn for being both a companion and guide for those who are in transition, and for anyone who feels lost or lonely.

Julie Lupien
Director of From Mission to Mission
(2002 – 2018)

NOTE: The Foreword to the First Edition can be found in Appendix IV.

# Introduction: My Own Journey, and the Process of Transition

> The geographical pilgrimage is the symbolic acting out of an inner journey. The inner journey is the interpolation of the meanings and signs of the outer pilgrimage. One can have one without the other. It is better to have both (Merton, *Mystics*, 92).

At *Home in the Journey* grows out of my own experience of transition. I spent over twelve years in the Democratic Republic of the Congo, then called Zaire. I loved its great forests and rivers, the thundering sound of the rain, like galloping hooves as it grew closer and closer, the sights and sounds of its river boats, and the bustling towns and cities. I even loved the red clay that turned to mud in the rainy season. Above all, I came to love its people: their strength and sheer determination to survive against all odds, and their joy and laughter in the midst of incredible hardship. They lived–and still live–in my heart.

It's no exaggeration to say that letting go of the Congo was possibly the hardest thing I've ever done in my life. When I returned to the United States, I embarked upon a difficult "re-entry" experience, moving through different phases over a period of several years. *That transition, which also involved the discernment and ultimate decision to leave my religious community of almost twenty-five years, is what gave birth to this book.*

Before continuing, a word about Zaire. In 1997, the government reclaimed one of the country's former names, the Democratic Republic of Congo, or DRC. During the 1980s, when I lived there, however, under the dictatorship of Sese Seko Mobutu, the country was called Zaire, as was its currency, its citizens (Zaireans, in English), and even the Congo River had been renamed the Zaire River. Because of the narrative nature of this work, the emotional substance that the name "Zaire" carries for me, and in order not to be anachronistic, I will, throughout these reflections, refer to the DRC as Zaire. I do so with the utmost respect for the Congolese people, children of that beloved country.

Once back home in the USA, one of several significant people to support me during my transition was Larry Lewis, a Maryknoll priest who had spent some years in China. His doctoral dissertation was entitled "Waiting,"[1] and it was with his help, through spiritual accompaniment and many tears, that I learned how to *wait*: to wait patiently, but *actively*, is like being on "night watch," waiting for the dawn. This initial "liminal" time in my life was a long night, at times confusing, startling, anxious, awesome. But after almost a year of discernment in darkness, a glimmer of dawn appeared on the horizon. I cannot remember the exact moment, but gradually the light grew brighter and stronger, until a sense of clarity came. It was as though a "cloud lifted," and I could continue on my journey.

This cloud was not a cloud of *unknowing*. Rather, it was a cloud of *intuitive* knowing, a consciousness of the Divine's presence enfolding me. The book of Exodus tells us that when the cloud settled on the meeting tent of the Israelites: *the glory of the Lord filled the Dwelling. Whenever the cloud rose from the Dwelling, the Israelites would set out on their journey. But if the cloud did not lift, they would not go forward; only when it lifted did they go forward* (Exodus 40:34-38).

I did experience some "unknowing," because I did not know which way God would lead me or which door would open. Still, somehow,

I knew that God was "in that cloud, and that sooner or later I would
know *the way in which I should walk* (Psalms 31: 8). I finally felt that
I could move, and I realized the Divine was leading the way all along.
*In the daytime, the cloud of the Lord was seen over the Dwelling;
whereas at night, fire was seen in the cloud by the whole house of
Israel* in all the stages of their journey (Exod 40:38).

   This book is about those "inner journeys" the experiences of
"coming home"–not only geographically but psychologically and
spiritually. It is for the religious and non-religious, clergy and the
secular. Life is continual change, and we humans are always in some
kind of transition.

### Life is a continuous process of consolidation and detachment (Hall, 23).

   Yet at the same time, we have the need to be at home in the midst
of this change. We need a certain sense of security or homeostasis,
especially during a transition. Human beings cannot *always* be living
in a perpetual limbo, belonging neither here nor there.

   I believe this is especially true for missioners, who understand
themselves to be pilgrims, always "on their way" to the Kingdom. I
wrote the first edition of this book from this perspective, as a missioner. In this second edition, I want to broaden that perspective: We
all have a need to belong somewhere, to have a sense of home in some
way. Living in liminality, a continual state of in-betweenness, implies
imbalance, insecurity, inconsistency, and ambiguity. To remain there
throughout one's life, it seems to me, would be psychologically and
spiritually unhealthy.

   As Gittins notes, van Gennep's classic study on the rites of passage[2] did not romanticize the pain of transition, even going so far
as to say that "in a liminal phase, one is a threat to oneself and to
the group" (Gittins, "Communities of Concern," 322). Typically, the
onset of transition is triggered by some sort of crisis, which can be
both painful and confusing. Yet ironically, while sometimes danger-
ously risky, authentic crisis also provides an opportunity. For those

who have entrusted their lives to the Divine, expending themselves for the fullness of God's Spirit in this world, this can be a time of incredible growth. In the following pages, I suggest that a time of transition–moving from the familiar to the new, grieving through times of separation and loss, experiencing anew one's limitations and loneliness and one's feelings of alienation or anxiety–all of this can be a process of *coming home*. This implies, above all, discovering (or perhaps uncovering) one's deepest self, that privileged place, sacred womb, where we encounter the invisible Divine. And this meeting happens, not apart from nor even because of, but precisely *in the midst of the journey*.

## Re-entry and Culture Shock

Shortly after my return from Africa, I met my sister on the coast of Maine, and we spent some time in Acadia National Park. One early morning, as we sat on one of Acadia's rugged cliffs watching the rising sun glisten across our little piece of the Atlantic's waters, a group of rock climbers approached a neighboring cliff, not far from where we were seated. We watched them as they set up their ropes along some difficult cliffs that jut out over the ocean.

It was the first time I had seen any rock climbing at close hand, and I was fascinated. I asked myself, what is it that motivates people to undertake this kind of sport? The sense of adventure? The risk involved? The thrill of arriving at a mountaintop after a challenging climb, or the breathtaking views that one would never know without being able to scale the slick sides of that mountain? Or was it simply the challenge of being able to say, "I did it!" As I examined the composition of the group more closely, I realized that they probably were a *family* of climbers. We approached an older member of the group and he confirmed it. He and his wife were lifelong climbers who had initiated *their* children into the sport, who, in turn, were initiating their children! We spoke a little, then let them get back to leaning over the cliff and watching one of their sons scale the granite wall below us.

My sister Angela, having done a little amateur climbing, knew more about the sport than I did. She explained some of the techniques involved in what they were doing: the skillful handling of the rope (the climber's wife was learning how to hold the rope for him, tightening up on it or giving him slack); the handholds and footholds; the importance of the lead climber knowing just the right crevices in which to pound the spikes, called pitons. She told me how exciting it is to hear them call to one another with special codes and signals, their voices echoing up and down the mountain. She said, "Climbing has its own special language–it's like another culture."

She talked me into attempting a little climb ourselves. We would go up to a spot called "Bubble Rock." She had done it a few years earlier and assured me that it was an easy climb. Having embarked on our little adventure, however, and the farther we got along the trail, she realized that this was *not* the same one that she had taken before. Actually this approach to Bubble Rock was much more difficult and risky than she had expected, demanding skills that neither of us had–certainly not me! As we progressed, the climb became more steep and treacherous. We both realized that even though the climb was becoming more and more strenuous and challenging, to turn back and try to return the way we had come would have been even more treacherous. My sister knew there was an easier way down–*if* we could just make it to Bubble Rock. As we got closer to the top, we came to what seemed to be an impasse. We rested while trying to find a way to continue.

Finally, Angela went first and managed to hoist herself up to a plateau near the top. After looking at the rest of the path ahead she called down to me, "If you can just make that one climb, we're home free." She reminded me to be sure to have a good, firm handhold on the rock I was moving to, before letting go of my foothold on the rock where I was presently standing, and where I felt secure. I made several attempts, but I felt like my legs weren't strong enough to pull me up to the next landing. I realized I was really afraid. I didn't dare look behind me, which was straight down. Angela was afraid too, but she kept encouraging me, knowing that there really was no turning back. We just had to keep going and get through this scary moment. She kept coaching me with the limited knowledge she had, "Lean into the rock. Get a secure handhold on the same rock I used. Take your time. Just keep leaning in. You can do it. . . ." And finally, I *did* do it! Somehow I found a way to pull myself up to the next rock. At the moment, I was just so relieved to have made it. I kept going the short distance which remained. Upon reaching the top, though, I immediately became aware of some signs of the stress my body had been under: my heart was beating hard and fast; my hands—in fact my whole body—was trembling; even my liver (a weak point since my bouts with malaria and hepatitis while in Africa), was "in a quiver," as a friend used to put it. Yet as we sat there on top of Bubble Rock, taking in the spectacular view surrounding us, it felt good to know that I had summoned up (from somewhere!) the strength—both physical and moral—to make that climb, along with the courage to overcome my fear. I had *literally* been between a rock and a hard place, and I had gotten through it.

*It has its own special language. . . . It's like another culture.* My sister's words echoed in me, and I began to think about these cultural worlds of climbing and of mission. A person in the midst of a significant transition probably experiences what most climbers feel each time they attempt a new climb. Missioners, like climbers, are people with a sense of adventure, not afraid of risk, willing to accept the challenge of "a tough climb"—one, in fact, that sometimes seems impossible. Missioners have been "climbing" for centuries, and they keep on climbing, working their way to the heights—and sometimes falling into the depths. They live a life which, for most outsiders to this missionary culture, seems incomprehensible.

Each time we make a cultural transition, whatever it be, we face a new and different challenge than the one before. Granted, it's certainly not like that very first climb when *everything* was new. We have learned some of the skills of crossing cultures. Nevertheless, climbers say that no climb is ever the same. Even if you have taken the mountain before, each climb in itself is a new experience. Likewise, each move, each moment of *every* transition is both challenge and adventure, however "experienced" we may be. And perhaps the hardest climb of all is the climb inward, which I'm calling here *the journey home*.

## Transition

> **Implicit in the conflict and tension posed by the transitional experience lies potential for authentic growth and development, the transcendence from environmental to self-support (Adler, 14).**

For Christians, a sense of being "on the move" toward God's reign is an essential part of life; even more so for those who, within the mission of the universal church, are called to minister in a culture other than their native one. Yet how are they to live in this time and space called *transition* when returning to or while living in their "home" culture? It is my observation that more attention has been given to preparation for cross-cultural mission than to what is typically called *re-entry*.

I am indebted to From Mission to Mission (FMTM, originally known as F.R.O.M.) for their invaluable contribution in this area of re-entry; very little other systematic, well-researched material is available to address this particular topic. In addition, I often find that re-entry is equated with culture shock as something negative to be endured and overcome. My aim is to place this experience of cross-cultural transition–admittedly at times confusing, alienating, anxiety-producing, and ambiguous–in the overall context of something positive. I believe culture shock, or the crisis of transition, has the potential for transformation both psychologically and spiritually, leading to the personal growth and integration necessary for healing, wholeness, and holiness.

⁜    *Being missionary is an affair of the heart.* Part of the pain and the gift of a missionary life is knowing, on some deep level, that one has become a stranger in a strange land–whether in the host culture to which one has been sent or in one's place of origin. Once a missioner, always a missioner. However, being a stranger need not be understood as negative. In fact, it is one of the most important gifts the missioner has to offer, both as a guest abroad and as one familiar to the local church and culture back home (see Gittins, *Gifts and Strangers*).

At Home in the Journey was originally designed for those who have themselves been through the process of transition; i.e., returning from mission in other countries or from cross-cultural contexts within their own country. It might also be helpful for those who are on sabbatical or home leave, for those studying or in a period of discernment about ministry, or for those who have definitively completed their mission assignments in other cultural contexts.

Feedback from the first edition has shown that *At Home in the Journey* is also relevant for those who are experiencing *any* kind of transition in their lives; e.g., veterans transitioning from active service; those involved in marital separation or divorce, mid-life crises, or career change, etc. These reflections are intended to respond to the very real need of anyone who is betwixt and between, experiencing the fluctuations of an ever-changing life. As the body can go into a temporary state of shock for its own protection and healing, similarly does our psyche. And while cross-cultural transition is an integral part of every phase of a missionary life, this book is especially helpful for those in a stage of cultural upheaval, such as the pandemic of 2020 might have caused in so many lives. It is for those experiencing *separation* from any place of commitment, whether ministry or a job lay-off, etc. It is intended to help us *grieve through* an in-between period (for whatever reasons and for whatever period of time), and *move toward* a new perspective, a new vision, a new beginning. Sometimes the new beginning may be geographic, but it will most always be psychological and, potentially, spiritually transformative.

## In the Method Is the Meaning

These reflections come not only from my own personal experience but from the shared experiences of other cross-cultural sojourners as well. Participants of interviews and different focus groups that I conducted were made up of women and men, parents and children, members of religious congregations and those ordained. They have been racially, culturally, and ecumenically diverse, though all recognized themselves to be in a time of cultural transition. They were all experiencing its effects, albeit in different phases and forms. Together and individually, they reflected upon their past and present experience of transition, seeking to find meaning in it and support from others going through it. *I believe in the principle that what is most particular in human experience is also most universal.* It is my hope, then, that the few experiences and insights shared in these pages will find resonance and response in the lives of many, including *you*.

I hope to engage you in a holistic process of reflections, which unfold in five movements, represented by each of five chapters. The process is based on a method developed by Patricia O'Connell Killen and John de Beer. They maintain that a truly theological process of reflection *cannot happen* without being intimately connected to the *human drive toward meaning.* When these two processes merge, new meaning and insight occurs, leading one toward better *integration of one's past experience into the present.* You don't even need to embrace theology or a particular religion—but a *holistic* process of reflection will embrace the spiritual within us and the innate universal desire to seek meaning. This integration happens in the context of a larger elliptical *movement* that I will often refer to as simply "*from→through→to→from→through→to→ ...*" (a paradigm used by Maryknoll missioner Larry Lewis, in an integration seminar at Catholic Theological Union, which will be developed more fully later).

These movements intertwine throughout the process of transition, as various melodies flow in the background of a movie or the scenes of an opera. While each chapter treats each of these movements as though it were a separate happening, keep in mind that they are not so easily identifiable when one is in the midst of transition. Rather, like the stages of grieving, they flow in and out of each other, all mixed together within the person who—while sometimes *feeling* very fragmented–is still a whole person, seeking to reestablish his or her sense of self and equilibrium. This might be understood in terms of a cultural rite of passage.

## 1. Entering Experience

In Chapter One we enter into the experience of separation, leave-taking, and transition. We reflect upon identity; i.e., who and how we have been in a certain context. I both explain this process and illustrate it through my own autobiographical stories as well as those of other. Entering into one's experience is done primarily through focusing on some particular aspects of it. For example, I describe in detail an event from my life in Zaire, the particular place, the persons involved, etc., concentrating on the "who, what, when, where, and how?" The "why" of an experience is better deferred to a later moment, to avoid the tendency to make a premature judgment on what happened, rationalizing, or doing what I call "spiritualizing," which sometimes means repressing or ignoring one's feelings.

## 2. Attending Feelings

In the second chapter we are invited to pay attention to the feelings that we are *currently* experiencing, as well as to remember feelings from the past, possibly discovering unexpressed joys or uncovering unhealed hurts. Feelings are "clues to the meaning of our experience" (Killen and de Beer, 27-30). Naming and claiming feelings is not only a healthy psychological movement, but as Killen and de Beer suggest, a necessary "spiritual discipline." Some of the ways recommended for attending to these feelings are through journaling, creative imagining, prayer, body work (e.g., yoga, massage, exercise), and through dialogue with others in similar circumstances.

## 3. Exploring Images

Attending to feelings will naturally give rise to *images*, because images are capable of expressing our feelings in ways that words often

cannot. This is an area which is often neglected. "Images symbolize our experience. They capture the totality of our felt response to
reality in a given situation . . . they encourage multiple aspects of
meaning in an experience to come forth" (Killen and de Beer 37). In
fact, our ordinary, everyday language is full of metaphorical images:
"I feel flat as a pancake, dead as a doornail, higher than a kite." Or,
"Chill out, cool down, get fired up!" Or simply, "He's down today, she
seems up tonight," etc. "As a metaphor or symbol, the image is both
specific, referring to a particular event, and universal, connecting
that event to human experience at a deep level. The more it captures
a very particular experience, the more it invites resonance with the
experiences of others" (Killen and de Beer, 39-40). After exploring
some personal images, we turn to scripture, as a fertile source for
images related to the spiritual life of a sojourner. *The Pilgrim God*
(John of Taizé 1985) was my primary source for this particular scriptural exploration; in particular, the missioner's sojourn in the desert.

## 4. Probing the Heart of the Matter

The third chapter explores the power of images for capturing and embodying experiences and feelings, as we explore key images of others.
Articulating feelings through images helps us to notice the energy
we have around a key issue or issues, which may be unresolved or
perhaps have only recently surfaced. This significant issue is called
the "heart of the matter" (Killen and de Beer, 61). In Chapter Four we
are encouraged to identify and articulate our own heart of the matter. We help one another to do so by the sharing of images, by other
expressions of an identifiable pattern, or articulating a key issue or
concern that we have at this time in our transition. A turning point
occurs when we engage this heart of the matter in a conversation
with the resources of our spiritual tradition.

Genuine conversations are a reciprocal movement full of surprise, sometimes delightful, sometimes sobering. This is what we aim
for when we put the most energy-filled point of an event, or the heart

of the matter, into conversation with the wisdom of the Christian heritage (Killen and de Beer, 64-65).

This kind of dialogue actually calls one to a kind of transformation, or in the words of liturgist Mark Searle, "conversion." I recommend for your reading an article by Mark Searle, "The Journey of Conversion" (see Works Cited). Searle describes conversion as the successful negotiation of crisis or change as a form of "passage" or "transition," whereby a person may pass through to a new "lease on life" and enter into a new set of relationships with self, the world, and with life itself. Using the example of my own unexpected conversion, as well as the insights gleaned by others during theirs, I offer this perspective on the challenge of examining one's transition or re-entry: we are called to transformation. ☝

## 5. Integrating Insight

In the fifth and final chapter, we explore some of the spiritual challenges involved in this journey with self, others, and the Divine. The sometimes imperceptible movement through experiences, feelings, images, and issues—if faithfully carried out in dialogue with one's true self and one's sacred tradition—will usually enkindle *insight*. Insight occurs when "reasons of the heart are made known to the mind" (Dunne "Insight," 3). And each insight is an invitation to transformation. As we arrive at these moments of insight, I encourage ritualizing them in some way, personally or communally, which helps to integrate them into our current situation. This, in turn, enables us to move into new experiences and new life. One's integrative process, as I develop it in this book, consists in *being faithful to the unfolding of the movements of our own life*.

These five stages constitute the methodology of this book and the rationale for undertaking your journey with deeper awareness, and seeking understanding. After the Epilogue, I have included Appendices that are intended to help you put what you have read into practice. I hope your time spent along this transit will be eased and aided by what you read–knowing you are not alone. It is my sincere desire that in the following chapters you will recognize your own sojourn and that of every companion in transition. So I invite you now to put on your "hiking boots" and your "backpack" and dare to do a bit of "rock climbing" with me.

> *Jumping from boulder to boulder and never falling,*
> *with a heavy pack, is easier than it sounds; you*
> *just can't fall when you get into the rhythm of the*
> *dance.*
>
>                          JACK KEROUAC

**Chapter One**

# The Nature of Cross-Cultural Transition

It's not easy coming back to this country
[America]. It's not like any other country
in the world. Most of you don't know that,
because you live here, and you've never
been anywhere else, except maybe the
Caribbean, which is like a big beach, or
Europe, which is like going to an old mu-
seum. Europeans sit at tables with knives
and forks. They have beds and sheets,
toilets and garbage cans. Africa is different. The expatriates there will tell you that
the reverse culture shock of coming back
to America can be worse than the shock of
going to the Third World in the first place
(Dooling, 1).[3]

## Part I: Re-entering Experience: Welcome Home?!

"Welcome Home! How was Zaire?"

"Oh fine," I would numbly reply, not knowing quite what to say or
where to begin, not yet ready or able to describe the life I had been

living for half of my adulthood. Strangely, my simple answer seemed enough to satisfy most of those who asked!

How well I remember my initial days back in the United States, after being almost thirteen years outside of it. I arrived in the States in August 1992, and I remember that everyone was talking about the "Dream Team." When I asked, "What's the Dream Team?" the group stared at me incredulously.

"You haven't heard of the *Dream Team*?!?"

"Well, I've been in Africa for the last thirteen years," I would explain rather apologetically. (I don't think I really understood what the "Dream Team" was until four years later, when the *next* Olympic games rolled around.)

Many similarly disjointed moments threaded those first months, even years, together. "How does it feel to be back home? I'll bet you're in culture shock, huh?" How often well-intentioned friends and members of my family would ask me that question. I remember saying *I guess I'm in culture shock*, but I wasn't exactly sure what that meant at the time. Was it feeling totally disoriented, and equally stupid, about almost everything around me? Was it not knowing how–or sometimes simply not wanting or not having the energy to answer all those questions? Was it being overwhelmed by a new *language*? "If I'm not home, just leave me a message on *the machine*. Do you have voice mail yet?" *Voice mail*? "Are you online yet?" Am I *what*? Whatever culture shock was, I think that I must have been in it!

Family and friends are important at this time because they love us. But this is not enough. Although they try to be supportive and understanding, sometimes their attempts are more of an obstacle than aid to the challenge of *re-newing* oneself. Well-intentioned family, community, and friends want to be helpful and to help us adjust. But they want to "make it all right." They want us to feel and act "normal." They want us to be at ease, to be glad to be "back home." It is hard for them to listen to our stories–they don't understand that strange world from whence we've come–and to which they usually hope we'll never return. They just "can't relate" to where we've been and what we've experienced—and most importantly, to what we're currently experiencing at this critical time. For many of us, we just kind of fold up, like a flower at night, keeping inside that other world, that other life, that other *self* that has become an integral part of who we are. And if we ever open up enough to dare to say that we hope to return—others are usually dismayed. They just don't get it! Why would anyone want to go back to *that*!? "All that we're hearing about that place in the news—what about all the violence? There's lots of mission work for you to do right here at home." Sometimes what they say is objectively true. But that's just not what we need to hear at that moment.

When I returned to the States, I was fortunate to have been advised to take a class at Catholic Theological Union (CTU) in Chicago, entitled "Mission/Ministry Integration Seminar." This class, facilitated at that time by Larry Lewis, M.M., taught a powerful methodology that sparked the beginning of my own long journey *home*. The method can be described in three key movements geographically, but also psychologically and spiritually: *"from→through→to→-from→through→to→ . . ."*

→ FROM → THROUGH → TO → FROM → THROUGH → TO →

**Figure 1.1**

I began my explicit theological reflection on my own departure *from* Zaire, *through* transition, *to* integration. This integration of one's past life into one's current experience does not usually happen in a tenweek seminar! It might take months or even years before one begins to see a glimmer of light as to what one is about—or more accurately, what God (or the Cosmos, Universe, Karma, or however you understand that Other reality) is about, in our seemingly disrupted lives.

A fundamental principle of that Integration Seminar was that *every* experience, no matter how small or insignificant it may seem, has the potential of becoming a *formative* experience. In order for this potential to be realized, the experience must be the subject of reflection. Reflection enables us to discover, as much as possible, that which can be revealed in the experience. Some experiences in our lives are like flowers. It is as though one gently observes petal after petal of the rose gently unfolding, revealing its splendor in color and fragrance. Others may be more reminiscent of the ripping off an old bandaid, or a hard scab that didn't want to go away. Understanding still others happens like the peeling of onions, layer after layer, in order to fully know the whole of it.

As many of us know, in onion peeling the process is not without its sting. I have found that the movement and growth involved in honest reflection on my life can often bring tears. But through those very tears comes new awareness and insight, new life, and growth. And it is in moving *through* that transition, acting on our new or rediscovered insights, that integration can happen. We begin to know ourselves to be strangely "at home" in this journey of life, in which we are continually moving *from→through→to→from→through→to*.

As mentioned above, this movement is not only in a physical, geographical sense, but it is also the psychological, emotional, and spiritual movement *from* places where we have come to feel settled, comfortable, at home. The movement *through* can mean, in the same way, many types of in-betweenness or liminality, which we will discuss more fully in the next chapter. And the moving *to* represents direction *toward* new psychological, emotional, spiritual—and sometimes geographical—spaces, in which we begin again to feel at home. Theological reflection—or spiritual reflection, for those not familiar with theology—on our experiences makes us more insightful. This final movement toward *insight* will be explored in Chapter Five.

With *from→through→to→from→through→to* . . . we become more aware that our life is a continual journey in which we are already at home, in whatever space we find ourselves. Yet ,at the same time, we know ourselves to be pilgrims, sojourners, and our sometimes dark and difficult journey reminds us that we have not fully arrived.

For missioners, this knowledge also comes with awareness that the goodness of God's reign similarly is not yet at hand.

How long did my transition last? It's hard to remember. I know that the initial days turned into months, and the months to years. Mine also happened on multiple layers. Somehow, gradually, I began to be able to both let go of and embrace differently, all that had become so familiar: the places and people in Zaire whom I had grown to understand and love; the country which I had learned to call home for over twelve years; and my religious congregation and community of over twenty years. I only know that after many years, I am truly able to call this place and space where I am now living home.

How did this movement from disorientation through transition to a new sort of homecoming happen? Well, that's what this book is all about. I know that it happened with the support of many others, and certain people who were providentially in my path. They were willing and patient enough to *listen* to me as I struggled to tell my story, over and over again, in many different ways, scene by scene, narrating the drama of my own journey.

There were various stages to my movement: leaving a new home for a strange land, crossing cultural and psychological boundaries, slowly breaking down barriers, exterior and interior, of my own making and of those of others. Missioners, veterans, and service personnel, those seemingly without "a home," or anyone who is in the midst of significant change and upheaval in their lives–all need others who can in some way understand our journey, who can "watch and wait" with us until we are ready to move on again.

As I write this, I am conscious of having spent many years in transition (and all that implies), because for a time it seemed as though I did not know how to move nor which way to go. I like to believe that I am still and will always be *en route*. The difference is that I am now "at home" in that journey. Perhaps it is valid to say that we, as seekers and sojourners, will in some ways always be in transition, ready for a new transformation, a special sign of embracing that which is "already," yet at the same time, open to that which might yet come to be.

## *Liminality: Some Characteristics*

The heart of any transition is living through a "spaceless space" and a "timeless time," often referred to as "liminality."[4] This is an ever-present state of "in-betweenness," or "liminal" time, when we must attend to what we are feeling–a very important and often neglected part of an integrated reflection on our human experience. The term *liminal* was made almost commonplace among anthropologists through the pioneering work of Victor Turner, who in his turn built on the seminal work of Arnold van Gennep (*The Rites of Passage* (1909)).[5] William Bridges, in his popular work, *Transitions* (1980), referred extensively to van Gennep's stages (separation, liminality, reincorporation) and their accompanying rites of passage. He speaks of them as "Endings," "Neutral Zone," and "Beginnings." Evelyn and James Whitehead also make use of this structure for their description of an adult crisis as a religious passage in *Christian Life Patterns* (51-53, (1979)). For a more recent treatment of liminality during the Covid-19 pandemic, see Richard Rohr's "Daily Meditations," which offered online an excellent week-long series on the topic of Liminal Space, at the Center for Action and Contemplation, April 26-May 1, 2020.[6]

I prefer the word liminality to other terms, because it seems to express well that "betwixt and between" reality that informs this part of the transition. Turner also refers to this time as "mid-transition" (*The Forest of Symbols*, 105). Missioners see this liminality expressed clearly, even in simple terms of place and time. Separated from their mission, but not yet reassigned to another, a missioner literally is a person "without a country," with no place to call "home." In his essay, Turner points out certain characteristics of this liminal phase of the transitional process as contrasted with the "status quo" (see Figure 1.2 below). Although Turner's research is in an entirely different context (Turner's research in ritual, myth, and symbol took place primarily among the Ndembu people of Zambia in central Africa), some of his insights and conclusions might help us to deepen our own understanding of the situation of the "passenger," in order to better facilitate the "passage" through transition.

During this liminal period "the state of the ritual subject (the "passenger") is *ambiguous* and passes through a realm that has few or none of the attributes of the past or coming state" (Turner, *Forest*, 94). The pain of this liminal state[7] occurs because one is neither what one was before, nor what one will eventually be. Ambiguity is something with which few people are comfortable.

Most of us prefer clarity in our lives—we like to be able to define things for ourselves. Most of us are happy when things are relatively one way or the other; living in the middle is, at best, challenging. Many people have, perhaps unconsciously, defined themselves by their role, precisely as missioners, nurses, teachers, etc. or by their identity with a certain place, country, or population. The need to do so is even stronger when we are in this time of transition.

## LIMINALITY CONTRASTED WITH STATUS SYSTEM

Transition/state
Totality/partiality
Homogeneity/heterogeneity
Community/structure
Equality/inequality
Anonymity/systems of nomenclature
Absence of property/property
Absence of status/status
Nakedness or uniform clothing/distinctions of clothing
Sexual abstinence/sexual activity
Minimization of sex distinctions/maximization of sex distinctions
Absence of rank/distinctions of rank
Humility/just pride of position
Disregard for personal appearance/care for personal appearance
No distinctions of wealth/distinctions
Unselfishness/selfishness
Total obedience/obedience only to superior rank
Sacredness/secularity
Sacred instruction/technical knowledge
Silence/speech
Suspension of kinship rights and obligations/kinship rights and obligations
Continuous reference to mystical powers/intermittent reference to mystical powers
Foolishness/sagacity
Simplicity/complexity
Acceptance of pain and suffering/avoidance of pain and suffering
Heteronomy/degrees of autonomy

**Figure 1.2 Turner's "Liminality contrasted with status system"[8]**

If the pairs of characteristics listed above are seen as being on opposite ends of a continuum, one can envision many transitional states in between—as well a variety of continuums occurring simultaneously. I remember when I began studies at CTU in Chicago after a few months back from Zaire. Each quarter, at the beginning of every class, the participants would briefly introduce themselves. I would never identity myself as being from Georgia (although that was indeed where I was born) but from Zaire. I struggled sometimes with what to say when people would ask, "Where are you from?" If I replied, "Zaire," often they might laugh and say, "Were you born there?" It took me several years to let go of identifying myself as having "worked in Zaire for over twelve years."

On the other hand, there is, as Turner puts it, "the peculiar unity of the liminal: that which is neither this nor that, and yet is both" (*Betwixt*, 99). He reminds us that the Latin root for *liminal* means "threshold" (*Ritual Process*, 94-95). In liminality, we are indeed "standing on the threshold." We are not what we were nor what we will be. At the same time, we are what we have become, and what we are becoming. I always wince when someone introduces me or someone else as a "former missionary." I've never been comfortable with that term. It tends to identify one with a role at a given place and in a given time. I rather think that mission has more to do with a quality of being. If we have a missionary heart, no matter where we are, no matter what we're doing, we will always be a missioner. All those qualities that we have acquired and fostered in another cultural context, we bring to whatever we do in the future.

Another aspect of this liminal process is its *invisibility*. "The subject of passage ritual is—in the liminal period, structurally, if not physically—'invisible'" (Turner, *Forest*, 95). Turner points out that "the structural invisibility" of liminal *personae* ("threshold people") has a twofold character. They are at once no longer classified and equally not yet classified. The former is frequently represented by symbols involving death and dying. The latter, by symbols of gestation and birth (Turner, *Forest*, 96-97). (We will discuss symbolism in more depth in the next chapter.)

For missioners in transition, as well as for friends and family who surround them, this "invisibility" or not being "classified" is at best, awkward; at worst, devastating. When I would come to the States on a home visit every few years, I was always "the missioner." "This is my daughter, JoAnn, the one who works in Africa." It takes time and patience for all of us to get used to one's no longer being "the one who works in Brazil . . . Taiwan . . . Bolivia. . . .

Turner also tells us that liminality may be described as a *stage of reflection*:

> **[Those undergoing this passage] are withdrawn from their structural positions and consequently from the values, norms, sentiments, and techniques associated with those positions. They are also divested of their previous habits of thought, feeling, and action. During the liminal period, neophytes are alternately forced and encouraged to think about their society, their cosmos, and the powers that generate and sustain them (Turner, *Forest*, 105).**

Transitional people, says Turner, *have* nothing. "They have no status, property, insignia, secular clothing, rank, kinship position, nothing to demarcate them structurally from their fellows. Their condition is indeed the very prototype of sacred poverty" (*Forest*, 98-99). Similarly, missioners in the transition of "re-entry" often *have nothing*." They have been stripped, as it were, of all that was familiar, of all that gave meaning to their ministry, their vocation–and sometimes to their life. Indeed, at times this transition is an invitation to live in poverty as we have never lived it, even though we may have slept in the simplest of huts or walked the most rugged of roads. Oftentimes, living in liminality, with all of its ambiguity, is the most radical and rugged "faith walk" missioners have yet had to make in their missionary life. How can one be helped to name and claim these elements of liminality: ambiguity, invisibility, and being in a stage of reflection, in order to work toward transformation? This question leads us to consider the meaning of *communitas*.

## Communitas

> *I spent the first year of my "sabbatical" feeling angry, closed, bitter, almost antisocial. It was only after a year or more that I began to realize how angry I was, and that somehow I had to deal with it. . . . I began to journey with a group of missioners who were also on sabbatical, studying, regrouping, returning, moving on. . . . Gradually I began to gain trust in this group, having my experiences accepted, my feelings understood. I began to gain the confidence I needed to look within myself, to begin this inner journey. . . . the most difficult I had ever made* (Eileen, 1997).[9]

Transition, and particularly the liminality that is the heart of it, can become transformative *if* we are given the time, space, and accompaniment that will enable us to reflect seriously, even theologically or spiritually, about *our* world, our reality, and the powers that generate and sustain us. Many today, upon returning from their place of mission or during a period of sabbatical, are indeed given this opportunity. But what I want to emphasize here is the need for intentional community to accompany us during this time of potential confusion and crisis.

As Gittins puts it, van Gennep did not romanticize the pain of transitional states. As previously mentioned, Gittins noted that in a liminal phase one is a threat to oneself and to the group (Gittins, "Communities," 322). Turner also recognizes what Mary Douglas called "the potency of disorder" in this transitional state. At the same time, van Gennep, Douglas, Turner, and others building on their insights, all acknowledge that this disorder can also be potential for creativity and growth. Two important factors will influence the way in which this potentially dangerous phase will enable transition to become, in fact, transformation: ritual and community–and in particular that spontaneous form of community which Turner calls *communitas*.

Turner differentiates *communitas* from the more common form of society, *community*. The latter is "structured, differentiated, and often hierarchical." By contrast, the communitas model "emerges recognizably in the liminal period as an unstructured or rudimentarily structured and relatively undifferentiated community–or even as *communion* of equal individuals who submit together to the general authority of the ritual elders"(*Ritual Process*, 96). So we understand that communitas often arises spontaneously among those in similar situations of transition, ambiguity, and stress, and in particular during the liminal or in-between phase of this transition process.

What I really want to emphasize here is the need for a *community of support* during this time, the kind that missioners experience especially when they are with "their own kind." How many times have we sat in a circle while someone recounted their experience, feelings, confusion, etc., and all of the heads in the circle are nodding with affirmation?

"Yes," we're saying to one another. "Yes! That's exactly how it feels."

"Yes, I know what you mean!"

"Yes! I understand."

Tony Gittins suggests that "if the liminal person is encountered and embraced in suffering, not primarily by functionaries or persons of a particular status or authority, but by the right kind of significant others–peers, fellow campers . . . or community–there may well be a deep and salvific experience, a real conversion which will redirect the individual and set a new course for the future. It will also modify the community and exemplify real co-ministry, ministering with, rather than professionalism or ministering to" (Gittins, "Communities," 326).

We all need to laugh together at the crazy moments. I recall one of our group relating her experience of wading through a Bolivian swamp. At one point, she saw what seemed to be the head of a snake poking up through the water. Before she knew it, she literally jumped into the unsuspecting arms of one of her Bolivian companions–who was at least a foot shorter than she–and clung for "dear life." Similarly, we can also cry together at the pains, the losses, the hurts, the injustices, the oppression that we have sometimes witnessed, sometimes even been a part of. Again, traumatic events have often shattered the sense of connection, the trust, that one would normally have with others. Gradually restoring or rebuilding that sense of trust can be an important part of this process of those traveling together through transition, trying to make their way to that safe place again, found both within and outside themselves, which they can call *home*.

## Part II: Identity

> **A person's identity is never static because personal history is always unfolding, and there is no self-understanding apart from an understanding of the historical horizon or tradition which serves as the context to the interpretation of identity (Stroup, 108-109).**

So, who is this strange breed of human we call a *missioner*–and how can our understanding of *missioner* today the broadened? The on-looker might undoubtedly look at missioners in much the same way as I looked at those rock climbers, wondering, "What makes them do what they do? Why take such risks? Does he really enjoy scaling that bluff? Looks like nothing but hard work to me." I remember one time while I was on a few months home leave from Zaire, when I was visiting my aunt and godmother in Atlanta. As we were driving across town, my aunt said to me that sometimes her friends asked her why I did what I did. She told me how she had explained to them one day, "Well, it's kind of like garbage collecting–somebody has to do it!" I have no idea how I responded in that moment. My aunt doesn't remember ever saying that, but obviously it made an impression on me. I have since thought about what she said. We all attempt to make sense out of things we just don't understand. Her explanation satisfied her–even if it seemed a bit incongruous to me!

Mission, and missioners or missionaries, have been variously defined and understood over the years by outsiders and insiders alike. Webster's pocket dictionary puts it this way: "Missionary: a person commissioned by a church to propagate its faith or carry on humanitarian work. Missioner: a person undertaking a mission and especially a religious mission" (319). Perhaps this would be put differently today, but Webster is not far off the mark. This simple, two-sentence "secular" definition seems to include the essentials: a person *commissioned*; i.e., a person called and sent, given, as it were, a mission, which the missioner *undertakes*. Most missioners are impelled to do what they do because they believe that they have been *called*, and *sent*, by God and usually by a church or community And what is the nature of that mission? It is explicitly or implicitly *spiritual*: i.e., *evangelizing*, and/or some form of *humanitarian work*.

Michael Collins, in his *Spirituality for Mission*, summarizes a list of the most common motives that seemed to characterize the spirituality and lifestyle of missionaries over the last three centuries. This might be referred to as the old missionary myth. Their motives include glorifying God and acting in service of Christ; being called by God and commanded by Christ; pitying and/or feeling compassion for "lost souls," as well as undertaking humanitarian acts for their temporal well-being; establishing and nurturing the church, along with–consciously or unconsciously–one's cultural "civilization" (Collins, 129-31). David Bosch has a listing of similar motifs that shaped missionary thinking since the middle of the eighteenth century: "The glory of God, a sense of urgency because of the imminent millennium, the love of Christ, compassion for those considered eternally lost, a sense of duty, the awareness of cultural superiority, and competition with . . . missionary efforts–had blended together to form a mosaic" (Bosch, *Transforming Mission*, 342).

## *"Missionary Myth"*

But this mosaic has begun breaking into pieces. The last half of the twentieth century and the post-Vatican II era brought about a significant change in the world of mission and missionaries. There has been a growing feeling in the church worldwide of what Bosch refers to as a "missionary malaise" (*Transforming Mission*, 345) due, at least in part, to the old myth unraveling within a church that had been permeated by the myth. In fact, Protestants and Catholics, religious and lay alike, have been living through a powerful and transforming "identity crisis" in mission since the 1960s.

As an anthropologist, Gittins uses the term *myth* not in its technical anthropological sense, but more because it was a perceived reality in the lives of both missioners and non-missioners alike. They *believed* in the myth, and believing in it, they continued to create and sustain it. In this context myth was perhaps more like a sub-culture. Per Gittins, *myth* here is:

> **A portmanteau term embracing the explanations, projections, and rationalizations shared by missionaries explicitly or implicitly, and serving to bind them together as a unitary group with common work, aims, and understanding . . . the web of relevancies which largely unconsciously, missionaries wove around themselves and each other, and within which they survived and grew, despite and sometimes because of, other worlds of meaning or patterns of relevance which abutted or threatened theirs (see Gittins, "Missionary Mythmaking," in Scherer and Bevans, 1994).**

The history of humankind reveals that we need myths to live by. It seems inevitable, therefore, that the old missionary myth had to give way to a new one, more in keeping with a radically changing world. The economic, political, ecological, and technological revolutions that characterize our planet today demand an equally revolutionary understanding of mission, both from within and without the church. Such competitive concepts as numbers of conversions, baptisms, and newly established churches have been called into question. Although mission would nevertheless remain highly theocentric, Christocentric, and ecclesial, Vatican II (1962-1965), and later Pope Paul VI's extraordinary *Evangelii Nuntiandi*, ushered in a new era in missiology, marked by such concepts as inculturation, contextualization, development, ecumenism, and dialogue. More recent examples are the writings of Pope Francis, such as his encyclical "*Laudauto Si*" ("Care for our Common Home," 2015) and his pastoral letter "*Querida Amazonia*" which flowed from the Special Synod of Bishops for the Amazon (2019). "The traditional forms of mission embodied a response to a world that no longer existed, and even if we do not have to negate the traditional mission as such, we are challenged to respond in a very different way today" (Bosch, 345 (1991)).

## *In a World of Violence*

In addition to this kind of "missionary malaise," missioners today must contend with many other factors that may make their time of transition more difficult or even traumatic. One of these factors is the reality that today we all live and work in a world strongly marked by violence. We need only glance at or listen to the morning news. When I was working on the first edition for *At Home in the Journey*, thousands of Rwandan refugees were on the move in fear of being caught in the cross-fires of violence; over seventy hostages had been held in Lima for over two months; bloodshed was escalating in Algeria and Sudan; youth and hundreds of other citizens had been marching in the streets of the Serbian capital, protesting the non-recognition of their new leader by the old regime, and the list could go on.

Today there are many more subtle or overt forms of terrorism and violence that touch our lives. Many are being increasingly affected by this upheaval in varying degrees. As I work on the second edition, the entire world is living through a global pandemic. At the same time, new demands for justice are erupting across the USA, in the "Me Too" and "Black Lives Matter" movements. In Hong Kong and countless other regions of the world, people fight for their rights or live in fear from day to day, *not knowing* what might happen next in their village, town, or neighborhood. All sorts of political and social unrest exist: being "on a list," suspected of collaborating with "the enemy"; knowing that others are "disappearing" around you, whether from illness or violence; living with the confusing guilt, anger, or shame of having been molested, raped, tortured, kidnapped, or imprisoned; or sometimes living with mixed guilt and relief, wondering why you have been spared. We have wars on drugs, poverty, crime, and terror—not to mention the numerous military conflicts around the globe.

In journeying with groups of "transitioning" missioners over the last few years, I and others have increasingly found the impact of terrorism and violence on our lives to be powerful and sometimes deeply painful. One friend had worked in Peru for over twenty-five years and was there during the height of the reign of terror of *Sendero Luminoso* ("Shining Path") during the late 1980s and early '90s. He had been almost a year in the States for study, when he began to have recurring post-traumatic symptoms, not unlike he had experienced before in the midst of the terror, when close friends and parishioners were being *disappeared* or killed, and he was privy to a lot of information and consequently, a lot of fear and pain.

In a workshop of returning missioners sponsored by From Mission to Mission (FMTM), another friend shared with us an excruciating experience that he had not been able to talk about with anyone until that moment, although he had been back in the US for almost a year. Although a "foreigner" in a Muslim state, as a teacher and priest he had been invited by some of his student friends to be part of a rally and an evening of dialogue for peace. An informer had leaked their gathering location. This young man had been witness to an overt and intentional massacre of hundreds of people who had been gathered. He had helped gather the wounded and carry them to the hospital. He had to walk through hundreds of dead bodies strewn across the plaza where they had been meeting. The next morning, the massacre headlined the morning news. And yet because of the tense political situation, and his own paralyzing fear, until that moment he had never been able to share with anyone—not even members of his local religious community—that he had been present at the event.

So many patterns of violence have been with us for generations, for centuries, so that today we even talk about inter-generational trauma; for example, as in American violence against Blacks or global violence against our planet. "Malaise" no longer seems an adequate description for the multitude of reactions we experience.

## *Self-images of a Missioner*

As the missionary myth has begun to crumble in our midst, and the global situation becomes increasingly more violent, many missioners find that maintaining self-understanding and a sense of purpose has become more complex. What is the missioner's self-image today? In an article entitled "Seeing Mission Through Images," Steve Bevans[10] maintains that theologies of mission are concentrated in various images of the missionary. He acknowledges that missionaries have always seen themselves through various images, some of which remain valid today "if properly understood." But he says that in the twentieth century, "times and attitudes changed." He points to the US Catholic Bishops' 1986 pastoral statement, "To the Ends of the Earth," noting that, since Vatican II, "we have been living in a world that provides a new context for missionary activity." Bevans maintains that "missionaries need to go about mission work differently, and they have to understand themselves and be understood by others through different images" (Scherer and Bevans, 159). He then goes on to reflect upon eight different images through which a modern church might understand its missionaries. These are:

"(1) treasure hunter, (2) teacher, (3) prophet, (4) guest, (5) stranger, (6) partner, (7) migrant worker, and (8) ghost" (see Scherer and Bevans, 158-169). These titles in themselves reveal a bit of the complexity of what it means to be a missioner in today's world church.

Here I want to look at one of these images more closely, namely that of stranger.[11] Part of the complexity and pain of the missioner's life is knowing, on some deep level, that one has become a permanent stranger in a strange land, whether in the host culture to which one was sent, where one is always a "guest," or in the home culture from which one has been sent, where one often feels strangely different than before leaving. This latter reality can be a very disorienting discovery for those who are returning to their countries or cultures of origin, either definitively or even for a temporary time. Furthermore, those who once have been missioners will *always be missioners.* In this sense we find ourselves in some way "misfits" (see Lewis, *Misfit*), and it is painfully disconcerting not to quite fit in anymore. As Gittins puts it, "So many of us wriggle or fidget as we resist the discomfort" (*Gifts,* 112).

One of my favorite descriptions of a missioner says a lot about this image of "stranger." It was written over sixty years ago, yet it seems amazingly relevant today. It comes from Maryknoll Bishop James Walsh. (*Note: I have taken the liberty of changing singular pronouns to plural.*)

**The task of a missioner is to go to a place where they are not wanted, to sell a pearl whose value, although of great price, is not recognized, to people who are determined not to accept it, even as a gift. To do this they must so conform to the place as to make themselves first tolerated, then respected, finally esteemed; and yet their conformity must not be total, for all the time they must conserve that precious**

foreign clan that will unceasingly nerve
their campaign . . . until the people begin to
see some value in their offering. They must
become Chinese while remaining American,
thus conforming and resisting at the same
time. It is easy to become wholly oriental,
and it is easier still to remain wholly occi-
dental; but the adaptation needed by the
good missioner is a judicious combination
of the two, and that is a feat. They must
absorb a new and fascinating civilization,
while eschewing its philosophy; they must
adopt new view points, while retaining
old ones; they must learn and wield a new
language, while clothing it in, not its own
shopworn tags, but their own vigorous foreign thoughts. They must absorb not only
the language itself, but what lies behind the
language: the mentality that made it and is
at once expressed and revealed, and even
at times disguised by it. They must know
and adopt many customs that are quite
strange . . . some others they must know
without adopting. They must doff all sorts
of habits and prepossessions, and must don
many others, so that they find themselves
obliged to maintain through life a flexibility
of both mind and body that makes them a
perpetual gymnast" (Walsh, 3-4).

Though difficult and challenging, such "gymnastics" are not to
be understood in a negative way. They are, in fact, taken as a whole,
one of the most important gifts that a missioner has to offer, both to
the local church in which they have been serving as a "guest," or to

the church back home, as well as to any new reality in a new context. Bevans points out a growing phenomenon in the worldwide church today: "Returned missionaries, by sharing their experiences abroad and their continuing strangeness in their home culture, can perhaps help their brothers and sisters contribute more actively to the church's mission to the ends of the earth (Scherer and Bevans, 165). But this kind of "reverse mission" is easier said than done. And it first must be negotiated within that sometimes long and arduous process of "transition." In this next section we will explore this in conversation with sources from psychology, anthropology, and the humanities.

## Part III: Transition: The Experience of "From → Through → To"

> *From birth to death, life is punctuated by separa-*
> *tions, many of them painful. Paradoxically, each*
> *separation forms a foundation for new stages of*
> *integration, identity, and psychic growth* (Hall,
> 223).

### *The General Nature of Transition*

Transition has become quite the popular term in some circles, especially in the Western world. It is not uncommon to hear that someone we know is "passing through a transition." We know that we all go through many natural, developmental transitions in our lives: from childhood through puberty to adolescence; from adolescence to adulthood, and so on. The Whiteheads call these "scheduled" changes. "The change may not be desired or preferred, but it is known to be inevitable or at least highly likely" (*Christian Life Patterns*, 35). There is the now infamous mid-life transition, more often called the mid-*life crisis*. We must move through later adulthood into our senior years—and, even if we are blessed with a long and healthy life, we eventually pass through that final transition called death.

As the Whiteheads point out, when these transitions happen "on schedule," as it were, they are much easier to negotiate. Although they may be critical and significant, the upheaval of the "crisis" associated with every transition will be less severe. They make reference, however, to other kinds of transitions that are worth mentioning here, namely the "unscheduled," the "misscheduled" and the "overscheduled." The *unscheduled* or unexpected life transitions would include those induced by the loss of a spouse or another loved one, or the change or loss of a job. As one might expect, these kinds of crises usually make the transition a much more turbulent and dark time. A *misscheduled* transition might be a premature marriage or a couple dealing with their own intimacy issues after their children leave home. *Overscheduling* refers to those kinds of transitions that one is expected to make at a given age, in a certain lifestyle, in a given culture, etc. The Whiteheads give the example of young adults in the USA being *expected* to get married in their early twenties, whether or not they feel ready for this personally (Whiteheads, *Christian Life Patterns*, 36).

There are several other terms that it would be well to clarify concerning this subject. Again, Bridges, in *Transitions*, makes an important distinction between *change* and *transition*. While every change implies a transition, he notes that *they are not the same thing*. A change in jobs or mission assignments will inevitably spark a transition, because every change means an *ending* and a *beginning*. Change may happen abruptly, or slowly, but it happens and it's over. But every change implies a *loss* of some sort or other: this is where the transition begins. As Bridges puts it, "Every transition begins with an ending" (Bridges *Transitions*, 11). This may seem rather obvious, but sometimes it's very difficult to pinpoint when something has ended, and something new has begun. That's often because of the space or "non space" in between the beginning and the end. And this is, as we will see, the core of the transition.

Another term that is sometimes used in connection with transition is *crisis*. For many of us this term probably sounds more formidable or foreboding than *transition*. We often hear the term crisis in a negative context; e.g., the sudden illness of a family member becomes a crisis; a country stricken by famine, war, or a deadly virus is in crisis; domestic abuse sends out an alarm for "crisis intervention," etc. However, Michael Amaladoss offers another view. He points out that crisis has the potential to be something positive, that "Crisis can be a time for growth" (Amaladoss, in Jenkinson and O'Sullivan, 359).

## *The Missioner in Transition*

The connotation of crisis, therefore, like its character in written Chinese, can mean both danger *and* opportunity. I like to think of crisis as a crossroads, where we have an opportunity to make a new turn, take a new path, follow a new route–but we have to choose. Initially we have to "cross the road," and this moment of crossing can be risky. And once the route is chosen, it can be a long, long way before we arrive at a new destination–or sometimes even at another crossroads! Being in crisis is also risky–and sometimes one has reached an impasse and cannot decide which way to turn. A crisis is often the moment or event which ignites a transition. Sometimes a crisis is precipitated by a series of decisions or intuitions of some sort which lead up to it. For the missioner in transition, this precipitating event is often changing mission assignments or what is even harder, leaving "the mission" altogether.

How do we experience times of change and transition, especially if we are in between cultures; i.e., moving from one assignment to another, discerning the next phase of our life? A missioner, you might say, is used to change. As a missionary friend of mine would say, "Hey, pal, it's what we signed up for!" Missioners leave home; they leave their base of identity. Often they spend a few months or a year in one place learning the language. Then they move on to their first real assignment. The children of lay missioners (often referred to as "MKs" or missionary kids), often grow up with constant change: new schools, new neighborhoods, new friends. They are no strangers to the crises and transitions that these changes often evoke. Most of us need at least a certain degree of security or stability, even in the midst of change, and often missioners have had to deny or sometimes repress that simple human need.

Leaving a job, ministry, or assignment is rarely easy–no matter how pleasant or difficult, successful or unsuccessful it was. This is especially true because of the motivation or calling that prompts us to traverse cultural and often geographical boundaries in the first place. For military veterans and other retirees, this is often equally true. And in today's global socio-economic and political environments, many experience in between assignments; leaving one job, region, country, or continent for another; retiring or re-turning home definitively–each may undergo a uniquely complex or confusing transition.

In addition, some changes are less expected, and sometimes less welcome, than others. I'm finding that this sense of the expected or unexpected plays an important role in transition. Those who have in some way anticipated the change, or missioners who have known that ultimately, they will return home–while yes, they will have to move through the experience of transition–but it may not be as dis-ruptive or devastating as for one who has not anticipated it or denied an inevitable change. Sometimes the move is abrupt or forced upon us. The recent Covid-19 pandemic precipitated this for many who were, in some cases, hardly at their place of mission. The unusual rapid spread of the virus forced them to abruptly return home while they could get flights.

And what about the missioner who had planned to stay for life, but is asked to leave by their congregation; or those who sense that they are no longer needed by the local community, or are themselves no longer able to endure the climate or the lifestyle? What about the minister who contracted for ten years, but is asked to leave after three? Or those who sense from the local people or co-workers that they have overstayed their welcome? And then there are those ser-vice personnel or missioners who must be evacuated from their mis-sion in a day or even an hour's time, because of a sudden eruption of violence or a natural disaster in the country; not to mention the transition of one who later discovers that a companion left behind has died, been disappeared, or killed.

My own experience, as well as that of others, reveals that this can be a very traumatic time in one's life, precisely because it is so unexpected. In my own case, I left my mission in Zaire for what was intended to be a time of study, or sabbatical. I was tired, "burned-out" I suppose, and quite confused, with a sense of uneasiness about the future. Nonetheless, I left fully expecting to return to my mission after a year of study and rest. Upon my return, however, I found myself plunged into an emotional whirlpool of questioning and discernment. Unexpectedly, I needed to re-evaluate everything: my ministry, my vocation, even at times my life's meaning.[12]

## Reverse "Culture Shock"[13]

> **Culture shock has traditionally been thought of as a form of anxiety which results from the misunderstanding of commonly perceived and understood signs and symbols of social interaction. . . . [It] is primarily a set of emotional reactions to the loss of perceptual reinforcements from one's own culture, to new cultural stimuli which have little or no meaning, and to the misunderstanding of new and diverse experiences. It may encompass feelings of helplessness, irritability, and fears of being cheated, contaminated, injured, or disregarded (Adler, 13).**

An identity crisis at any age, under any circumstances, is difficult. The identity crisis of the missioner can be even more challenging due to the simultaneous experience of culture shock. They who are supposed to be home, find themselves instead in a *strange* environment, feeling unable–or unwilling–to adjust to this new way of doing things. As missioners we expected to find ourselves in culture shock when we left home, even if we didn't know what it would look like or how it would feel. *But few of us really expect such a shock when we return. This lack of expectation or readiness is what makes it disorienting.*

What some of us don't fully realize, even though we may know it intellectually, is that when we return from mission, *we are not the same person who left for mission* however many years before. Inevitably, we have been *fundamentally* changed by our mission culture, often depending upon the degree to which we inserted ourselves into that culture. It is a presupposition of cultural psychology that the person and the culture are continuously *mutually* influencing each other, a "making each other up," as it were.[14] We human beings, as such, are continually in the process of changing, adapting, growing.

Let us consider someone who has been serving in a highly context-dependent or, as some would say, "holistic" society, one in which relationships and the group are the strongest factors influencing one's understanding of oneself and one's purpose in life.[15] In an African context, a person's perspective might be, as Kenyan philosopher and theologian John Mbiti has put it, "I am because we are; and since we are, therefore I am" (Mbiti, 141). I remember once a young Zairean in his early teens, telling me about the technical school his parents were sending him to. I asked him, "Is that what you want to do?" I recall him looking at me with an almost bewildered expression, saying "I've never really thought about what I *want*. It's just what I'm going to do. It's what's best for the family."

The point is that we may have been living in a culture with a fundamentally different worldview, a different conception of life, a different anthropology, psychology, spirituality. We may have been influenced by a different system of values, of individual-social relationships, of understanding one's "self" in relation to the other, to environment, to the Divine, etc. When changing to a low-context, highly individualistic, capitalistic society, is it any wonder that we feel lost, confused, hesitant, vulnerable, etc.? An American friend recently said to me, having spent over thirty years in Taiwan, "My family members don't really know me anymore." I'm sure that many of you reading this have felt the same way, or at least known someone who has. Sometimes this creates a deep loneliness, as well as a sense of powerlessness, not only in oneself, but often on the part of family and friends as well.

We need to be convinced—and actually comforted, that as "returning" missioners (or whatever our particular cultural transition may be), we are really entering a new cultural reality. We are feeling again that sense of disorientation or alienation that comes from culture shock and the array of emotions that come with it. (See Figure 1.3.) We will explore these feelings more fully in Chapter Two.

## SYMPTOMS OF REVERSED CULTURE SHOCK

- Homesickness
- Boredom
- Withdrawal
- Need for excessive amounts of sleep
- Compulsive behavior (eating, drinking, cleanliness, etc.)
- Irritability
- Marital stress
- Family (community) the tension and conflict
- Chauvinistic excesses
- Stereotyping others (nationals of a former host country or country of "re-entry")
- Hostility toward others (especially toward current host nationals)
- Loss of ability to concentrate or work effectively
- Unexplainable fits of weeping
- Physical (psycho somatic) illnesses (headaches, colds, muscle pain, etc.)

**Figure 1.3. A list of some typical symptoms that may occur in relatively severe cases of culture shock** (adapted from Kohls, *Survival Kit for Overseas Living*).[16]

The computer revolution is one good example of a "new" culture. Today's exploding technology and social media platforms offer amazing opportunities but also challenges. In the fast pace of this evolving world, one can easily be overwhelmed and feel inadequate to cope—literally "lost in cyber space." I recall when I returned to the States to study, I was quite content to find an *electric* typewriter at my disposal! (In Zaire, I had grown accustomed to using an old, portable manual typewriter, sometimes with a few well-worn sheets of carbon paper for copies.). Friends kept telling me to learn to use a computer! "It's so easy!" they would say. "Once you get used to it." Of course, they were right, but it took me about six months and lots of persuading before I finally attempted it. Then a few more months and many frustrating battles before the computer and I began to call a truce!

## Unpacking Our "Baggage"

We do not, however—and must not—remain in culture shock forever, as though in some sort of perpetual time warp. To the contrary, Peter Adler proposes that the alienating experience of culture shock, the time spent "betwixt and between," can be transformed into a "transitional experience," a privileged time of growth.

> **Although culture shock is most often associated with negative consequences, it can be an important aspect of cultural learning, self-development, and personal growth. . . . The problems and frustrations encountered in the culture shock process to an understanding of change and movement experiences. . . . transitional experiences [which] can be the source of higher levels of personality development. . . . Implicit in the conflict and tension posed by the transitional experience lies the potential for authentic growth (Adler, 14).**

It is the presupposition of this book that transition can become, in fact, *transformative*. This kind of growth, however, does not usually happen automatically. It can be a long, slow, and sometimes painful process before we find ourselves capable of feeling at home and useful again. It means rediscovering the skills and gifts that first enabled us to adapt to a new culture, and reinvesting ourselves "back here, as we once did "over there." We need to be patient with ourselves in this process, as we begin to "unpack the baggage" we've brought with us.

There may be different kinds of baggage that we carry around, heavy burdens often well packed away within us somewhere, as we return for a sabbatical, discernment, a vacation, or maybe "for good." The significant emotional and cultural upheaval in our lives is even more profound and life-changing, because of the genuineness with which missioners have usually tried to invest into the adopted culture, in spite of the many ambiguities and hardships this often causes. At the same time, within both secular society and the church–local and universal–there is a widespread growing ambivalence, from critics and supporters alike, toward the very concept of mission and "missionary." This ambivalence only weakens and confuses an already unsteady "missionary myth." The depth and challenge of a missioner's tumultuous transition might in some way seem to threaten the commitment that has marked their lives, the very essence of being faithful to their call.

## *Need for Support*

There is a legitimate need for those "in transit"–be it geographical, psychological, spiritual, or all of the above–to be able to share their story with someone who "gets it." Often that someone has, in some way or another, "been there" too. Sometimes others such as family, friends, or a religious community are unsuspecting and unaware of what their loved one might be experiencing. A clearer understanding of the impact of the profound changes that have occurred may help others grasp the nature of their transition better. It is because of these and many more factors that we propose that missioners and veterans–despite their frequent reluctance–be strongly encouraged to enter into some program or support group, a workshop or retreat, rehab or a time of reflection, which will help them process their transition or reentry.

Whatever the framework, it exists in order to help the missioners get in touch with their own stories and their feelings–often repressed–about their mission, their successes and failures, their pain and anger, their fear or disillusionment. Many testify that it is in sharing these stories and feelings with those who can understand and empathize with them that they are strengthened, consoled, and paradoxically, they are also most challenged. It is especially this kind of peer support, which helps them arrive at new insights, new or renewed feelings about themselves, and about mission in general, even in the midst of profoundly shifting paradigms. Today, as often in the past, veterans and service personal returning from combat zones often experience an ambivalent culture upon returning home. All the more, they need strong peer support and a community of trust which understands what they've been through.

## Part IV: The Narration of One's Experience: Telling the Story

*The memory is a living thing–it too is in transit. But during its moment, all that is remembered joins, and lives–the old and the young, the past and the present, the living and the dead* (Eudora Welty, quoted in P. Sullivan, 103 (1991)).

Patricia O'Connell Killen and John de Beer remind us that any kind of serious reflection on one's life begins with entering one's experience. We enter that experience by recalling it and describing or narrating it with as much descriptive detail as possible.

**A narrative description of a concrete
human experience intensifies that experience in a way that makes it begin to
resonate with and relate to the stories of
others. This resonance does not occur
on the level of the particular topic of the
story. It sounds on a deeper, symbolic level
where the quality of the particular event,
conveyed in the dominant feelings that
were experienced in it, relate us to the
humanness of all events characterized by
such feelings. A narrative description of an
event, then, can reveal the profoundly symbolic and interrelated quality of our lives
(Killen and de Beer, 24).**

The first step for moving through transition is telling one's story.
The Whiteheads' advice for narrating an incident for reflection is to
"tell enough for ourselves and others to see what we saw, feel what
we felt, smell what we smelled, experience the fear, joy, peace, that
we knew" (25).

> *A conch shell blew to signal that things were about
> to start. We all gathered around the "Banis" (an
> enclosure built of dried palm fronds). The com-
> mentator said a few words of introduction, and the
> drums began. . . . The singing began at something
> like a low hum and increased gradually in volume
> and speed. As the singing increased in intensity,
> first one side of the enclosure began to shake, then
> another, then another. One side fell, then the other
> three. It was as if the sides of a gigantic cardboard
> box collapsed outwards. And there in the middle
> sat Peter Kamposi, looking cool and relaxed. . . .
> The drums began another rhythm, one to walk*

*and dance to. The drummers and singers began a*
*stylized movement toward the Cathedral, followed*
*by the concelebrants and the consecrating bishops*
*and Peter (the first Papua New Guinean bishop).*
*Then came the throng of people in the typical*
*local style of procession. Formless as it may have*
*appeared to some overseas visitors' eyes, the clear*
*awe and wonder on the children's faces showed*
*that something special was going on. I could feel a*
*sense of anticipation all around (Rick, 1992).*

The above excerpt was the beginning of a long process of transition and healing for the missioner who wrote it. It seemed unassuming enough at the time of its first writing, but in his own words:

*The experience I relate above did not seem to me*
*to have any formative implication at first glance.*
*We had been asked to pick an experience that we*
*would not mind sharing with the group, and to*
*avoid any experience that was too personal or*
*soul-searching. Fine. But through guided reflec-*
*tion upon this "innocuous" experience . . . a lot of*
*thinking and praying over it . . . I have, much to*
*my own surprise, come to recognize that God is*
*working in my life even when I am not aware of*
*it. . . . Gradually in the reflection process, it became*
*clear to me that I had been measuring my self-*
*worth according to how much I accomplished and*
*according to how much affirmation I was receiving*
*from people whose good opinion I valued. The more*
*items I could check off on my "to do" list, the better*
*I used to feel. . . . I began to discern a pattern in*
*my life that I had not been consciously aware of.*
*Instances where I was not in control were becom-*
*ing more numerous in my life, and I was becoming*

*more and more resentful toward others, and with
my own inability to live up to my own expectations
(Rick, 1993).*

The process is not an individual one, although it will be intensely personal and unique. In my experience with missioners recently returned for study or sabbatical, one of their greatest needs is to know that they are not alone in their journey. Together with a much-needed time of solitude, they also need guided reflection, to be able to *tell someone* what they're thinking and, especially, what they're feeling. And they need to see others nodding their heads in understanding, silently saying, "Yes, I've been there too." A group of missioners in transition grew precisely out of that need to be with others who had experienced in some way what they had. Even though we might have been in entirely different cultures or continents, what they had in common produced a sense of solidarity: they were travelers together on this journey, looking for the way "home." Not unlike those rock climbers or soldiers, missioners have a sort of culture that they live and move in. As we saw earlier, perhaps this is partly because of a common myth, whatever shape it may be taking at the present moment. This is all the more true with missioners who find themselves in some sort of limbo, when they are between assignments.

I invite those who find themselves in this sort of "limbo," while transitioning, to intentionally get in touch with their experience. Exactly when this is best begun is different for everyone. From Mission to Mission recommends that ideally people be back from their assignment at least six months before joining a re-entry retreat or workshop. This allows time to recover from the initial "reverse culture shock," which can be a time of extreme fatigue, hyperactivity, or sometimes just being "spaced out." (Recall your first months in your new mission culture.) It can take some time before we come to *recognize* that we are disoriented, still living in the place we left behind, or simply not quite "right." For some, this recognition may never come. For others, for one reason or another, a sense of disorientation may never be felt. This may be related to the degree or period of time a missioner was integrated into the local culture in which they served, but not necessarily. In most cases, however, whether we know it or not, some process of reflection will be invaluable for an integration of our past experience into our present and future. We now take a look into that process.

## *The Nature of Experience*

> **"Life history," like personal identity, is an interpretive concept used to bring order out of a person's unstructured past, and in so doing to imbue it with a particular significance or worth. The identity of any person is an interpretation culled from that individual's personal history (Stroup, 106).**

Killen and de Beer describe experience in a broad sense as "the flow of interaction between an individual and the people, places, events, material conditions, and cultural factors that make up that person's identity, context, and world" (Killen and de Beer, 58). They speak about all of this "flow" of interaction as "Experience" with a large "E"–which, in turn, can be separated into many "experiences" with a small "e." There are four categories which make up our experiences, each an integral part of all of human Experience:

- **Action:** one's lived narrative, which we normally think of as *experience*;
- **Tradition:** the religious, philosophical, or spiritual wisdom that one accepts as authoritative;
- **Culture:** ideas, social structures, and ecological environment; and
- **Positions:** standpoints, attitudes, opinions, beliefs, and convictions (see Killen and de Beer, 54-60).

Action                                              Positions
*(lived narrative)*                                 *(attitudes, values, etc.)*

# THE ELEMENTS OF EXPERIENCE

Culture                                              Tradition
*(symbols, mores,*                                  *(scriptures, theology,*
*rituals, etc.)*                                     *etc.)*

**Figure 1.4 The elements of experience** (Killen and de Beer).

Implicitly, and sometimes explicitly, I deal with all of these experience sources throughout this book, because they are, in reality,
inextricably interconnected. The smallest, seemingly insignificant
moment in our experience is inevitably influenced by all of these
sources. They are, like the air we breathe, always a part of us, and
we exist by inhaling and exhaling that air, though most of the time
without any particular awareness that we are doing so. That air, fresh
or polluted, stormy or still, is a part of every movement we make,
every thought that we think. So too are our lives informed by our
culture, religious tradition (or the absence of one), and our beliefs,
convictions, attitudes, values and standpoints. We might say that the
"action" of our experience *embodies* the culture, tradition, and positions by which we have been formed and informed. It is primarily on
the actions, the *lived and living narrative*, that we want missioners
to focus as they begin their own process of reflection.

But these actions, events, or incidents do not happen in
a vacuum. They take place in a context, a context which is also
part of our broader "Experience." I have found it helpful to
begin the process of narration by situating oneself in the context of vocation, mission, or ministry–or life's work. There are
many ways to do this, formally and informally. One that has
been used in the Mission/Ministry Integration Seminar was
to invite participants to think of their cross-cultural or mission experience as a sort of novel, or at least in story form.[17]

We cannot reflect, however, on our vast experience "in general."
As Killen and de Beer have put it:

**In order to reflect, the flow of experience must be stopped. We cannot reflect on experience in its entirety. We need manage-able pieces of experience in order to reflect, so we take a single event or issue and focus on that for reflection. We freeze Experience in a moment of time and separate it into aspects or sources (Killen and de Beer, 58-59).**

It is in focusing on specific experiences that we can begin to dis-cover the issues that may be hidden within. We have come to believe, from our own experience and from working with others, that if we *recall any experience*, however small and seemingly unimportant it might be, it is a like a microcosm of all of our Experience. That is, within that one experience are contained the same key issues or concerns, which Killen and de Beer call "the heart of the matter" (61), that we would find if we recounted ten experiences, or better, one "major" event or incident that *we judge* to be of great importance. One might say *that in every acorn there is an oak*.

## The Importance of Narrating Our Experience

**In the field of religion, a paradigm shift always means both continuity and change, both faithfulness to the past and boldness to engage the future, both constancy and contingency, both tradition and transfor-mation (Bosch, *Transforming Mission*, 366).**

Those who have left their previous life status or a place of mission, either temporarily or permanently, might ask, "What's the point of recalling the past? Rehashing old events? Digging up buried hurts? Remembering good times that are no more?" I'd like to argue that there is much to be said for those in transit, taking the time and the space they need to tell their story, first of all for themselves, and then for others who are there, wanting to receive it.

Such stories don't need a plot. Often a sojourner might somehow realize that they are being called to "move" in the mysterious journey of their own vocation, their own sense of purpose, and yet don't see at all clearly what that "new movement" is all about. This takes numerous forms:

- A missioner who is being asked to leave or change assignments, after years of learning a language or a culture
- Anyone who doesn't know how to deal with the tension and stress of a new approach to life, or with physical limitations due to age, sickness, or the general "wear and tear" of another climate or culture–or even just everyday life
- A person who has been living amid overt or subtle violence and is beginning to experience the physical and emotional signs of its impact
- Someone experiencing what is called "burn-out," who is simply physically, emotionally, and spiritually exhausted and needs a change of environment?
- Veterans or missioners who come home from abroad and unexpectedly begin to discover some neglected inner needs or emotions that are demanding attention.

Allow the story to unfold. Whatever the circumstances, I am convinced that telling one's story is vital to a positive integration of the past with the present in order to move into the future with courage, confidence and hope.

## *Narrative and Identity*

Perhaps the stories of those who are in transit in their lives express a searching for personal and/or vocational *identity*. Some find themselves asking questions like: What should I do now? Is there anything I *can* do? Has what I've been doing made any sense? Is there any purpose to my life? Have I been wasting my time and energy? What am I doing here? Should I continue? Should I go back? Where am I going? etc. These are identity questions, which may coincide with the issues arising at mid-life as well as during transitions. They are questions that *demand* to be answered, issues which–once raised–will be buried no more, presenting challenges to be addressed for the articulation of personal identity. In this regard, George Stroup asks a relevant question:

> **Is narrative simply an imaginative way of entering into theological reflection, or is there something about the nature of human being and the structure of human experi-ence that makes narrative the appropriate and even necessary form for the articula-tion of personal identity (Stroup, 100).[18]**

Using the work of Hans Georg Gadamer, Stanley Hauerwas, and Stephen Crites, Stroup leads us to understand that if one's identity is bound up with one's past, it is also bound up with one's memory.

> **By means of the memory an individual selects certain events from his or her personal history and uses them to interpret the significance of the whole. The claim that human beings are inextricably tied to history simply means that they search for meaning and unity of self in some pattern of coherence in their personal history. . . . Personal identity, therefore, is always a pattern or a shape, which memory retrieves from the history of each individual and projects into the future. . . . The identity of any person is an interpretation culled from that individual's personal history (Stroup, 105-106).**

He further points out that Crites takes an even stronger position, believing that the very quality of experience through time is *inherently* narrative. Crites holds that the "past, present, and the future are the 'tensed modalities' which are *inseparably joined in every moment of experience*" (Stroup, 112). It is the fusion of these modalities that is expressed in our stories, whether they be mundane or sacred, whether expressing the ordinary day-to-day unfolding of our history or the deeper meaning found in patterns of "internal coherence." The person moving *from→through→to→from→through→to→* . . . is experiencing the "fusion" or coming together of past, present, and future in this present liminal moment–all of which is "transition."

-> FROM -> THROUGH -> TO -> FROM -> THROUGH -> TO ->

**Fig. 1.1**

In the midst of transitional upheavals as described above, many will find themselves struggling to renew–or in some cases retrieve–personal identity and even vocational or ministerial identity. The very act of telling one's story, of putting together a narrative of one's life, in particular one's mission history, is a way for missioners to articulate and affirm their identity–especially at a time when we are feeling disoriented and estranged. In the simple act of selecting (even unconsciously) the events and moments that will go into our narrative, we begin to find a pattern. Finding meaning in the past helps make sense of the present, and this has the power and momentum to carry us into the future. "To tell a story," says Hauerwas, "often involves our attempt to make intelligible the muddle of things we have done in order to become a self." (See Stroup, 112.) And being able to tell one's story may be the beginning of a new way to live it out. This may involve a confirmed, renewed, or in some cases, *transformed identity, inherent in the process of new growth*. Let us take a look at some particular elements of storytelling that facilitate this process.

## 1. Non-judgmental Narration

In narrating our experiences, it is important to be non-judgmental; i.e., avoiding evaluation or premature interpretation. When describing an event, we often tend to interpret it as we go along, even for ourselves. This robs it of its original impact. The time for interpretation and evaluation will come later. It is important first to simply try to relate the stories as they come to mind, as we remember them. Killen and de Beer give us an important rule for non-judgmental narration. First, they remind us of what most of us learned in language or writing class; i.e., the classic questions of Who-What-Where-When-How. At this point we don't yet ask the question, "Why?" This will be asked later on as we seek understanding and insight.

> **Answering why yields an interpretation of the event. Whatever our interpretation is at the beginning, it is most likely inadequate and unsatisfying, or we would not be reflecting on the situation. Answering why too soon smothers the actual experience. It prematurely distances us from the event and rationalizes what happened. This short-circuits the revelatory power of the experience (Killen and de Beer, 25).[19]**

But sometimes this description of our lives is not as easy to construct as it might seem. Irving Polster in *Every Person's Life Is Worth a Novel*,[20] stresses paying attention to the "ordinary" details of one's life. Not many of us do this very well, nor very often. And yet these very ordinary things, described in vivid color and in the context of the dramas of day-to-day living, are the very stuff that good novels and movies are made of. The importance here is not in the "objective accuracy" of the narration, but in its meaning and significance for the rememberer. Besides, there is no totally objective memory.

Experiences are subjective as they happen, and as they are recorded in the memory or suppressed in the unconscious. They will always be subjective when they are recalled and narrated.

## 2. The Power of the Written Word

Another point I want to stress here is the value of *writing* one's story before orally sharing it with others. The emphasis here is the need to recollect memories first by letting them flow from the head to the fingers. Paula Farrell Sullivan emphasizes this in her work on autobiographical writing, "Writing stimulates memory and thought, memories and thoughts stimulate writing. . . . Whatever comes through our fingers, trust that it is truth as each reader of this book has experienced it"(P. Sullivan, 8-9).

This has been my experience over and over again when working with people in transition. They need time and quiet space, first to get in touch with their experiences and events of the past that come to mind, and then to allow them to flow, as in a written "stream of consciousness." They are sometimes amazed how the act of journaling seems to jar memories that they had not originally thought of or intended to record. The act of writing stirs the creative imagination to "fill in the blanks" that may be left by memory. When we come together in a group (or with a counselor, director, or friend,) we can usually recount only a small part of what we have written, often simply due to time and logistics. At the same time, as we tell our story or event, it is difficult not to begin to alter it, often interpreting it, making explanations or judging our actions or those of others. The narration might be influenced by the self-consciousness of the narrator, or one's degree of introversion or extroversion. It might also depend on the amount of confidence that the members of the group have built up in one another.

I'd like to note here, in this age of computerization, that the creative and therapeutic response is not the same when typing as when *writing by hand*. Unfortunately, this kind of writing is becoming a lost art. Handwriting analysts tell us that there is much more expressed in and through our handwriting than merely the content of our thoughts and words. The *way* we write, the force, the slant, the size, the way we dot our i's and cross our t's—all of this is an expression of who we are and what we have to say.

## 3. Creativity in Expressing One's Own Experience[21]

Writing may not be the best method for everyone, although it is the most common. It has long been a pedagogical principle that *the more senses one employs in the learning process, the more one learns.* A student learns from listening in class, but even more when also interacting through questions or discussions. One learns from taking notes; still more from reading the material ahead of time and going over it afterwards. And finally we optimize learning when we creatively put the material into practice through actions; e.g., art, skits, role-playing, etc. Some of us may want to re-enact our coloring or finger painting days, or prefer to do modeling with clay. These can often be meaningful and powerful ways of expressing ourselves, in addition to the written word.

Another tool that may be helpful in giving our memories or creativity a jog is that of using films or fiction. Through these media, stories are told that we can relate to and can often be both a reminder and a validation of what we have lived through. Because these fictitious or autobiographical accounts are in narrative or story form, they can help us give shape and voice to our own stories. Call to mind examples of autobiographies, novels, or film.[22] What is especially helpful is the stories and struggles of others like ourselves who have attempted to live and minister cross-culturally. One missioner commented after viewing the film, *At Play In the Fields of the Lord.*[23]

> *I found the whole film frightening as well as thought-provoking. The total defeat in the end is very telling, "It would have been better for this people not to have known us. . . . We are getting out of here!" Meanwhile, the village of the native people*

*is ravaged by an epidemic. . . . The film, however, is*
*powerful. It emphasizes for me the need to ap-*
*proach mission and ministry with a sense of hu-*
*mility and reverence. At the same time it urges me*
*to examine my style of doing mission. Do I confuse*
*the message of the faith with material things, for*
*example, the students passing their exams at the*
*end of the year? While this cannot be neglected, I*
*have to be careful to ensure that I am establishing*
*the bonds of human relations, and building bridges*
*across cultures* (Kate, 1995).

## *Moving On: Some Concluding Comments*

Perhaps Chapter One has seemed a bit theoretical and abstract. In fact, we have laid the foundation and outlined the framework that will unfold in the rest of this book. We introduced the broad concept of transition, and in particular cross-cultural transition.

Looking at the process of so-called "re-entry," we saw how it closely correlates with the same kind of culture shock we experience when we enter a new and unfamiliar cultural context. We are often living in an in-between space, called *liminality*, and this kind of ambiguity is uncomfortable and sometimes quite confusing. Living in a liminal space of transition can lead to a loss of identity: we are no longer that "missionary" or "soldier" or whatever role we had come to identify with.

At the same time, we have to find a way to navigate our way through this space: described in this book as an evolving process, "from→through–to . . .," a term coined by Maryknoll missioner Larry Lewis (see Works Cited).

I believe that one of the best ways to wade through these sometimes murky or tumultuous waters is through the telling of our story– to think of our experience as a sort of short story or novel, keeping in mind, of course, that our lives are far more than any novel or a film. They are, in fact, a living " history," the story unfolding in ourselves and in the lives of those around us. The shaping of that story is perhaps the first and best place to look for the mysterious action of the Divine. Probably, for most of us, the thought of seeing the Divine working through us in our ministry or acting in the life of those we serve, is not a difficult one. But how often do we think of our own life as an actual living example of God's "salvation history" or for others, the unfolding grace of karma?

This narrative process begins by reflecting on one particular event or incident in our past experience. This does not have to be a spectacular event. It can be quite ordinary, long or short, humorous or serious, etc. Keep in mind that it doesn't matter whether you perceive it as positive or negative. What is important is that it is an event that spontaneously comes to mind when you're invited to think back and choose a particular moment. This experience, together with the feelings and images that accompany it, will be the source of further reflection throughout the process, and often will reveal the entire "plot" of one's personal story. The narrated event is the key for the integrative process that unfolds in the following chapters: naming feelings, identifying images, and discovering the primary issues (the "heart of the matter"), often the *source* of the transitional "drama" in one's life. In telling the stories, and attending to the feelings, images, and issues they elicit, we will begin to integrate the insights gained throughout the process, and hopefully begin to feel "at home" again in our life journey. Let us now see how the process unfolds in the next chapters.

## Chapter Two

# Attending Feelings:
# "Betwixt and Between"

*The world is falling apart.*
*I want things . . . the way they were.*
*How do I mend this broken world?*
*How do I hold on to the Past . . . yet move into the Future?*
*How do I change, without changing,*
*Die without dying?*
*How do I get New Life . . . without giving away the Old?*
*How do I accept New Wine Skins . . . when I like the old*
*ones better?*
*I rebel . . .*
*Against others . . . against God . . . most of all, against*
*myself.*
*I am confused, disorientated, frustrated, lost, and helpless.*
*Help! My world is falling apart* (Jim, 1992).

In this chapter, we will examine more closely the *feelings* involved in the experience of transition or liminality, as described in Chapter One. We've been invited to recall and "re-enter" experiences *from* our past, when we were in our mission home, as well as what we are experiencing in the present, as we pass *through* transition. Now we notice that when we enter our experience, if we observe it non-judgmentally and attentively—we are filled with feelings. In addition, these feelings may sometimes be associated with experiences of violence, trauma, or other forms of psychological and physical abuse in varying degrees. We need to be prepared for such possibilities.

## Part I: Getting In Touch with Feelings

> *One day Peter, a friend and fellow missioner studying at CTU asked me to trim his hair. (Having spent many years in India where his wife was his "hairdresser," he didn't worry about my lack of expertise in the area!) We proceeded to lay sheets of newspaper on the floor and got on with the haircut. As I was clipping his straight, graying wisps of strawberry-blond hair I was—without realizing it at the time—careful to put the cut pieces into the wastepaper basket as I cut, trying to keep it from getting on the floor, or even on our carefully spread-out newspaper. When finished, we carefully folded up the sheets of newspaper and put them into the trash basket. After we had cleaned up and he had gone, my eyes fell on the wastepaper basket with the freshly cut hair lying in little mounds amid the crunched newspaper. As I looked at those strands of hair, I recalled another haircutting session one day in Zaire, about twelve years ago at this time.*

I had only been a few months in the village of Iboko in equatorial Africa, when I and an American friend visiting for a few days, took the opportunity to give each other a haircut. We installed ourselves outdoors, so that there wouldn't be any hair to sweep up later. In the midst of our cutting, two of our Zairean sisters came out to join us. As they watched, they were shocked. "No, no! You mustn't just let each others' hair be picked up by the wind and carelessly blown away in the open like that! You must be careful to bury or burn it! Hair is sacred!"

I can't recall if they explained their reasoning to us at that time. If they did, it didn't make an impression on me. It would be several years before I would come to understand the significance of "hair" in their culture, and the implications of allowing hair to be carelessly carried off by the wind. I learned that hair is an important symbol in many African cultures, believed to possess the life-spirit of the person. One indication of the power of hair is that it is commonly used in witchcraft. Often the sorcerer demands a lock of hair of the person to whom harm is intended. Or in an altogether different context, friends might exchange locks of hair much as they exchange blood, in ritually confirming kinship.

As if coming back from a moment in time, I said to myself, "JoAnn, you're in Chicago now. No one here worries about cut hair!" As I looked at the wisps of hair in that wastepaper basket, I realized that I was feeling as though I had committed a sacrilege, treating something sacred without proper respect. There I was looking at "the embodiment of my friend's spirit" lying crumpled in that waste can. How could I just walk away and leave it there, in full view of a passerby!? I knew that I just couldn't leave it like that. For some reason within myself, I had to attend to it in some more "sacred" way.

I then carefully proceeded to gather the little wisps and mounds of "Peter's spirit." I carefully wrapped them in paper toweling, folding it into a package so that nothing could be seen or fall out. Then I gently laid the wrapped package back into the wastepaper basket, somehow feeling that "it was enough." I felt that I had ritually disposed of the hair in an appropriately respectful way and so appeased my own spirit.

There were many similar moments in my life after I returned to the United States from Zaire. Over time I realized, reflecting on my own behavior, that somehow in some fundamental ways, *I had changed*. Oftentimes many of us are not at all in touch with what we are feeling, and find it very difficult to articulate. We can usually say what we *think*, but what we *feel* is another question altogether. Killen and de Beer suggest that naming feelings, accurately and non-judgmentally, is a necessary spiritual discipline (Killen and de Beer, 30). One way to face and explore these feelings evoked by transition is through dialogue, especially with others who may be experiencing–or possibly repressing–similar feelings. Exploring those feelings and what might be their origin is the work of this chapter.

## *Defining "Feelings" and "Emotions"*

Feelings can generally be defined as "embodied affective and intelligent responses to reality as we encounter it. . . . *They are clues to the meaning of our experience*" (Killen and de Beer, 27). I like thinking of feelings as clues. I'm a mystery fan, and any good mystery writer gives subtle hints, clues to help the reader figure out "who dunnit." We must be very attentive to the clues, often hidden or found in unsuspecting places. So too in narrating our personal stories from the past or present, we–and those who walk with us–must be attentive listeners to the clues our body and emotions give us. When we are speaking or listening to one another, what are we *feeling* within ourselves?

While Killen and de Beer refer to "feelings" in a general sense, some authors prefer to make a distinction between "feelings" and "emotions." I find some aspects of this distinction helpful as we look at different phases of the transition process. Magda Arnold[24] describes feelings as the physical or somatic signs which accompany an appraisal of something as good or bad, but refer to the *person* doing the feeling rather than to the object of appraisal. Feelings, in this sense, are like reactions, either pleasant or unpleasant, painful or delightful. For example, one can say, "I feel good" or "I feel sad." These feelings are like the perceivable "envelopes" for the emotions which usually accompany them; e.g., love, anger, fear.

Emotions, on the other hand, are the "action tendencies" produced by the appraisal, rather than the "felt" physiological signs. For example, a "positive" emotion is a felt tendency *toward* something that we intuitively appraise as good for us. A "negative" emotion moves us *away* from anything which we intuitively appraise as bad or harmful. According to Arnold's theory, this attraction or aversion is accompanied by different patterns of physiological changes organized toward approach or withdrawal. Sometimes the *same feelings* can accompany very *different emotions*. For example, "I feel good because you love me," and "I feel good because I finished my work." Obviously, there are different appraisals of desirable objectives in these two cases. Another example might be a "flushed" feeling: red face, fast heartbeat. What emotion is the person experiencing in this case? It could be anger, embarrassment, or maybe love. Whatever the case, emotions and the decisions we make because of them are always connected to our self-esteem. In most situations of conflict between two or more parties, if we look carefully, we will find that *an issue of self-esteem is almost always at stake*. Our emotions are geared toward *enhancing or protecting our self-esteem* as we perceive it in relation to some intuitively appraised "object" (Solomon, 140-141).

I think that this might have some bearing on understanding the *felt* reactions and responses we experience in transition, especially as we try to identify exactly what it is we are feeling. I recall several times a counselor asking me, "How do you feel about that?" or "What are you feeling as you tell me this?" I would respond, and often enough she would say, "That's what you *think*, but you still haven't told me what you *feel*." Gradually I began to distinguish between the two, and to articulate better what I was *feeling*; i.e., the sensations and emotions involved. These would, in fact, gradually give me a clue as to the *meaning* of an experience, situation, dream, etc. My mixed feelings during the hair-cutting experience (recounted a few paragraphs above) is a good example of this. Feelings I sensed, yet initially couldn't identify or articulate, ultimately became the clue to understanding the internal displacement or disorientation I was not consciously processing.

Once in a small group, one of its members was recounting an experience from her time on mission. As she was speaking, I found myself feeling chilled. Later when I was responding to her, my gut was actually trembling, as was my voice. I recognized that energy had gone out of me in listening and responding to her story. This apparently simple sharing on her part had generated strong feelings in me. This was more than an empathic response. Something in her story was connecting to something in mine, evoking a feeling response within me. At this point the reason for such an emotional response was not yet apparent. It would eventually reveal itself as I remained faithful to the process: *attending my feelings, exploring the images they evoked, moving through the "conversion"* that was demanded, and eventually embracing and *integrating the insights* revealed along the way. We will explore this process now more fully.

## *Encountering Feelings from the Past*

One evening in a group sharing, Kathy recalled a night in Brazil, when one of the women from the base communities had come to talk with her, to share with Kathy her heavy feelings related to poverty. This sharing had a weighty impact on Kathy. In her words:

> *I don't know how to describe it except that I felt this woman's pain. Poverty and oppression were no longer a nameless face, just another "poor person." The poverty, the injustice, the oppression took on a face, a name, a reality that I could never forget. I felt overwhelmed by it all. I was angry. I felt powerless. I can't exactly say what happened, but I knew from that moment on everything had changed . . . I had changed and would never be the same.*

> *After the woman left, I found my two companions in the sitting room still up that night. I began to tell them what had happened and how I felt. I began to cry—for the first time since I had been in Brazil. They listened, but they must not have been comfortable with my tears. They began to give me*

> *advice about how I must learn to distance myself*
> *from these things . . . not to get too emotionally*
> *involved* (Kathy, 1997).

Kathy can't exactly explain what happened to her in that moment with the woman, and her memory of the talk with her companions is even less vivid. She only knows now that her community companions couldn't receive her tears, her pain, her vulnerability—and that something within her "turned off." With a wrenching gesture toward her gut, she continued with a trembling voice:

> *That night, something within me shut down. I knew*
> *that from that moment on I had to become hard,*
> *tough, invulnerable. From then on I became "the*
> *crusader." In my fury, I began a stream of ceaseless*
> *activities aimed at changing the situation. Even*
> *if no one else would help them, even if they don't*
> *seem to want to help themselves, I will help them!"*

And for the next nine years, Kathy spent all of her energy organizing, strategizing, developing, doing. She concluded:

> *Toward the end of my time there, it dawned on me*
> *very forcefully—so forcefully that I was once again*
> *brought to tears—that all of my work, plans, strat-*
> *egizing were not one bit helpful. It was changing*
> *nothing—and keeping me at a distance from those*
> *whom I was trying to help. All my effort was not*
> *alleviating the pain of what I saw and, at times,*
> *experienced with those who suffered. I could not*
> *help the situation either. The tears were tears of*
> *useless time spent on too much activity, and tears*
> *of compassion as I identified with the futility of*
> *their lives and my own. All I could do was "get*
> *out." I was "a mess" and so angry* (Kathy, 1997).

Kathy acknowledged that when she left her mission to come to the States for a sabbatical, she was indeed "a mess." But at the time, she wasn't fully ready to recognize the degree to which she was seriously struggling, much less the reasons why. She spent the first year of sabbatical feeling angry, closed, bitter, almost antisocial. It was only after over a year that she began to realize how angry she was, and that somehow she had to deal with this anger. Angry at whom? About what? At her religious congregation? Her companions? The injustice of "the system"? Herself? God? She needed to get to "the heart of the matter," the key issue or issues which were causing her so much anger, so much pain.

In this liminality, Kathy began her "journey," beginning with meeting with a group of missioners who were also on sabbatical. Gradually, as her experiences were accepted, her feelings understood, Kathy gained trust in this group. She also gained the confidence to look within herself, to begin her *inner* journey–possibly the most difficult she had ever made. She realized her need for spiritual guidance and counseling and began to pursue both. This movement *from* past events and her lived narrative, *through* her feelings and the images and other feelings they evoked, led *to* a certain liberation from all those feelings that had been "shut down" for over ten years. It was only after two more years, however, that she really began to see some light in her darkness, to get some clues as to what was happening to her and within her. Gradually these clues became insights, which would begin to further free her to move on, into some new light, new clarity and insight. This would spark the transformation that enabled her to discern new initiatives, to make decisions, and to take action about her future.

Kathy's journey, although uniquely her own, is not unlike the journeys of countless others who live with "unfinished business" or carry "baggage" that still needs to be unpacked. So many of us muddle through changes in life, rather than deal with the unprocessed wounds of our past. We often just push the bag under the bed, or put it down in a basement somewhere, hidden from everyone's view, even our own. Yet something within us knows it's there, that unpacked bag. It keeps reminding us—in subtle or obvious ways—that we have to eventually deal with it. A friend told me that he *literally* shoved a full trunk under his bed when he first returned from a mission assignment. He didn't unpack it until six years later! Some say, "Let it go" or "Forget it," but I believe we will never be fully at home or readjusted to a new situation until we unpack that bag.

This chapter is all about that baggage. We may have been carrying it around with us for a long time, or maybe only for a little while. For some, this baggage may represent a very complex reality, while for others their bags may be relatively light. Certainly, for most if not all, the liminal stage of transition, betwixt and between, carries with it a vast array of feelings that might be attributed to any number of factors. In addition to a primary change in status, for example, a person might also be facing other challenging life crises: health problems, family difficulties, the death of a significant person, radical changes in what once were familiar surroundings, etc. Again, while some of what we feel during transition may be closely connected to the past, for others it's what they anticipate or fear regarding the future. It's very common to have mixed feelings about that which awaits us beyond the horizon.

The emotions driving us, and the feelings expressing them, are obviously all interconnected. They are not neatly divided into categories: past, present, future, or loss, grief, trauma. For our purposes in this chapter, however, and for the sake of better understanding this aspect of transition, we will treat each of these emotionally charged time frames and categories as though they were experienced separately. But we know the transition affects the *whole* of one's self, including spirituality. Since we cannot possibly address all of the many feelings which may be experienced during any given transition, I have tried to focus on what I consider to be three major pieces of baggage often weighing us down during a liminal time, namely: loss, grief, and trauma. I have found that the many-faceted process associated with the act of *grieving* provides an especially appropriate prism for understanding the dynamics and feelings experienced by anyone in a major transition. I invite you now to take a look through that prism.

## Part II: The Nature of Loss

> *The art of losing isn't hard to master; so many*
> *things seem filled with the intent to be lost that*
> *their loss is no disaster.*
>
> *Lose something every day. Accept the fluster of lost*
> *door keys, the hour badly spent.*
>
> *The art of losing isn't hard to master.*
> *Then practice losing farther . . . faster: places and*
> *names, and where it was you meant*
> *To travel. None of these will bring disaster.*
>
> *I lost my mother's watch. And look! My last or*
> *next-to-last, of three houses went.*
>
> *The art of losing isn't hard to master.*
> *I lost two cities, lovely ones. And vaster, some*
> *realms I owned, two rivers, a continent. I miss*
> *them, but it wasn't a disaster.*
>
> *Even losing you*
> *(The joking voice, a gesture I love) I shan't have*
> *lied. It's evident*
>
> *The art of losing's not too hard to master,*
> *though it may look like (Write it!) like disaster.*[25]

In *All Our Losses, All Our Griefs*, Mitchell and Anderson discuss six major types of losses, as well as several possible variables (36-51).[26] I believe these losses are worth mentioning in some detail here, because the missioner in transition is usually affected by not merely one or two, but often all of these different kinds of loss. (In my own experience I can now identify that when I returned from Zaire, I was dealing with each of them in a significant way.) I will name and briefly define each, using Mitchell and Anderson's schema and complementing it with Sullender's perspective. At the same time, I'll give a few examples of these kinds of losses using my own and others' experiences.

## *Material Loss*

"Material loss is the loss of a physical object or of familiar surroundings to which one has an important attachment" (Mitchell and Anderson, 36-37). Sullender refers to this as "loss of external objects [which] can be losses of such things as money, pets, special mementos, home, or even homeland" (15-17). He goes on to say:

> **The loss of one's homeland, even if by choice, is a complex phenomenon that also involves the loss of roots, identity, support, and familiarity. . . . The loss of one's home can also be by disaster, by changing homes, or by leaving homes. "Home" often involves more than just a building. It also includes one's family, security, childhood, familiarity, etc. (16).**

Material loss is perhaps the easiest to identify for those in transition. I remember when I first came back from Zaire, I surrounded myself with all kinds of material objects which seemed to bring Zaire "close": I liked to wear my *limputa*, that piece of bright African cloth that is not only the basic clothing for women there but also serves at least a dozen other purposes. On my dresser was the carved African Madonna that spoke to me of the elegant simplicity of the people. I listened endlessly to homemade copies of popular Zairean music or the vibrant liturgies that had become my way of worshipping. Depending upon many variables, missioners may actually be engaged in uprooting themselves from that which has actually become "home:" the length of time spent by the missioner in the host culture, the emotional investment in relationships and work, the effort at acculturation, whether or not the decision to leave is voluntary or involuntary, the age and experience of the missioner, etc. (See Storti, *Crossing Cultures*, 70.) This kind of transition necessarily means dealing with questions of identity and the loss of a part of oneself and one's sense of rootedness.

I longed for the sights and sounds of Zaire: women calling to one another across the road or marketplace, "*Mbote! Okei wapi?*"; the drumbeats of a distant celebration; the children always and everywhere laughing, singing, hopping, and jumping with the games I could never master. I missed the equatorial sun burning through the morning haze of the dry season, the distant sound of the rain approaching, moving across the lush forest like the hooves of a galloping herd coming closer and closer. I longed to place my feet again on Zairean soil, and look up at night into the vast, diamond-studded African sky. Instead, I had to be satisfied with listening to vague news reports about the refugee crisis there, the "rebels taking over one-fourth of the country," the endless television scenes of gaunt faces of hunger, starvation, and death in the land I had come to love.

## *Relationship Loss*

> **Relationship loss is the ending of opportunities to relate to, talk with, share experiences with, make love to, touch, settle issues with, fight with, and otherwise be in the emotional and/or physical presence of a particular other human being (Mitchell and Anderson, 37-39).**

I believe relational loss is the most significant and often the most difficult to accept of all losses. Sullender puts this category first in his discussion, since when we mention loss and grief, we most readily think of separation from persons. He simply calls this the "loss of a person," whether by death, divorce, or separation of any significance (see Sullender, 7-12).

> **In recent years, I have had reason to do much more traveling than I might wish. I have relieved the boredom of waiting in airports by engaging in the wonderful pastime of "people watching." I've become quite a keen observer of humankind. Through this pastime, I've become convinced that one can learn a great deal about grief in airports. At every [departure] one can find embracing couples, crying children, and weeping parents. The pain of separation, however brief, is the pain of grief. Every good-bye, however temporary, is a prelude to the final good-bye. We fight off that pain with "promises to write," gestures of affection, gift exchanges, taking pictures "to remember her by," and so on. Yet all of these assorted rituals only point to the reality of the loss and the inevitability of grief feelings (Sullender, 12).**

The loss of relationships is inevitable for those transitioning to and from mission. We indeed try to console ourselves with promises to keep in touch, but we know that the relationships that we have formed in our adopted culture, the familiarity and intimacy with which we have lived them, will never be the same. One missioner, after several months back from Brazil, shared a part of a letter he received from a friend:

> *Listen to me, Frankie, every friend who has entered into our lives always takes with themselves a little*

*bit of us and lets a piece . . . stay with us. A piece of you, which is here with me, makes me remember that which has gone away. . . . For three months I have been waiting for some words from you. . . . I am very sad and also, maybe more, worried about you. . . .*

The missioner reflects:

*All of the letters I receive express clearly their grief and also my grief. I have also written many letters to some of them in the same tone. Many times the grief comes strongly whenever we think that this separation is a permanent one . . . no more opportunity to get together, no more working as a team* (Frankie, 1995).

My first Zairean friend was also my tutor. She eventually became my "kinship sister." It was especially my Zairean community companions who unlocked for me the door to many aspects of the culture. Other Zaireans became my "sisters and brothers," many of them affectionately called me "*Mama leki*," which means "maternal aunt" in Lingala. I can still see the brave, long-suffering women, wives and mothers, workers of the fields and the marketplaces. I also can recall some proud and hardworking fathers, who did their best to provide for their families under impossible circumstances. I remember the "forest people" of Iboko, who taught me much more than the literacy and life skills I tried to teach them.

One of the strongest people I knew was Mama Anna, who bravely raised her three grandchildren in conditions of extreme poverty and in the face of unbelievable obstacles. It was on a routine visit to one of the base communities in Mbandaka that she asked me to take a look at her youngest grandson, Gaylord. When I entered the small, dark room where he lay in bed, I could barely believe my eyes. Gaylord was almost two years old, but he was shriveled up like a little old man. He was suffering from general malnutrition and *kwashiorkor* (an extreme

lack of protein). Mama Anna was doing her best to fill him up with
*kwanga* and *mpondu* (cassava bread and greens)–the only diet that
most Zaireans could afford. She didn't understand what was wrong
with him.

She only lived about three blocks from the general hospital,
Mama Mobutu, but she had no money and was afraid of taking
her child there, afraid of what would happen. Together with Sister
Jacqueline, one of my Zairean companions and a pediatric nurse
at the hospital, we were able to convince Mama Anna to take him
for the consultation that would be the beginning of Gaylord's almost
miraculous road to recovery. When I left Mbandaka about six years
later, he was a robust, husky eight-year-old who could hold his own
in any scuffle, and was also doing well in school! I remember the day
he and his grandma came to say good-bye. She literally knelt before
me on the red-clay floor of the little pagoda outside our house, tears
in her eyes and a basket of papaya and pineapple in her hands. She
thanked the Divine for me and our intervention. I was humbled and
overwhelmed with a sense of unworthiness, compared to this coura-
geous, long-suffering woman. From time to time I would get a letter
from her, handwritten in her broken Lingala. It is I who am grateful.
I shall never forget Mama Anna and little Gaylord.

## *Intrapsychic Loss*

**Intrapsychic loss is the experience of losing
an emotionally important image of oneself,
losing the possibilities of "what might have
been," abandonment of plans or a particular future, the dying of a dream. Although
often related to external experiences, it is
itself an entirely inward experience. An external event may be paralleled by a significant sense of inner loss. What makes such**

> **a loss intrapsychic is that what we lose**
> **exists entirely within the self (Mitchell and**
> **Anderson, 40-41).**

Missioners today deal with intrapsychic loss constantly–on two levels. As we saw earlier, the very meaning of *mission* is being continually reconfigured; e.g., a "foreign" missionary, a "home" missioner, a cross-cultural minister, etc. Then add to this the complexity of being "an individual in the midst of a *personal* transition." Intrapsychic loss involves our self-image, which for many missioners is intimately connected with their role as missioner or minister in a particular context. Sullender refers to this as loss of "some aspect of self":

> **"Self" is defined as an overall sense of**
> **identity or self-image. We all tend to define**
> **ourselves by those ideas, roles, things, and**
> **relationships to which we are emotionally**
> **attached. In a sense then, all losses involve**
> **a loss of some aspect of the self. Yet, in this**
> **category, I want to focus in particular on**
> **those non-physical losses, such as the loss**
> **of status, an opportunity, an anticipated**
> **outcome, or an ideal. These losses can be**
> **very powerful and subtle (Sullender, 12-13).**

Becoming a "self" involves the unique patterning of perceptions and values centered around our lifelong task of creating, sustaining, and actualizing ourselves (see Switzer, 78). Given this understanding of self, we can see how a missioner "without a home" or confused about a sense of purpose, about their "lifelong task," is at risk of a serious crisis of identity and of threat to their sense of self. As we saw when we looked at the dynamics of grief and of reverse culture shock, this perceived threat to self creates anxiety. One missioner writes, reflecting on this part of her process:

> *Probably the biggest intrapsychic loss that I had to*
> *deal with when I got back was the loss of the image*
> *I had had of myself as the wife of the guy I was*
> *engaged to before I left for Africa. I had grieved the*
> *loss to some extent after we broke up, but I had to*
> *come back to the issue on the spiral. . . . I had to*
> *deal with the dying of the dream I had about being*
> *married* (Susan, 1995).

My own case involved several layers of loss which could be called intrapsychic. The robbery of our fledging cooperative/credit union (an "inside job") had triggered within me a significant loss of meaning, purpose, and motivation. I was depleted of energy for several weeks, if not months. At this same time, no doubt connected with my psychological and emotional state, I found myself struggling with issues of intimacy. Confusing and challenging at any time in one's life and in one's own familiar culture, how much more so when compounded by cultural and language differences, loneliness or spiritual desolation.[27] Because of my emotional fatigue and the upheaval in my life at that time, I had asked to leave Zaire for what I thought would be a one-year sabbatical. Once back in the States, I knew that I had some serious "inner work" to do.

### Functional Loss

> **Powerful grief can be evoked when we lose**
> **some of the muscular or neurological func-**
> **tions of the body; we call this functional**
> **loss...Functional loss often carries with it a**
> **loss of autonomy. . . . Gone is the sense that "I**
> **can manage"(Mitchell and Anderson, 41-42).**

Sullender includes this under the category of loss of an aspect of self. It may be that a missioner has experienced an incapacitating illness or accident, literally lost a limb or the function of an organ. One missioner shares, "I had to learn that I am not as physically, spiritually, or mentally strong as I thought I was. I'm not even as good at language learning as I thought I was" (March, 1996). In my own case, in spite of continued preventive quinine derivatives (which have their own lasting side effects), I still had many bouts with malaria. I also contracted a severe case of hepatitis. In addition to the months it took for me to regain my normal strength and energy after the hepatitis, my liver was damaged, and I still experience it as a vulnerable point in my body. I have to be conscious of what I eat, getting enough rest, etc. If not, I feel–as a friend says–"a quiver in my liver," and I have overall reactions . . . headache, nausea, fatigue. It's nothing "serious," I can readily say, which is objectively true. Nonetheless, I have to live with a certain "functional loss."

Sullender also discusses the inevitable losses one encounters as one advances in age. Much has been written about the loss and transition which accompany mid-life changes, for both women and men. There is also some significant study and literature being written concerning the later adult years.[28] To quote just one of many authors in this area: "At mid-life, a part of us is dying and changing. We are no longer who we used to be. A part of us feels dead, and in fact, a part of us is dead. . . . The task is to *discover* and to *grieve over our losses*" (Faucett, 50).

I mention this here in terms of functional loss for missioners in transition because I believe that for many, though certainly not all, the change in mission or the return to one's country of origin often coincides with the transition of mid-life or entering the "golden years." So, while missioners are having to negotiate losses and changes associated with aging, they may also be dealing with the significant separation from all that has been familiar for ten, twenty, or thirty years. This not only involves psychological changes and losses, but these are usually related, as we know, to actual physiological changes and "functional losses." A woman in her fifties may not only be grieving the separation from her adopted home of many years, but she may also be experiencing the physical and

psychological turbulence of menopause. She may be asking herself
those mid-life questions such as, "Is that all there is?" Likewise a
male in his mid-forties will typically pass through a difficult transition of reevaluating his entire life course, as he begins to note
the ache in his back or legs and the decline of his youthful energy.
This can be very threatening to a one's ego and acquired sense of
identity—more so for someone who has prided himself on his virility
and strength, or the miles he could trek through the forest or over
the mountain, as he visited the people of a remote church or parish
territory. One missioner reflects:

> *Many, many times what I expected or predicted
> turned out to be very different. Even things I had
> been taking for granted began to change, and in
> the process, upset many of my plans. One of these
> was my health. I had always enjoyed walking and
> exercising and was proud of my physical fitness.
> Then in March of 1991, I got a sore ankle. I thought
> nothing of it at first, but the pain lingered on. The
> more I tried to exercise it out by walking, the worse
> it became. I tried pain-killers; I tried gout medi-
> cine; I went to see a doctor. Nothing worked.
> With the loss of my ability to walk for exercise, I
> also began to notice myself taking out my anger
> and frustration on others more and more. Then
> I began to apologize for my behavior more and
> more. I didn't like what I was seeing in myself. . . .
> I was becoming discouraged with what I was not
> accomplishing, with others who were not meeting
> my expectations, with life in general. What was
> happening to me? . . .*
>
> *The physical problem I was having with my ankles
> kept on getting worse in the middle of all this,
> compounding what was going on. Sometimes I*

> *would try to hide it, trying to "brave it" through*
> *situations that required a lot of standing (such as*
> *teaching catechists). And a few times I even used*
> *the pain to get sympathy by exaggerating my limp,*
> *so that I could just withdraw and be alone* (Rick,
> 1993).

For those who feel bodily or sometimes mental capacities literally breaking down, compounded with the fact that they had to leave—for whatever reason—the mission they have literally *spent their life for*, mid-life or aging processes can easily cause confusion and grief. As we have seen, the symptoms or emotions involved in "reverse culture shock" are similar or often identical with those of the grieving process.

## *Role Loss*

> **The loss of a specific social role or of one's**
> **accustomed place in a social network is ex-**
> **perienced as role loss. The significance of**
> **role loss to the individual is directly related**
> **to the extent to which one's sense of iden-**
> **tity is linked to the lost role (Mitchell and**
> **Anderson, 42-44).**

Role loss is one of the most applicable and relevant for those in transition. Sullender reminds us that we are continuously changing (intellectually, physically, socially, spiritually, and psychologically), but at certain transition points we become *aware* of *how* we have changed and of the issues involved (see Sullender, 18). Such "transition points" for a missioner can be home visits and furloughs (although these are still temporary "visits" and usually one doesn't have to adjust except to being, as it were, "on vacation"). Even when we must "work" or do mission appeals, we are still fundamentally relating to others in our role of missioner. It is clear. We have a sense of security in who we are and what we do. To others back home, we are something of a celebrity. We are usually introduced as "daughter . . . brother . . . friend . . . the *missionary*, the one who works in . . .".

But in a time of changing mission or job assignments, or definitive re-entry, when we are actually facing the future, or trying to envision a new one, we find ourselves suddenly like a musician without an instrument, no longer clear about who we are and what we can do. For a while, one might be a student, as I myself was, and often enough transitioning missioners have the opportunity for a time of sabbatical or study. Not everyone making a life change has this opportunity. Being a student (especially after ten or twenty years in another cultural context or in the bush or the mountains!) is already a significant change in role–quite a feat in itself, as many a back-to-school missioner knows! We have seen in the previous chapter how often we tend to strongly identify ourselves with the work that we do, our skill set, ministry, our *role*–in the community, the organization, the church, even our family, at times. Often it is this role which defines *who we are*. One young missioner, upon returning from a year of pastoral internship, put it this way:

> *Probably the loss that most hit me on coming back*
> *from Senegal was the loss of a role. I was no lon-*
> *ger an American as before I left, and I wasn't a*
> *Senegalese. Yet I had characteristics of both. At first*
> *I was left without a sense of how to behave in my*
> *society. Now I am struggling to decide who I am–*
> *what values do I hold, and how do I maintain those*
> *values in a society that doesn't easily accept some of*
> *those values? How can I be myself when I don't even*
> *know who I am anymore? Or maybe I never knew,*
> *and I'm just beginning to finally understand. But I*
> *find it very hard to be myself, because it doesn't al-*
> *ways seem to fit what I'm used to. It's like I'm trying*

*on new clothes. I like what they look like on me,
but they feel different from the clothes I'm used to
wearing. So I go back to my old style, but that style
no longer fits, and I feel more uncomfortable and out
of place than I do in the new style. How long does it
take to get used to this new style? What do I have to
do to make it fit* (Mary, 1995).

## Systemic Loss

**To understand it [systemic loss], we must
first recall that human beings usually
belong to some interactional system in
which patterns of behavior develop over
time. Even without a strongly personal
relationship to others in the system, one
may come to count on certain functions
being performed in the system. When those
functions disappear or are not performed,
the system as a whole, as well as its individual members, may experience systemic loss
(Mitchell and Anderson, 44-46).**

In some ways, this loss could entail that of homeland and culture. Culture, it has been said, is a term with a thousand definitions and no definition. One image that I have found helpful is that of a "net" or "web" of common understandings, meanings, or values which reside within a group or society on some conscious or unconscious level, and are expressed in that group or society's structures, symbols, etc. Steve Bevans has defined it simply as "a set of values and meanings that informs a way of life" (*Models*, 7).

Most missioners have learned to live in at least two cultures (sometimes more), which we often call our "home" culture and our "host" culture. If culture is a way of designating the web of value and meaning within these "systems," missioners, then, must learn to function in these different systems of meaning. This is a skill that we must have if we are to survive, and thrive, in our mission countries. Because of it, however, when the time comes to leave or change an assignment, we will inevitably find ourselves experiencing "systemic loss."

How often in our countries of origin do we find ourselves feeling helpless, useless, stupid, or clumsy? We are overwhelmed by the aisles and aisles of choices in the supermarkets. We don't know how to order in a fast-food line, much less online! Sometimes we don't know how to pay for gas–that is, if we're brave enough to take a car out on the multilane freeways! We might know how to maneuver around muddy potholes or stubborn animals, or align tires onto a two-log "bridge"–but cars and busy traffic, well that's another thing all together! We've been in and out of airports and customs; we can manage without running water or electricity. Yet "the Web" or a smart phone can be intimidating, or even paralyzing for some. We find ourselves lost in a complexity of new systems, and begin to long for the security of the challenging ones we had learned to navigate with relative ease.

One missioner's return from Latin American illustrates painfully her sense of systemic loss. She had come to the hard decision that it would be best to leave her "beloved Bolivia" after fifty-two years of service there. She was getting older and felt less able to cope with the changes and new ways of doing ministry, as well as with the difficulties of travel, climate, etc. After a few months in the United States, she was encouraged to take a re-entry workshop, which she did. It was evident that she was struggling with re-adaptation to the country she used to call "home." She wanted to be of service, to be of use to her religious congregation. But the systems involved, however simple or complicated, whether in parish ministry, chaplaincy, even simply visiting the sick–everything seemed to be so different. Just "getting around" (shopping, transportation, leisure activities, etc.) in the United States implies "knowing the system." She didn't "know" the members of her congregation in the United States anymore; her friends were in the communities of Bolivia.

In denial at first, later in a stage of "bargaining," she thought more and more about going back rather than trying to stay in *this* country. What could she possibly do here? She was intimidated by this fast-paced American culture. She hated working with computer technology that she didn't understand. She was trying to know enough to get by–because *that* was a strategy of survival in *this* system. What she really knew had to do with village-based communities and a Latin-American mentality. The teaching and methods she knew were for a different context and language. She simply had no desire to readjust to life in the USA.

*When one is in the process of grieving what one has lost, one cannot invest oneself emotionally in what there might be to gain.* This is precisely why the returned missioner or person in transition *needs time and patience with self* before it's even possible to begin thinking creatively about what one might do or how one's gifts might contribute to society and church in another context.

## Part III: Grief and Transition

> *I had spent almost twenty years as a missionary...*
> *Just returning to the States was enough of a shock.*
> *I had no choice . . . everything had suddenly col-*
> *lapsed. Like some strange quirk of fate, everything*
> *had turned upside down. I felt disowned, a failure.*
> *The only choice I could make was to leave. Yet,*
> *leaving mission life was like cutting away half my*
> *heart, half my life. Death in any form is difficult to*
> *accept. Dying often comes slowly . . . sometimes,*
> *breath by breath* (Tim, 1993).

One of the main components of what is often referred to as "re-entry" or "reverse culture shock" is *grief*. As we noted in Chapter One, transitions involve endings before they lead us into new beginnings. And endings involve leaving, losing, letting go, dying. And as the testimony above reminds us, "death in any form is difficult to accept."

Consider a couple who mutually agree to divorce: the letting go of the other and of "how things used to be" is still not easy. It's a slow and often difficult process. This is equally true of missioners, even when they have voluntarily decided that it is time to move on. Moving on is easier said than done. It involves a certain kind of dying to an old way of life, and oftentimes multiple and complex changes.

The adjustment that caused me the most trouble and grief was the great amount of loss and change I was forced to experience suddenly. The only thing that did not change in my life was a few pieces of clothing and a few articles I brought with me to America. Everything else . . . was either altered or completely lost. Everything: people, relatives, friends, cars, climate . . . nature–Everything! It was almost as if I was (and I believe I was) dealing with thousands of deaths at once, including my own (a young returnee, in Storti, *Coming Home*, 176).

Letting go of the life one has known and lived is one of the most challenging tasks for those in transition. This letting go is, in effect, a sort of dying. But most of us aren't too eager or too well prepared to die. Elizabeth Kübler-Ross, in her seminal study, *On Death and Dying*, found that people go through stages in the dying process (denial, anger, bargaining, depression, acceptance).[29] These might also be considered as stages of the grieving process *after* a loss, as well anticipatory grief when one knows a loss is imminent and begins to grieve *before* the loss. Much has been written in recent years about grief as a necessary response to any significant loss in one's life.

> **Grief is a normal emotional response to significant loss. Grief is universal and inescapable, even when its impact and its existence are denied. . . . It is a composite of powerful emotions assailing us whenever we lose someone or something we value (Mitchell and Anderson, 18).**

When one has lost a loved one, a spouse, good friend, parent, or child—even a beloved pet, one is *expected* to grieve. Family, friends, neighbors, and society in general are sympathetic (if not always empathic) to one's sometimes erratic behavior. Granger Westberg in *Good Grief*, insists, as the title suggests, that grief is not only normal and necessary, but that it is *good* for the bereaved. However, when one is in transition from one mission to another, no one really thinks of them as *grieving* the loss of the mission. Yet one has lost, in a very real sense, everyone and everything that had come to have meaning during X number of years. Of course, as with any loss, its nature and the length and kind of relationships involved will influence the degree of grief experienced and the time necessary for grieving. In fact, there are many variables affecting transition and reentry. The kind of missionary engagement, the time spent, the degree of acculturation to the host culture, all of these will influence the missioner's need to grieve.

This is all the more evident if a family and children are involved. Everyone doesn't grieve nor move "from→through→to . . ." at the same pace nor in the same way. When a spouse or children are in the transition, this can be even more painful and confusing, since we feel we are not on the same page, not aligned as we were in the past, at least in our idealized selective memory of it. On the other hand, being a couple or a family can have its advantages during a time of transition and grieving, since they share common experiences and are an immediate support group.[30]

## *Defining Grief*

> **The most significant affective element [in grief] is anxiety, identical in its dynamics with any acute anxiety attack. . . .The anxiety of grief is an experience of separation from or loss of a significant other, perceived as a threat to the life and integrity of the self" (Switzer, 179-80).**

According to many psychologists, grief is primarily a form of separation anxiety.[31] It is not difficult to understand grief in these terms for missioners in transition, especially given what has been said earlier about the changing identity of mission and missioners today. We might assume that missioners may experience this kind of separation anxiety at least twice, and possibly several times, during their lifetime. First separated from family, friends, country, and culture, missioners have probably done some grief work during their initial adaptation and efforts at acculturation to their mission country. Many attest, however, that the second adaptation, the reverse culture shock, is worse and more difficult than the first.

This could be true for varying reasons: the difference in age and experience, a mellowing of the usual idealism and early fervor of the initial missionary call, or simply the fact that, for the first mission assignment, one is usually somewhat *prepared* for an initial culture shock and the difficulties of adapting to a new environment. (In my own experience, though, the difficulties one *expects* are rarely the most difficult!) One is also highly motivated for the first mission assignments, while one is rarely motivated for the return or even for a change in mission. At best, one's feelings are usually ambivalent under these latter circumstances. And no matter how much one is intellectually prepared for the reverse culture shock or for a life-changing transition, the impact of what is happening often doesn't become real until well after one has left the local mission and has been through some months of initial shock, numbness, and return "euphoria."

Scott Sullender speaks of grief as "a process of . . . 'making real' the fact of the loss." When the griever has been able to do that, to make that loss real, in some way reaching a certain acceptance, then "the new reality no longer hurts" (Sullender, 38). This involves a new kind of "letting go," a living through a time of "liminality," and finally a "moving on" with a new hope and an ability to invest oneself again in new relationships, work, and life in general.[32] Negotiating a transition is essentially "grief work." Grief work actually spans the entire transition of from→through→to . . ., but it is most evident, and most essential, in the beginning, because it is necessary to *name the loss* (and in the case of many, this can be complex and entail multiple losses) in order to begin to let go.

The grieving process, according to Mitchell and Anderson, is "the *intentional work* grief-stricken persons engage in, enabling them to return eventually to full, satisfying lives." Then they add a sentence which I find relevant for us here: "It [the grieving process] can be avoided, though at a very high cost to the one who refuses it" (*All Our Losses*, 19).

I have lived through and seen others live through this process of grief work. Symptoms typically include homesickness (nostalgia for the host country that has become "home"), excessive tiredness and the need to sleep, irritability, episodes of crying, withdrawal, and lack of interest or caring about life. To recognize one's feelings as being symptomatic of reverse culture shock (and of grief ) only adds to one's sense of helplessness or uselessness. Acknowledging these feelings could bring a general sense of confusion, moments of inexplainable sadness, panic or depression, even guilt or shame. In journeying with missioners in transition, first of all, what we need to be aware of is that at the heart of every significant transition is a profound loss (*Whiteheads, Christian Life Patterns*, 37).

I remember the day when I finally accepted the reality of all my losses. My spiritual director had said to me on several occasions, "It's over, JoAnn, it's over." But I hadn't been able to hear or accept that reality until *I was ready*. Once I could say to myself, and to others, with a heavy sigh of relief, "It's over," then—and only then—was I able to begin to remember with joy and celebrate all the years I had spent in Zaire, all the relationships, the ministry, the life, the love. I also remember the poignant words of one companion in a From Mission to Mission workshop when she had finally moved to a new phase in her process. Not with exhilaration, nor with resignation, but with a certain serenity, she said to me as we hugged each other during a ritual celebration, "Yes, there is life after Tanzania."

I believe that often missioners returning home or changing assignments do not allow themselves to grieve for many reasons. First of all, many of them do not recognize that they have suffered significant loss and are experiencing grief. For those who belong to missionary organizations in which "sending" and "being sent" are an ordinary part of the routine, the return or change can be viewed as something more or less customary. There has been much material written on grief and grieving, so our purpose here is not to re-explore that territory. It is rather, as mentioned earlier, to help us relate it (more explicitly than we have seen it done elsewhere), to the reentry or transition process of a missioner.

## *Stages of Grief and Transition*

Usually the most characteristic initial reaction to loss is some form of disbelief, on a spectrum from stupefaction to exhilaration. Different authors call this stage by different names, but they all express a similar phenomenon. Kübler-Ross referred to it as "denial" (38); others call it "shock" (Westberg, Oates); Anderson and Mitchell refer to it as "numbness," which Oates also considers a second phase after the initial shock (see Figure 2.1). Sullender reminds us that, in psychological terms, denial and/or repression is a defense mechanism, and it is one of the most common employed in the grieving process, as it is in the transitional or reentry process.

If we consider the reverse culture shock characteristic of missioners in transition, the initial phase is typically one of euphoria, just as we experienced an initial euphoria when we first arrived in our mission country. Storti calls this stage in the transition the "honeymoon" (*Coming Home*, 57). Do you remember having experienced that? As Larry Lewis puts it, "After the glow of 'everything's new and everything Chinese is wonderful,' which faded after about two months of language study, I knew enough to have an idea of what I didn't know" (Lewis, *Misfit*, 86). Most missioners experience a similar "honeymoon" when they first come home (or when they arrive at a new mission assignment.) It's good to be able to stand under a hot shower or soak in a warm tub! Inevitably, family and friends invite us over and ask what we'd like to eat. I remember just savoring a glass of cold milk! Being asked to speak here and there, people are interested in what we have to share—at least for the first few minutes. Storti has captured this "honeymoon" stage well:

> **This is also the time when you do all the things you've missed doing while you were gone: You go to that favorite restaurant and have your favorite dish; you have a picnic in the park you love; you go to a decent book-store, fabric shop, garden center, or com-puter store and stay for hours just looking; you drink all you want of a favorite drink and eat all the strawberry ice-cream or rainbow trout you can stand; you can't get enough of golfing at your favorite course or working in your garden (*Coming Home*, 57).**

This is often the experience of missioners when they first return on furlough or for a few months home.[33] One veteran missioner in our group was assigned to the States for formation work. He was just exuberant the first few months. He'd say, "Wow, I feel great! Good food, plenty of rest, time to study, a community to pray with . . . Not many guys to worry about . . . This isn't so bad—in fact, it's really a good assignment!" But after a few more weeks went by, we noticed that he gradually began to speak more and more about his former mission. He began to reveal his anger and frustration at being brought back here for a few guys who really didn't need much attention, when he had just begun some important work back where he had been. At that point, he began to throw himself into a serious program of study. Then we heard him beginning to "bargain" with his superiors for time. "I told them I'm just here for two more years, then my time's up. They'd better start looking for someone else, 'cause I'm going back."

I used to return to the States from Zaire every few years, for about three months. I remember feeling like I was on a train all of the time, just sort of gazing out of the window as everything rolled by

me. There were many things that bothered me about this society, but
I didn't have to engage myself in it. I knew I'd be heading back soon,
where I felt I belonged. I let my family and friends pamper me a little,
take care of me. I enjoyed many of the delightful simple things this
life had to offer, including some privacy and time to just be quiet and
really relax. I had left the constant demands and responsibilities of
my ministry behind me for a while.

But when I *really* returned and began to realize that *this time
it's for good*, life began to take on a different color. As Storti puts it:

> **The vacation-like unreality of the first part
> of readjustment will start to fade...By now
> your novelty value has started to wear off;
> people are used to your being back, though
> you are far from used to it. Moreover, people
> expect you to have settled in now and as-
> sume that you are happy being among family
> and friends again. They don't ask you how
> you're doing during this stage—they think
> they know—and more or less leave you to
> your own devices. At a time when you may be
> suffering the most, everyone assumes you're
> fine (*Coming Home*, 59).**

Most researchers agree that the stages involved in the grieving
process are in no way neat and orderly, as the name "stages" might
indicate, and that the emotions described in the stages are all "mixed
up" (Sullender, 55). (See Figure 2.1.) Nevertheless, there seems to
be common agreement that *there is a process*, and these "stages"
sometimes help the griever give a name to an experience that might
otherwise be difficult to articulate. We all know how much it helps
when we read, described in a book, or when someone else puts into
words, "exactly what I've been feeling!"[34]

These stages are very similar to the descriptive phases that we
find in most "re-entry" literature. In many cases, we notice the pattern

"from→through→to . . ." If we consider the process of a missioner in transition, we see phases very similar to those first named by van Gennep in his classic *The Rites of Passages*. A study by Asuncion-Lande, in 1980, also suggests "distinctive patterns of response" to re-entry(Austin "Reentry Stress," 519):

- shock;
- excitement;
- re-establishment or frustration;
- sense of control; and
- re-adaptation.

Storti also describes four stages: leave-taking, honeymoon, reverse culture shock, and re-adjustment (*Coming Home*, 60-65). Jack Sullivan, a Maryknoll missioner, prefers to refer to re-entry as "rediscovery." He speaks simply of a three-stage process: "letting go . . . letting be . . . letting begin" (Sullivan, 30-38). Some of this terminology, while quite true, may be a bit deceptive. As we have already begun to see, this "letting go" is often quite complex and painful. Even more, the "letting be,"or liminal, phase of transition is anything but neutral in the emotional context of the term. It can be the most difficult and confusing part of the process. All of these phases, including "letting begin," involve dynamics of grief and grieving. (See Figure 2.1 on the following page.)

## *The Dynamics of Grief*

As we saw above, Kathy had spent nine years of her life dedicated to working for the people of Brazil. Yet these few words, expressed spontaneously at a sharing session, contain the most common elements or dynamics found during the transition. They are the expression of one missioner's grief, associated with both the experiences in the *past* as well as with her feelings in the *present*. There are perhaps as many expressions of grief as there are people living with losses. Innumerable variables make descriptions of its dynamics very generalized. With missioners, transition adds even more variables of possibility to the kinds and circumstances of losses and subsequent grieving one might experience. Nevertheless, much research has revealed that certain major dynamics seem to characterize most expressions of grief. There is no order or chronology to these, although some may be more obvious signs of grief than others.

### STAGES EXPERIENCED IN THE NORMAL PROCESS OF GRIEF

| ELIZABETH KÜBLER ROSS | WAYNE OATES |
|---|---|
| Denial | Shock |
| Shock | Numbness |
| Anger | Mixed belief and disbelief |
| Bargaining | Depression |
| Depression | Selective memory |
| Acceptance | Commitment to living again |

| MITCHELL AND ANDERSON | GRANGER WESTBURG |
|---|---|
| Numbness | Shock |
| Emptiness, loneliness | Expression of Emotion |
| Anger | Depression, loneliness |
| Fear and anxiety | Somatization |
| Sadness and despair | Panic |
| Guilt and shame | Guilt |
| Somatization[1] | Anger and resentment |
| | Resistance |
| | Hope |
| | Struggle to affirm reality |

Figure 2.1 Comparison of stages of grief according to several authors.

## *Tears and Sorrow*

Tears are perhaps the most easily recognizable sign that a person is grieving, although they could be reflective of several different emotions. They may be tears of regret, anger, or loss and separation. They may also be empathetic tears for the suffering of the people we have left behind. When they are linked with sadness or sorrow, they serve a profoundly necessary and healing function of grieving. Tears, weeping, and wailing are all healthy releases of grief. They literally and psychologically "cleanse the soul," sometimes releasing a storehouse of pain. In some societies, tears are an unacceptable form of behavior, especially for the male gender in Western society (although this is beginning to change slightly as we enter the twenty-first century.) Oftentimes we, especially men, have been schooled not to cry–and certainly not for such "silly" reasons as the leaving of a mission. After all, isn't this just part of our life? But for everyone–those who leave and those who stay behind–leaving hurts, especially if someone has invested a significant amount of energy and/or years into the ministry, having formed significant relationships. It is important to encourage missioners in transition to get in touch with their pain. Sometimes they need to allow themselves to just "cry it out." But I've known missioners who prefer not to say good-bye, sometimes "sneaking away" in order to avoid emotions or emotional scenes. Sooner or later they will find themselves grieving, and let us hope they are accompanied in their grief by others who understand and care.

One of my own experiences may serve as an example. When I left Zaire in the summer of 1992, I thought I would be returning a year later. So I left without bringing closure to my twelve-plus years there. Much would transpire in my life during the following two years, changes and adjustments to country, community, ministry, lifestyle, relationships, and family. These had not allowed me to adequately grieve my separation from Africa, and the life and people I had served and loved. This transition entailed many losses. I think I first began to realize this in the spring of 1994. Civil war had erupted in Rwanda, after the plane crash that killed its president. It was the beginning of what would become one of the world's worst, known genocides: several million Tutsis, as well as hundreds of thousands of Hutus, would be massacred at each other's hands during the next few months. The refugees began to pour into neighboring countries, including Zaire, Tanzania, and Uganda. The crisis would shock the sensibilities of the world and would last for years. The impact of this genocide on Rwandans, Africans, and possibly all nations, would be felt for many generations to come.

Since Zaire was "in the news" for the first time since I had returned two years earlier, quite a few people were asking me about the situation. Some would say things like, "You must be feeling awful about all this" or "Do you know any of those people?" I would answer quite objectively, that this was taking place on the eastern border, while I had worked in the western side. The truth was that I didn't seem to feel anything. I found myself numbed by it. Then one particular evening I was sitting alone in my apartment in front of the television, watching an evening news special on the crisis. As I stared at scenes of slaughtered bodies and mass graves and the people fleeing their homes, I couldn't support it anymore. I suddenly broke into sobs and found myself weeping (and wailing, as do the women at an African wake), until I didn't seem to have any tears or energy left. Finally I was silent, and I just sat there for a long time, alone with my pain.

Later, I reflected that, although I was weeping for them, their pain, the horror of this devastation, I was also weeping for myself. This was perhaps the first time that I had been able to release the pain that was within me. Perhaps it was "survivor guilt" that I was expressing: being so far away, so removed from them and unable to do anything about their situation. I remember that this was the first time I felt like quitting what I was currently doing–"What *was* I doing here anyway?"–and volunteering to go to eastern Africa with some relief organization. But did I want to help, or maybe just run away from my own pain and theirs?

I didn't go. And I gradually came to realize the importance and necessity of that night of wailing. I lived through this time, and that evening's experience eventually led me into a deeper compassion, a deeper sense of suffering and of empathy with others–and with myself.[35]

Before turning to another aspect of the grieving process, I do want to mention that those of us living and working with transitioning missioners need to recognize when someone may be stuck in their pain. When tears become chronic, they may be a warning sign of serious depression, and perhaps more professional care is needed.

## *Stress*

I recall a commentary I once heard on National Public Radio. It was about the burgeoning phenomenon of stress. It's one of those words that has been incorporated, as is, into most languages on the globe. The editor was finding the English word "stress" popping up in the midst of a string of Japanese, Italian, or Swahili communications! His point was that stress means so many things, embraces so many different ideas, that it can fill a gap in any language for "that certain something." Sullender defines it as "a physiological response to a perceived danger or threat" (44). When a person feels threatened, the body prepares itself for what is called "fight or flight," i.e., for action!

> **Adrenalin is pumped into the blood system; muscular tension increases as blood is transferred from other organs to the muscles and the limbs; blood pressure goes up; the heart rate increases; breathing becomes shallow and more rapid; there is an increase of sweating and an improvement in vision; and excess energy is mobilized as glycogen and is converted to sugar (Sullender, 44).**

Sometimes, however, we sense the danger and prepare ourselves for action when there is nothing concrete to do about the perceived threat. Or maybe the fact that one *doesn't know what to do* increases the reaction of stress. It is in this way that individuals find themselves in a chronic state of stress. This state produces "wear and tear," which eventually begins to "break down" into different forms of sickness. Mitchell and Anderson describe this aspect of grief as "somatization." "Headaches, insomnia, loss of appetite, weight loss, fatigue, dizziness, and indigestion, are all common to the experience of grief" (81).

We have much reason to be under stress during a process of transition. We have already described the kinds of disorienting and overwhelming kinds of situations missioners can find ourselves in–including online options and digital technology, in general–when they return from or are discerning change in their life mission. It is not unusual that our psyche feels threatened by this new and unexpected environment. Oftentimes the future is unclear: Where do I go from here? What can I do now? How can I be a contributor to my community, society, church, etc.? How do I (and my family) survive financially? What if I can't adjust? What if I can't find a good job? What if I feel this way for the rest of my life? What if . . .? All this is stressful.

Nevertheless, from the point of view of such a "foreign" cultural perspective, when they have only just come back, plunging into a stress management workshop is probably the last thing they need to deal with. That would probably only increase their stress by making them feel more inadequate and out of sync! So they do need others who accompany them to understand their stressful symptoms–especially when they try to hide them. Those of us who have "been there" and may have picked up some stress management tips along the way, can support and help them as they navigate these uncharted waters *from→through→to→from→through→to→* . . .

## *Anger*

Anything written about grief includes anger as one of its most significant and almost universal dynamics. Anger is a normal and often spontaneous response to loss and separation. It is also an appropriate response to a perceived lack of justice, to feeling misjudged, mistreated, misunderstood, used, abused, neglected, and taken for granted. The list could go on. Most of us probably think of anger as one of those "negative" emotions, and we sometimes try to suppress it. Yet unresolved anger can be a dangerous volcano seething within a person for the rest of their years, while healthy, recognized anger can become a wellspring for healing and growth.

A friend of mine on sabbatical had been struggling with various issues regarding her mission and her presence there: an apparent incompatibility of her missionary vocation with that of her religious congregation, a lack of unity within the pastoral team where she worked, an anticipated lack of continuity when her small, local community left the mission.

Since she had been in the States, she had suffered in greater and lesser degrees from severe neck and back pain, colds and headaches, and even a chronic stomach disorder that doctors had called "ripe for an ulcer." She had been through acupuncture and massage therapy; spent money on x-rays of her esophagus and stomach. She was dealing with lots of ambivalence and confusing emotions. She was depressed and beginning to lose all sense of self-confidence.

She found herself not only unable but unwilling to pray for many months or seek counseling and spiritual direction. When she began to "climb out of the pit," as she described it, she finally was able to recognize the primary cause of it all: she had been *suppressing so much anger* for a long time and only within that past year had been able to get in touch with it.

Anger can be friend or foe, depending on how we approach it and what we do with it. I have heard it said that anger is not a nice nor a gentle friend, but it is a very loyal one. Anger, when it is recognized and expressed in a constructive way, can enable us to move *from→through→to→from→through→to→* . . . It can help us to be assertive and say what we must to whomever we must. It knows when injustice has been committed and raises awareness about it. Anger can help us overcome our fear and take initiative. It can help us seek creative options for the present and future.

But first *we must acknowledge it, own it, and befriend it.* Otherwise, it may become overtly destructive, or turn inward and express itself in another common form or grief; i.e., depression. We mustn't be afraid to share our anger with those we can trust. It will not let us down.

## *Depression*

> *I've been looking into myself, and I am not too*
> *happy with what I see. And that can still get me*
> *very depressed, if I seek the answer in myself,*
> *because I know now that there is no satisfying*
> *answer with myself. But there is hope, even for me*
> (Rick, 1993).

Probably some of us have gone through (and know others who have or are presently going through) periods of genuine depression. According to the standard clinical definition of depression, it is still best understood as "internalized anger" (Sullender, 49). The source of depression can generated from within or triggered from without. In relation to missioners in transition, they often experience the kind of sadness, lack of energy or enthusiasm, sometimes even lack of hope, which is a consequence of significant loss or separation, violence or trauma. This may or may not be clinical depression. It is in any case a state of melancholy which comes from without. Especially during the liminal time, when one is betwixt and between, it is not uncommon for missioners to feel isolated, lonely, and alienated from both others and even themselves, in this new "foreign" context.

According to a hypothesis by clinical psychologist Leroy Aden, alienation is one of the major problems that all humans wrestle with in life.[36] It is a feeling of being "cut off from the world above, below, and around. . . . Loneliness and isolation are not the only manifestations of alienation. The problem appears in other forms, chiefly in a sense of rejection, a sense of hate and disgust, a sense of dependency and self-alienation, and a sense of emptiness and despair" (Aden, 179). Mitchell and Anderson speak of a kind of sadness and despair, which can range from momentary feelings to long periods of prolonged sorrow (80-81). Often it seems to a grieving person that sadness comes in "waves," as does grief itself. These attempts to articulate aspects of the grieving process only confirm what all the literature emphasizes, namely that the signs and stages are all intermingled and not clearly defined one from the other, neither in content nor in chronology.

> **Most grieving people . . . will liken their pain to the rise and fall of waves hitting against the shore. . . . The waves of pain are alternated by lulls of momentary rest. Initially, of course, in acute grief situations, the waves are intense and frequent. Gradually, as one is healed, the waves are less intense, less prolonged, and less frequent (Sullender, 56).**

## Guilt

According to most research, the feeling of guilt also seems to be almost universally present in the grief process.[37] You might be asking why a missioner in transition would have to deal with guilt. Guilt has to do with responsibility—and missioners are some of the most responsible people you'd ever want to know! They are often persons of high ideals and expectations. It's not uncommon, during our life in mission, to let ourselves down, feeling that we have let others down: the local people, our religious community, friends, pastor, superior, co-worker, etc. We feel guilty when we have neglected to do something we should have or done something we shouldn't have. These "shoulds" and "shouldn'ts" can come from laws or norms exterior to ourselves, or *from internalized expectations we have of ourselves.* This latter kind of internal guilt, according to Aden, is the deepest and most important kind. It refers to the inner *gestalt* of the individual, "to the norms and demands of one's 'essential being' . . . to the individual's failure in the moral sphere of self-affirmation." (Aden, 180). One missioner shares about a disagreement with his local assistant:

> *There must be many ways of "losing face" in life. . . . In reprimanding [her], I took away a "good*

*face" . . . perhaps the only "face" she truly liked. I
robbed her of the little treasure she had, and did
not even notice that I had done it. I was that blind!
All she had left was the marred life she knew too
well. When her friends came, several days later . . .
I still did not realize what I had done. It was only
when they said, "Unless you go ask her [to come
back to work], she will never come back," that I
realized: [She] had "lost face" before her friends
because of what I had said.*

*All of my reading about the oriental value of "saving
face," and when I ran into it, head on, I did not even
see it! I missed it completely. In holding so strongly
to my own views of right and wrong, I missed seeing
an even stronger value of these new people. But
rather than admit my wrong, I still held on to my
own convictions. Inside I began to justify my actions
and condemn theirs. A proud, ugly "face" was beginning to rise inside me. I hid it as best I could from
their eyes, but I needed to get away! I got on my
motorcycle and raced off (Tim, 1993).*

Sometimes the very fact of leaving the mission or even *consid-
ering* it, for whatever reasons–including when one is asked to leave–
can, in itself, produce guilt feelings in the missioner. For myself, one
of the most difficult aspects of my own transition was feeling as
though I had abandoned the local people, in particular my Zairean
sister companions in the religious congregation to which I belonged.
I knew how much they loved and respected me. It was hard for me to
think they could feel that I had let them down. I remember imagining
them first getting the news that I wasn't coming back, then learning
that I was leaving the religious community. They would feel shocked,
dismayed, perplexed, deceived, abandoned. In fact, I *had* let them
down. And I couldn't sit down and talk with them about it. Due to

the postal situation, much less phone connections, in the country, I couldn't even be sure that my letters and attempts to explain had reached them. This was well prior to any internet connections. Not only was I dealing with my own loss of these significant relationships, but also with a lack of closure. There seemed to be no way to somehow alleviate my own feelings of guilt, my pain at their pain. "Guilt assumes responsibility" (Sullender, 51).

It is my hope that all missioners, through prayerful reflection on their own experience, will find the grace to forgive themselves the failings–real or imagined–that they're carrying around as excess baggage. Time to let that baggage go.

## Part IV: Trauma and Transition

In Chapter One we mentioned that we live in a world of increasing violence. One loss that is becoming more and more common today is the loss of a sense of safety or of basic trust: trust in other human beings, the environment, oneself, even in the Divine. And a common outcome of having experienced violence is trauma. Often one of the most common experiences of missioners today is that of having been traumatized by violence on some level while in the field. This third type of unfinished business or "unpacked baggage," that of trauma, is becoming increasingly prevalent in today's society.

### *The Nature of Trauma*

Trauma has been defined in many ways. Robert Grant[38] characterizes trauma as involving *overwhelming life experiences which cannot be integrated into one's belief system.* "Events are experienced as traumatic when they overload an individual's capacity to cope with, protect self/others, and make sense of overwhelming experiences" (Grant, *Trauma*, 73). Such events erode what Judith Herman calls "the ordinary systems of care that give people a sense of control, connection, and meaning" (33). The result is often feeling out of control or powerless, alone or alienated, confused and helpless. (As I update this book for its second edition, an immediate example of this kind of trauma is actually taking place all around me. It is the pandemic of 2020, the global outbreak of the novel Corona virus, which causes Covid-19, leading to a degree of sickness and death throughout the world, unprecedented in this century. This pandemic is without doubt an overwhelming stressor: physical, psychological, economic, and for some, even spiritual.) And in the words of Carolyn Osiek, in her short book, *Beyond Anger*, "the only way out is through."[39]

*The concept of "trauma" embraces two distinct but necessarily related aspects, that of the "external" event or stimulus, called a traumatic event or "stressor"* (Doehring, 1), *and that of the "internal" or "intrapsychic" response provoked by the event.* Traumatic events or stressors can also be of two kinds: what Herman calls either "disasters," when the force behind the event is that of nature, or "atrocities," when the force is other human beings (33). Natural disasters are those with which all of us are familiar, such as fire, flood, earthquake, hurricane, etc. People all over the globe on every continent have experienced various kinds of such natural disasters. Missioners working in these areas have not been immune to these.

A friend and former colleague is pastor of a small, rural parish with a largely Hispanic population. A few years ago, a fire broke out in their church building one night, destroying it almost completely. The entire church community was devastated, including its pastor, who at the time was pursuing part-time studies at CTU. He had planned to take a quarter off to go to school full time, but the fire changed his plans. He had to drop out of school altogether for the next two years. Temporarily traumatized and immobilized, he and his parishioners joined together in mourning their loss and seeking a temporary gathering place for worship and other activities. For several months, they shared worship space with another Christian congregation in the town. Then they moved into a makeshift auditorium. They lived in this liminal space physically and psychologically for over two years, as they gradually began to envision their future. Out of this traumatic experience they rebuilt their church: not only a place of worship but a *community* of strength and courage, renewed and deepened in its faith and commitment to be church for one another and for others.

The second kind of traumatic stressor is that which is caused, immediately or ultimately, directly or indirectly, by human beings inflicting harm to other human beings. Examples of such events are ecological disasters caused by humans, such as toxic waste spills, rain forest destruction, chemical and nuclear toxic poisoning, etc. Human disasters include car accidents and plane crashes, due to human negligence, carelessness, or error. What Herman refers to as "atrocities" are the kinds of traumatic stressors, even more devastating on the human psyche; i.e., those which are *purposely* designed and carried out by humans intending to inflict harm on other human beings. This would include war, bombings, shootings, disappearances, murders, massacres, terrorist intimidation, threats, and sexual, domestic, or other forms of physical and psychological abuse. Both Grant and Herman conclude that all such traumatic occurrences can lead to feelings of being unable to cope with reality; and *chronic* exposure to trauma can lead to a sense of losing one's self or identity (Grant, *Trauma*, 73). Given what we have already said about a missioner's sense of identity in today's world, and especially during times of transition in his or her life, this added experience of trauma in the mission field is a factor that needs to be taken seriously by missioners and by all who journey with them during such critical times.

Another aspect of trauma, equally significant, is called "psychic traumatization"; that is, "*intrapsychic* response to an acute or chronic life-threatening traumatic stressor" (Doehring, 1). Simply put, this is the *psychological (and physical in some cases) effects of the traumatic events on the human beings involved.* This vital dimension of trauma is very complex indeed, and in recent years it has received an increasing amount of attention, given how violence, civil war, and natural disasters augment trauma throughout our world and the human community.

While violence may come from without, the experience of trauma is always "subjective." Today when missioners return home, they are often carrying trauma as a part of their internal "unfinished business." While I don't want to exaggerate this point, neither do I believe that we should underestimate the impact that traumatic events may have had on missioners in transition today. (See FMTM's *Manual on Trauma*.) Oftentimes this only complicates what is already a difficult passage in our lives.

## *Post Traumatic Stress Disorder: PTSD*

Many of the kinds of symptoms associated with reverse culture shock (as we saw in Chapter One) are also those connected with what is generally known as Post-Traumatic Stress Disorder, or PTSD. Wilson defines PTSD as "a human reaction to abnormally stressful life experiences, which disrupt the physical and psychological equilibrium of the person" (29). This condition may be recognized by a set of symptoms, often referred to as PTSD, including trouble sleeping, recurring nightmares, withdrawal, feeling helpless, etc. According to the Mayo Clinic website, PTSD symptoms are generally grouped into four types:

1. intrusive memories; e.g., upsetting dreams or nightmares, flashbacks;
2. avoidance; e.g., trying to avoid thinking or talking about the traumatic event, places, or people that remind you of it;
3. negative changes in thinking and mood; e.g., feeling detached from family and friends, a lack of interest in activities you once enjoyed; and
4. changes in physical and emotional reactions; e.g., being easily startled or frightened, or always on guard.

(For more detail on symptoms of PTSD, see MayoClinic.org)

Another excellent resource on PTSD, the American Psychiatric Association, points out an important distinction between symptoms to be *expected* post trauma, and the actual condition diagnosed as PTSD.

**Many people who are exposed to a traumatic event experience symptoms like**

**those described above in the days following the event. For a person to be diagnosed with PTSD, however, symptoms last for more than a month and often persist for months and sometimes years. Many individuals develop symptoms within three months of the trauma, but symptoms may appear later. For people with PTSD, the symptoms cause significant distress or problems functioning. PTSD often occurs with other related conditions, such as depression, substance use, memory problems, and other physical and mental health problems.** (<u>AmericanPsychiatricAssociation.org</u>)

Two other related conditions worth mentioning, which might occur in those who have experienced traumatic events during their time in mission, whether a single overwhelming event or a series of cumulative traumatic experiences, are Acute Stress Disorder and Adjustment Disorder. Their primary distinction is the timing of the onset of symptoms, as well as the duration.

**Acute stress disorder occurs in reaction to a traumatic event, just as PTSD does, and the symptoms are similar. However, the symptoms occur between three days and one month after the event. People with acute stress disorder may relive the trauma, have flashbacks or nightmares, and may feel numb or detached from themselves. These symptoms cause major distress and cause problems in their daily lives. About half of people with acute stress disorder go on to have PTSD. . . . Symptoms of adjustment disorders begin**

**within three months of a stressful event
and last no longer than six months after the
stressor or its consequences have ended.**
(AmericanPsychiatricAssociation.org)

## *Secondary or Vicarious Post-traumatic Stress Reactions*

Today we are aware of the varying degrees and ways in which traumatization has also impacted the life of churches, and in particular
members of Catholic religious congregations of men and women
around the world. At the updating for the second edition of this book,
there is recent research and significant personal testimony which
suggests that religious women, both missionaries from abroad and
even more so those from local native congregations, have been among
those most often abused by priests, especially in developing countries. Transitioning missioners who have been traumatized by their
experiences may have little or no support, or because of their very
experience, they may feel that there is no one with whom to share.
Feeling alone and confused, perhaps dealing with post-traumatic
symptoms, unable to pray, separated from their network of friends
or colleagues, they might begin to withdraw, become depressed, even
begin to use alcohol or other substances, all in an attempt to escape
the pain, the memory, fear, or pervasive anxiety.[40]

Robert Grant's research makes an explicit connection between
trauma and the life of a missioner.

**Being a missionary can be very dangerous. . . .
In certain locations physical hardship, dis-
ease, and frequent exposure to violence are an
inherent part of the missionary package. . . .
Ministry can be peppered with years of direct experience with and exposure to crime,**

**psychological intimidation, military and terrorist threats, kidnappings, armed coercion, torture, mutilation, rape, and murder. Repeated robberies and home invasions by burglars, soldiers, and terrorists are also not uncommon. Similarly, daily conditions characterized by destitution, oppression, disease, and domestic, as well as street violence can wear down the most dedicated of missionaries (Grant *Trauma*, 72).[41]**

Elsewhere Grant writes:

**Senseless and brutal violence can destroy feelings of safety, beliefs in justice, as well as feelings of personal efficacy and faith in humanity. Beliefs in a just God are also seriously threatened. Doubts about mission, vocation and personal sanity are common effects of continual exposure to trauma and injustice (Grant, *Healing*, 148).**

"Vicarious" trauma is possibly most common to missioners who often work with victims of violence, oppression, and exploitation. Those working consistently with traumatized populations in cultures permeated by this kind of violence and oppression often unconsciously absorb the trauma of those with whom they work. Missioners working with oppressed or traumatized populations may tend to become either "over- or under-invested in those with whom they work." In addition to the other symptoms, they may experience guilt and feelings of helplessness or powerlessness in such situations (see Grant, *Healing*, 151-152).

These are common ways of dealing with the situation in order to survive. Have many of us not dealt with cynicism, withdrawal, or dissociation from situations we find beyond our ability to help? On the other hand, those who get over-involved, easily become caregivers, often creating unhealthy relationships of codependency. This can be played out in many ways, from exaggerated financial support to the "adoption" of homeless people or children. This over-investment is often appraised by the general population as emotional imbalance or transgression of appropriate boundaries. In the above example from Kathy, we can see both of these reactions operating.

Another way in which many missioners deal with this vicarious PTS is through activism. Building, or "planting," churches, schools, hospitals, and clinics, starting programs, etc., however well-intentioned they may be, are often ways of coping with trauma. They are, in some cases, well strategized–if often unconscious–defenses to keep us from dealing with the pain, the alienation, the fear, the guilt. If this happens while missioners are still on active duty, how much more difficult for someone who has no more work in which to hide. Again, we often make light of this kind of trauma because the "violence" has not been perpetrated directly or immediately to ourselves. But we may have been traumatized by living–vicariously–the tension, the pain, the agony of the situation and those around us. If missioners are not able to share this distress, or if they neglect the need to do so, plunging themselves quickly into new tasks and positions of responsibility, they may have to pay a high price physically, emotionally, and sometimes financially. Sufferers of PTS are especially vulnerable to times of change and transition, since this heightens their insecurity and need to be on the alert.

All of these secondary post-traumatic stress reactions are in some ways attempts at coping with feelings of anger or powerlessness in the face of situations of violence to our sense of human dignity. Recall also that trauma is not the *only* kind of psychological and physiological disequilibrium a transitioning missioner might be experiencing. Symptoms such as sleep disturbance, inability to focus or concentrate, fits of weeping, withdrawal, or detachment, may also be symptoms of unresolved grief.

Let us hear from a missioner as he writes about his own trauma while living in Latin America.

*I went to sleep that Friday night thinking about the catechism classes that we were going to have on Saturday. I fell into a deep sleep around 10:00 p.m. At midnight precisely (as I looked at the clock on my night stand to see the green glow of the numbers), I was awakened by a sharp noise, an explosion actually, which I thought was fireworks. I said to myself that it was strange to shoot off fireworks at this time of the night, although there were those who stayed out all night at the cantinas who launched some on occasion.*

*But then in rapid succession came more explosions. PA-PA-PA-PA-PA . . . BOOM! I knew it was not a celebration for the fund-raiser of the new home for the aged. That was next Saturday! As the explosions continued, I couldn't believe my ears! I realized these were the sounds of machine-gun fire, grenades, hand-held rockets, who knows what. I got up to look out the window and saw in the darkness above the police station, some flickers of light spitting out of some machine guns. My realization of what was happening was now confirmed. We were being attacked by the guerrillas! But why? What did they want? How many were they? How safe was anybody?*

*I felt so helpless and alone. I was in fact all alone in the rectory, as my cook left around 9:30. She lived back behind the courtyard of the parish compound. I did not stay too close to the window for fear of being detected and to avoid any stray bullets. Thoughts ran through my mind. What do I do? What can I do? Where can I hide? Are they going to come for me? I am a foreigner. What about the people in the pueblo? What about the police?*

*Where are the police? Are they responding—fighting back or in any way resisting?*

*As the outbursts continued, I kept asking myself the same questions. What can I do? Nothing—but pray. So I went back to my bed and began to say the rosary. I don't know how I said it or how many times. But I thought about my cook. I thought about some friends who lived next to the station and others across the street. How were they doing? Every once in a while after an explosion, I heard the scattering of glass and shrapnel on the pavement and rooftops. It made a zinging sound that came floating out of the sky. I didn't see anyone I knew. Not a soul from the pueblo was about. I imagined them hiding in their houses, cowering under their beds. Were the guerrillas entering the houses? What were they doing to the people? Does anyone know we're being attacked? Has anyone called for help? Why are they taking so long to come? Where was the army? How are Blanca, Hernando, Martha, Anna, and the others?*

*Every five, ten minutes—who could tell—I peeped out the window to see if anything had changed. The gunfire had ceased. There was an occasional outburst here and there. Then a few bombs. I felt a chill and put on my clothes and a sweatshirt. What's taking them so long? It was now past 1:00 a.m. No relief yet. I continued to pray. I wondered if they are now taking hostages? I knew from conversations with others that they usually leave the church and priests alone. I took some comfort in that. But I thought about the people. How were they doing? At one point I was going downstairs to*

*check again, for what I don't know, and I noticed
that the patio lights were out. That's strange, I
thought. Lights were on in the rest of the town. I
didn't continue down the stairs. Back in my room.
More prayers. As the night continued, that became
the pattern: Pray . . . look . . . pray . . . look . . .*

*It was around 1:30 when the most powerful ex-
plosion that I've ever experienced hit and rocked
the ground. The whole earth shuddered. What
was that? They're attacking the church, I thought.
Again the sound of glass, metal, and wood came
zinging down and collided with the ground. How
many died with that? I asked. When will this
nightmare end? I put on another sweatshirt. The
minutes slowly ticked by. . . . Finally—was it five
minutes or fifty?—I heard some commotion and
crept to the window to see distant light beams
approaching the town. One truck, then I saw two.
Were they campesinos returning from market? Or
were they police reinforcements? I felt some sense
of relief. But I still didn't feel safe.*

*Looking out again, I saw more people on the street.
It had been quiet now for about half an hour. I noticed some familiar figures standing around in the
midst of soldiers all over the place. The guerrillas
are gone, I thought. The army had finally arrived.
What do I do now? Do I stay here? Do I go out to
see what happened? What would the people want
me to do? As these thoughts continued, inter-
spersed with prayer, drowsiness took hold of me. . . .*

*At daybreak I arose and saw people still milling
about. . . . I readied myself for the day with morning prayer. Blanca, the cook, entered the house*

*before I was finished. She was racing up the stairs, and I met her halfway to let her know that I was all right. Questions were flying. Fears were relieved. Anxieties remained. She had knocked on the back door during the night to see how I was. I never heard her knocking. She was the one who had turned off the patio lights.*

*The police station was gone. The lieutenant in charge, Fabio, was dead. He had been killed in cold blood. One shot to the head. Another in the heart. He had been alone on duty in the station and apparently had tried to hide in the bathroom. He was only nineteen, two years out of high school and just starting his career. Fabio used to go with us on our visits to say Mass in the villages. He was a generous young man. . . .*

*How can one describe the scene? People were everywhere. Soldiers with their various types of hardware roamed the streets. Men, women, and children were looking, talking, asking, wondering. The police station was no more. Only the two side walls and back wall remained. TELECOM was a shell of its former self. Bricks, wood, and steel lay about as if a tornado had ripped them from their places. I saw the spot where Fabio was killed. It looked so ordinary. I saw the bullet holes in the back wall of the station, and the burn marks of a bomb that never exploded. . . . Men pointed out to me where the guerrillas had been hiding in the cafeteros, behind the banana trees and cisterns. . . . With rumors and fears in the air, they were concerned about my safety and thought it best that I not stay in the pueblo overnight. We arranged*

*that I go to the neighboring parish that evening. I*
*returned the next morning for the Sunday masses*
*in our parish. . . . What this experience brought*
*home to me is the reality that many live with every*
*day. There are always reports in the news about*
*this or that town that was attacked by guerrilla*
*groups. But the violence had never touched me*
*until now. Now I knew the terror that the people*
*live with. One feels very vulnerable living through*
*an experience like that. You have no control. You*
*are at the mercy of the aggressor. You feel helpless*
(Joe, 1996).

Though they are many and complex, as we have seen, trauma symptoms are interrelated and tend to cluster into groups. Let's explore some of these symptoms in the light of Joe's experience of the guerrilla attack. We will look briefly at three of them here: *physiological* hyper-arousal (or hyper-vigilance); *cognitive* intrusion (or re-experience), and *emotional* constriction (or numbing.)[42]

*Hyper-arousal* reflects the persistent expectation of ever-present danger. Because of a traumatic experience, such as the guerrilla attack, physical or sexual abuse, torture, terrorist threats, seeing others murdered or disappeared, the missioner's system may go into a state of "permanent alert." This hyper-vigilance is one of the most readily detected symptoms of post-traumatic stress. "The traumatized person startles easily, reacts irritably to small provocations, and sleeps poorly"(Herman, 35). Research shows that traumatized persons suffer both from generalized anxiety and specific fears, reacting strongly to unexpected stimuli, especially specific stimuli associated with the traumatic event. For example, someone who was tortured or threatened through electronic devices may have a fear or a strong reaction to the presence of such devices. One who has lived with bombings and gunfire, like Joe above, may startle at the sound of an overhead plane or the drilling of a manhole in the sidewalk.

*Intrusion* refers to a continual interruption or "intrusion" of the trauma into the life of the traumatized person. "The traumatic moment becomes encoded in an abnormal form of memory, which breaks spontaneously into consciousness, both as flashbacks during waking states and as traumatic nightmares during sleep. . . . Unlike ordinary memories, research shows that traumatic memories (or dreams) return in the form of "vivid sensations and images" (Herman, 37-38). The person seems to relive the moment of trauma over and over again. Another characteristic of intrusion is that the person often feels impelled to reenact the moment of terror, in some ways trying to gain control over it or in some way "integrate" it into one's world of meaning. At the same time, the person also makes great effort to avoid reliving the traumatic experience, because of the distressing emotional effect it has on them (Herman, 41-42).

*Constriction* is the third cluster, referring to a sort of "shut down" of the self-defense system. It is described in terms such as numbing, surrender, disconnectedness, detachment. Some complications from this state of constriction would be recourse to addictive behavior producing a numbing effect. Other symptoms would be withdrawal, alienation, or depression. *Any of these three clusters of symptoms– hyper-arousal, intrusion, and construction–indicates the need for professional help.*

Grant notes, "Many of these behaviors are not only self-destructive, but can also be life-threatening. . . . Without treatment, the more radical symptoms go underground within a few months of the original insult. The costs to health, prayer life, and interpersonal relationships for failing to receive timely treatment are tremendous" (Grant, *Healing*, 154-155). When we recognize symptoms of what might be post-traumatic stress, it is important to encourage and support seeking serious professional counseling. This is not always easy for them to do. It might seem foolish, wasteful, an exaggeration, or weak. There were no counselors and therapists available where I was for twelve years. (We were hard-pressed to find a spiritual director–that is, one who actually had some training or education as such.) And based on my experience with some missionary survivors of trauma, they tend to minimize their traumatic experiences. Remember, missioners are used to "toughing things out" and can be experts at repressing and denying very real needs. Oftentimes, others have no idea what we have lived through.

Those suffering from forms of PTS can easily be judged or misunderstood by others around them. Their behaviors often seem irrational or aggressive. My intention here is precisely to help us all be more aware and better informed about the strong possibilities of various kinds of post-traumatic stress symptoms in the life of missioners, especially those returning or transitioning from turbulent situations. One of the characteristics of traumatization is the *difficulty in expressing it or sharing it with others*. See Herman, 38) Rather, traumatized people re-live their trauma in their thoughts, dreams, and sometimes actions. Earlier we read about the experience of a friend who had witnessed a massacre of youth gathered for a peace rally. He had not been able to share that event with *anyone* since it had happened, over a year prior to his finally telling his group. He let himself cry that night, as he told us what had happened, and we cried with him. Our role at that moment was an important one: to receive his story and embrace his pain.

Some, however, will have the significant role of recommending *professional* help when it is clearly needed. *Today there are many helpful forms of therapy, especially since we know so much more about post-traumatic stress, acute or chronic forms of it, and other types of mental illness and brain disorders.* Three of the most common approaches to treatment are Cognitive Behavioral Therapy (CBT), Dialectical Behavior Therapy (DBT), and Acceptance and Commitment Therapy (ACT). As the field continues to grow, different modalities of therapy continue to emerge. In the fields of health and education, the concept of Trauma Informed Care (TIC) is becoming a standard approach to the well-being and self-care for staff, and to providing better support for those entrusted to our care; e.g., children or patients. For more on each of these and many other forms of therapy for PTSD and other related illnesses, there is much literature accessible on the web, in medical journals, and many other available resources. (See also FMTM's manual, "Trauma.")

In addition to these types of professional therapy, there are also so many ways to improve one's mental and physical well-being, through exercise, massage, meditation, guided imagery, healing affirmations, yoga, and other forms of energy work, such as tai chi or qigong and the Emotional Freedom Technique (EFT, developed by Gary Graig). EFT involves tapping acupressure points connected with meridians or channels of energy in the body. (See TheTappingSolution.com, and Capacitar.org.) Capacitar, an international network of solidarity and empowerment working in over 45 countries in the Americas, Africa, Europe, the Middle East, and Asia. Capacitar is especially committed to communities affected by violence, poverty, and trauma. (For more resources and practical suggestions, see FMTM's website, missiontomission.org. See also healthjourneys.com and Kaiser-Permanente's health website, KP.org.)

It is more and more likely today that missioners returning from their field of ministry will have been traumatized by violence, intimidation, instability, oppression or suppression, exploitation, ongoing situations of terror, etc. They may have been a target of continued threats, or aware of the threats of those with whom they served and lived. They may have been "warned" about the kind of work they do, forbidden to organize groups, or gather for any purpose (except, perhaps, prayer.) This form of stress results from "repeated exposure to events of a traumatic nature, often spanning a period of several years" (Grant, *Healing*, 150). Like Joe, who was awakened at midnight by a guerrilla attack, they have often lived on the brink of danger–for themselves and/or the villagers and townspeople around them. Some have had to flee in the middle of the night, leaving home and belongings. Others have had friends, co-workers, and parishioners "disappear"–which often entails not being able to adequately mourn, as well as trying to be strong for the bereaved. Often we are the confidants of guerrillas and generals, dictators and rebels. Another friend, home from over 20 years in Latin America, was plagued by panic attacks. He finally began to seek therapy, realizing that although he had left the country permeated with a terrorist, guerrilla presence, the terror and trauma of that presence had not left him. How many missioners today have lived through similar and worse kinds of trauma? Often they are coming from countries whose recent histories have been wrought with endless civil and tribal war, or even genocide.

A pitfall of many people of faith is to "spiritualize" their feelings rather than *really experience them*! How many of us have said, or heard said from a missioner filled with pain and anger, "Well, it must be God's will." *So what if my heart is breaking? So what if I'm damned angry at that superior? So what if I've been hurt, betrayed? So what if the people I left are still going to bed hungry and the babies continue to die? So what if I never got to say "good-bye"?* We must attend to those "so whats" if we are to authentically discover the Divine's presence in our experiences. Maybe missioners, like soldiers, have been too well-trained to be good "stoics": "Be tough." "Stay in control." This is not just part of a "spaghetti-Western" movie or a "macho" mentality. It's another very real part of the "missionary myth."

> **Anyone who has ever experienced the pain of grief could hardly be so insensitive as to ask the question concerning the need for healing . The most obvious reason growing out of the feeling of distress is simply that it hurts. It hurts desperately. Agony cries for relief. Normal life is disrupted. There are sharply unpleasant emotions, physiological distress, an inability to think clearly, a sense of the loss of meaning, the inability to perform one's usual job and engage in useful projects, a lack of enjoyment in activities that formerly produced pleasure. No one wants to live this way. We naturally seek healing (Switzer, 182).**

I have heard it suggested that PTSD should not be referred to as a *disorder*, as much as a *condition*; i.e., Post Traumatic Stress

Syndrome, or simply Post-Traumatic Stress: PTS. Statistics indicate
that an increasing number of those *returning from war zones* today
have *readily identifiable* symptoms of post-traumatic stress. And
a majority of returning or transitioning missioners have also been
victims of trauma-producing events in today's increasingly violent
world. *We must be vigilant, alert for the possibility of PTS, in ourselves or those we know.*

## Moving On: Some Concluding Comments

This process of healing and integration does not happen alone or in a
vacuum. Whatever might be the source or the cause of our feelings,
the important thing is that we are able to experience them, name
them, and share them with others who care.[43] Someone in transition,
especially during this liminal "non-space and time," needs a community. Unfortunately, many communities (be they religious, family,
local, governmental, etc.) are not well prepared to welcome returning
or transitioning missioners. Often in religious and other well-mean-
ing organizations, "the prevailing sentiment held by leadership is
that everything will 'work out' in time or as a result of a vacation or
some other type of renewal experience" (Grant, *Healing*, 60). But
often, more than time is needed to heal hurts, unresolved grief, separation anxiety, fear of the future, or the sometimes devastating effects of trauma. Attending a week-end workshop, support group, or
even a six-month sabbatical may be helpful. But one cannot assume
that this is enough. In fact, this could even be the opposite of what is
needed in the beginning. It could give the impression of being "sent
away" by the very community we need for healing and moving on. It
might also imply, to both the transitioner and the welcoming community, that the workshop or seminar will "take care of everything."

*Families and communities need to assure its transitioning and
hurting members that they are consistently supported and affirmed
and cared for in their quest for healing and new meaning.* The community holds the symbols with the power to strengthen communion.

It provides the rituals that dramatize major events, including the crises, gathering and expressing life commitments, and the faith, hope, and love of those who share a common lifestyle and mission. The Divine is with us in this journey. But just as God became completely human, we too must allow ourselves to *know and feel* our experience in its depths, from its most anguished suffering to its most profound joys.

Some lay missioners may have to struggle to find a community to support them. They often are not able to afford even a weekend workshop, let alone a sabbatical. They are forced too quickly by their circumstances to get out, find a job, a place to live, to begin rebuilding their "normal" life again. Financial security is often one of the factors producing added stress. The future is forced upon them before they have time to deal with the present, much less the past. But sooner or later, they too will find themselves still in the interior process of transition, struggling to incorporate their experience into their new normal, and learning to "let it be." The transition *from→through→to→- from→through→to→* . . . will not be denied.

Finally, in an entirely different but relevant context, Carolyn Osiek speaks of this liminal time and space as an "impasse," emphasizing that *"the way out is the way through"*:

**Depression, emptiness, and joylessness are symptomatic of the experience of impasse. There is a sense of having been abandoned: by friends . . . who said they understood; by those to whom one looked for leadership and inspiration; by God. All forms of support previously relied upon seem to have been pulled out. It is a death experience, a dark night, to which all the descriptions of such abandonment and desolation in the spiritual classics are applicable. . . . Is there any way out of this predicament? A**

way must be found, but it can only be found
by remaining in darkness, with the sense
of impasse. As with all suffering, there is
no resolution by dodging or attempting
to deny the pain. The way out is the way
through. . . . In this transforming process,
religious symbols and belief foundations
will inevitably change. The old ways that
were meaningful before the advent of darkness and impasse are dead and cannot be
revived. But eventually they will be re-
placed by new images and symbols, so that
what was once considered loss will begin to
appear as gain (Osiek, 23-24).

In Chapter Three, we will turn to these *transforming "images
and symbols."*

## Chapter Three

# Exploring Images: "In the Desert"[44]

In the Introduction to this book, I described my first close-up encounter with climbers, watching them as they hung suspended, literally "between a rock and a hard place," as the saying goes. It struck me at the time that this image is a fitting one for the life of a missioner, or anyone in transition, particularly when "in-between" jobs, relationships, or mission assignments. It can often feel like one of those climbers: having had to let go of one foothold or handhold, without yet having a secure grip on the one ahead. Sometimes it's hard even to know in which direction to go. The missioner quoted below describes his transition in precisely such terms.

> The image that I had during my time of transition
> to the States was that of being suspended by a rope
> attached somehow to the sky. I didn't know where
> to go or where to land, but was sort of swinging
> back and forth, not knowing where I was heading.
> At first I was anxious and uncomfortable, because
> I was surrounded by people who all had their
> ministry in place, and I envied them. I also felt
> somewhat out of place in the U.S. culture because
> of all the technology: computerized gas fill-ups,

> *computerized offices . . . and the language that all*
> *of this implied . . . I was in Bolivia for ten years and*
> *hadn't fully realized that ten years was a long time*
> *to be away from the fast-paced developments of*
> *U.S. society. I am sure all of this added to my sense*
> *of self, swaying in the wind. I don't think I ever felt*
> *that way before, in such a prolonged state of float-*
> *ing* (Harry, 1997).

Harry felt like a climber "suspended by a rope attached somehow to the sky . . . swinging back and forth . . . swaying in the wind." It's an image that seems to capture well the transitional stage of liminality, the betwixt and betweenness of it, a prolonged state of floating. Even the very term *liminality*, as we noted earlier, is the translation of an image, its Latin root, *limen*, meaning "threshold." A missioner in transition (for that matter anyone in a transitional phase of life) is indeed "standing on the threshold," having left one place behind, not yet having entered another.

This chapter is about those images through which we express ourselves. These images help us interpret our feelings and make sense out of our experience, both that of the past, as well as that of the present. In Chapter Two, I stressed the necessity of getting in touch with the feelings and emotions that are an integral part of our experiences. Now in Chapter Three, I want to show how images are *key* in helping us name those feelings, sometimes expressing what cannot be said in any other way. First I'll briefly discuss what I mean by imagery and how it has been expressed in both spoken language and literature. Then, using actual images of missioners such as Harry, described above, we will discover ways of exploring our own images, first of all in themselves, and then as they relate to the Christian tradition, particularly through images found in scripture. As indicated earlier, in outlining the process developed by Killen and de Beer, I am convinced that exploring our images will lead us into "the heart of the matter"–in this case, into the *heart* of our transition.

## Part I: The Power of Images

> To many people, "metaphor" is merely a
> poetic ornament for illustrating an idea or
> adding rhetorical color to abstract or flat
> language. It appears to have little to do
> with ordinary language until one realizes
> that most ordinary language is composed
> of "dead metaphors," some obvious, such
> as "the arm of the chair" and others less
> obvious, such as "tradition," meaning "to
> hand over or hand down." Most simply, a
> metaphor is seeing one thing as something
> else, pretending "this" is "that" because
> we do not know how to think or talk about
> "this," so we use "that" as a way of saying
> something about it (McFague, 15).

### *A Spontaneous Form of Human Expression*

In our language, we unconsciously use imagery.[45] I have found this to
be true in conversation with others, both in groups or on a one-to-one
basis. Most of us naturally tend to speak in images, especially when
we are describing an event or an experience. "It was like she just
shut the door in my face." "He reads me like a book." "Your talk was
fantastic–you hit it out of the park!" "I'm so excited I could burst!"
"Let's just chill." Our conversations, news media, and all forms of
literature are filled with images and metaphor. McFague would insist
that "metaphorical thinking constitutes the basis of human thought
and language" (15).

From the beginning of this book, I've used images to speak of
transition: journey, mountain climbing, unpacking baggage, crossing cultures, being on the threshold, a burden lifted from our shoul-
ders. And still more intentional are the "missionary images," such

as treasure hunter, migrant worker, etc. But often we don't even recognize the metaphor in the words and expressions we use, because
those words have become commonplace and their meaning is widely
understood. One missioner, Susan, wrote to me recently, "Without
going into a lot of detail, I share with you that when I returned from El
Salvador I was at a very low ebb–physically, emotionally, spiritually."
Perhaps some of us reading her sentence have never seen the ocean,
or, if we have, we may never have experienced the tide at its "ebb."
Still, we know what Susan is talking about because this metaphor
has become a part of our vocabulary.

I point out the spontaneity in our use of imagery and metaphor
to illustrate the important role it plays in integrative reflection. As
we attempt to recall experiences and memories, grapple with loss,
answer unanswered questions, deal with "unfinished business" (another metaphor!), describe often ambivalent feelings of both the past
and present: images will surface. One missioner writes, "Helpless,
insecure, and frustrated, I feel like a bloody stump, a broken mask,
a blind man. . . ." (Tim, 1993). Images are powerful tools. They say
what often cannot be expressed in any other way–particularly since
so many of us have not had parents or educators who were able to
model a creative vocabulary for our emotional experiences.

## Packed with Meaning

When we begin to "unpack" our narrative, moving from experience,
through feelings, to images that, in some way, express both our experience and feelings, we are already in the reflective process of making
meaning out of our experiences. *This "meaning-making" is one of the
essentially human acts.*[46]

> **Images symbolize our experience. They
> capture the totality of our felt response to
> reality in a given situation. That felt re-
> sponse is potent with meaning, but we often**

> **are unaware of it. Indeed, the sensations
> that accompany our felt response in a situ-
> ation embody that unacknowledged mean-
> ing. By symbolizing our experience beyond
> the level of physical sensation in our bod-
> ies, our images move us toward discovering
> their meaning. They direct our awareness
> toward the experience in novel ways (Killen
> and de Beer, 37).**

One of the reasons that images are so helpful in articulating, and especially of interpreting and understanding, our feelings and experiences is that they provide an "alternative" form to our conscious cognitive activity. They emerge from our unconscious. They are the stuff of our dreams and imagination. Images are symbolic, sometimes representing realities that our consciousness is not yet aware of. As we explore their images, we can learn from them about the inner dynamics of our transition, *the inner journey, which is really where the heart of the matter lies.*

> **The geographical pilgrimage is the symbolic
> acting out of an inner journey. The inner
> journey is the interpolation of the meanings
> and signs of the outer pilgrimage. One can
> have one without the other. It is better to
> have both. History would show the fatality
> and doom that would attend on the external
> pilgrimage with no interior spiritual inte-
> gration, a divisive and disintegrated wan-
> dering, without understanding and without
> the fulfillment of any humble inner quest. In
> such pilgrimage, no blessing is found within,
> and the outward journey is cursed with
> alienation (Merton, Mystics, 92-93).[47]**

Missioners in transition need to be concerned about that "inner journey," that "interior spiritual integration." Without it, as Merton intimates, the exterior journey, the outer crossing of continents and cultures, will always be a time of exile in which we are never fully "at home"–neither with self, with others, nor with God. Let us explore, then, some images of people who are in transition, images which emerge from both their outer and inner journey, bridging the conscious and unconscious worlds, between which, perhaps, the greatest of all "cross-cultural" journeys takes place.

I approach these images first of all from a more psychological perspective. We will look at Robert Johnson's *Inner Work* (1986), a very concrete and simple approach to the inner world through both dream work and the work of "active imagination."[48] In a second phase, we will apply some of Johnson's processes by exploring three different missioners' experiences. Finally, as part of one integral process, but making our reflection more explicitly *spiritual*, we will turn to biblical images. Coming from the classic authoritative texts of the Christian tradition, these scriptural experiences and images may serve as prototypes of our own.

## *Unpacking the Images*

In *Inner Work*, Johnson suggests "a four-step approach" to dream work, and a similar approach to the exercise of "active imagination," carefully leading the reader through these processes.[49] While negotiating transition does not depend upon his methods, I would encourage the reader to engage in these distinct kinds of "inner work" if comfortable with it. With the careful use of a guide such as *Inner Work*, and if needed, with the help of a therapist or counselor, the missioner would no doubt benefit from these kinds of exercises.

What I am suggesting here, however, is that some of the different methods that Johnson offers might be helpful in aiding to get in touch with one's feelings and inner dynamics through the exploration of one's images. Images surprise us with their richness and their many-layered aspects of meaning. I'm not talking specifically about dreams, although there is no reason why some important images might not come from dreams. Similarly, I'm not necessarily invoking the use of "active imagination," but there's no reason why those experienced in the ways of meditation and contemplative prayer could not feel comfortable exploring their images through this art form.[50]

What we primarily want to emphasize is that we *be attentive to our images*. When images come to us, they often come from some part of ourselves of which we are usually unaware. In the midst of an unexpected, unwanted, or simply jostling experience of leaving a mission and going to a new place, wherever it be, our conscious minds, our thoughts and memories may be too occupied to pay much attention to unconscious dynamics within. But our unconscious has something to teach us. It wants to help us in our transition, and in one way or another, it *will* be heard. One of its most common ways of expressing itself is through images. Johnson makes the point:

> **This experience, to be sure, is symbolic. The images with whom we interact are symbols, and we encounter them on a symbolic plane of existence. But a magical principle is at work: When we experience the images, *we also directly experience the inner parts of ourselves that are clothed in the images.* This is the power of symbolic experience in the human psyche when it is entered into consciously: Its intensity and its effect on us is often as concrete as a physical experience would be. Its power to realign our attitudes, teach us and change us at deep levels, is much greater than that of external events that we may pass through without noticing (Johnson, 25).**

## Invitation: "Opening Our Baggage"

The first step in approaching Active Imagination is the "invitation" (Johnson, 165-178). It's necessary to "invite" some images to come to us from our deepest self. Taking Kathy's example (Chapter Two), we perceived from her narrative how deeply she *felt with* the women with whom she was working. When I first met Kathy, she was, in her own words, "a mess and so angry," but she would not have been able to articulate it at that time. Perhaps on some level she knew she was angry–but why? At whom? And what was she to do about it? Ordinarily a "helper," for almost a year she kept much to herself, not at all her usual extroverted self. About a year after her arrival at CTU, the first Missioners-in-Transition group was formed. As she gained trust in that group, Kathy began to reveal more and more of her anger and frustration. I recall another night when she briefly mentioned an image that seemed to express how she was feeling, namely, like she was in a "deep pit." We all seemed to resonate with her experience and to understand at some deep level what Kathy was feeling. She had used an image which symbolized something that the group also could relate to.

This moment is a good example of what Johnson is referring to as "invitation" (165). It is something that I have experienced on many different occasions with different groups. ("The more [an image] captures a very particular experience, the more it invites resonance with the experience of others" (Killen and de Beer 40.)) It was over a year later when Kathy was able to share a little more about that image.

> *[In Brazil] powerlessness became very real, so*
> *that I was no longer able to function, even within*
> *myself. The result was a growing depression and a*
> *realization that I needed to move away in order to*
> *see. Returning to the States and beginning to see,*
> *the overriding image that dominated most of my*
> *time during these three years is a deep pit. I was*
> *in the pit, trapped and powerless. I am caught in*

*the pit, almost paralyzed, and there seems to be no
way out (Kathy, 1997).*

## Association: "Examining the Contents"

As we know, a dream may contain persons, objects, situations, colors,
sounds, speech—and each is a distinct *image*. Johnson invites us to
focus on *each image* appearing in the dream or active imagination,
and write out every association we make with each of them. An *association* is a word, idea, mental picture, feeling, or memory—literally
*anything* that spontaneously comes to mind when we sit with the
image. We sort of brainstorm about the image, asking such questions as: "What do I feel or think about it? What or who pops up in
my memory?" (See Johnson, 52-58.) We then record our associations in whatever way we choose. Written notes or recordings are
the most common forms. But as Johnson suggests, some people may
be more comfortable with "dance, playing music, drawing, painting,
sculpting, or speaking the dialogue [with the image] out loud" (163).
In FMTM workshops, missioners are invited to express themselves
through modeling clay or other art forms; others brought to the group
a symbolic object connected with their personal journey. Sometimes
it's something in nature that seems to capture what we were feeling.
After staying with that object for a while, we are invited to share our
associations with that symbolic object: an autumn leaf rich in colors,
a broken reed, a hard stone, a flower; the imagery is rich and powerful.

It is important not to force the process. It happens spontaneously.
What is important is to be open to alternative means of expression
through symbolic images. Let us recall that in our process, the *image*
is often the best way—and sometimes the only way—in which we can
express our *feeling*.[51] In making associations, Johnson counsels us
not to discount "colloquialisms." For example, the color "blue" in an
image might be associated with the colloquialism, "I've got the blues"
(Johnson, 55) or "once in a blue moon." Songs are often full of images,
hovering in our unconscious, or just beneath the surface; e.g., "Blue

Moon, you saw me standing alone. . . ." or, "I guess that's why they call
it the blues. . . ." But there's also, "Blue skies shining on me!"

We can see how the meaning of an image is very personal, depending upon one's experience and associations. In Kathy's image, a
colloquialism that she might associate with it is "the pits" meaning
"as bad as it gets." Or perhaps the image might call to mind the word
"*pitiful*." Though originally pitiful meant "full of pity," or something
fully worthy of pity, it is now commonly used to describe something
as quite bad, awful, and sad, in addition to deserving our pity. This
kind of exercise; i.e., making associations, is actually a creative way
of analyzing the image, of exploring it in order to find out more about
it. Every image can have many layers of meaning, involving a sort of
"archaeological dig," and each layer tells us something more about
ourselves and our transition.

## Inner Dynamics: "A Closer Look"

This leads us to another step in Johnson's approach: exploring
"inner dynamics," which he defines as "anything that goes on inside you, any energy system that lives and acts from within you . . .
It may be an emotional event, such as a surge of anger. It may be an
inner conflict, an inner personality acting through you, a feeling, an
attitude, a mood" (Johnson, 65). Images that surface symbolically
represent something going on inside of us. In a certain sense they
have *already given a name* to some inner dynamic. Let us remind
ourselves that the point of this kind of inner work is to "build consciousness" . . . to gain insight into the conflicts and challenges
that our life presents . . . to discover and draw on our own inner resources (Johnson, 13). At the same time, as Killen and de Beer point
out, "the image helps us avoid distanced analysis of our experience
that disguises premature interpretations of it" (39). We attempt to
discover the quality, emotion, movement, inner person, or "space"
within us that relates to a dominant image. This is a unique way of
moving toward a greater awareness or consciousness of the "why"

of our feelings or behavior, and in turn gaining insight as to how to interpret and deal with them, beginning to have a sense of where to go from here.

## Part II: Images and Our Experience

We will now "unpack" three different pieces of "baggage" by reflecting on some concrete images which missioners have shared. Our reflections have three different focus points: (1) A Personal Narrative, (2) A Cultural Text, and (3) A Scriptural Text. Regardless of these points, however, each reflection *ultimately begins in one's experience*.

## 1. Beginning with a Personal Narrative: "Unpacking Kathy's Images"[52]

Earlier we heard Kathy's narration of her experience, and the images that enabled her to put that experience into words: *Powerlessness . . . moving away . . . trapped . . . almost paralyzed . . . no way out. . . .* Another important image is that of "many forces coming down on me." Then there is Kathy's "overriding image" of *THE PIT*. This primary image is what McFague calls a "model," i.e., "a dominant metaphor or a metaphor with staying power (23). "I am caught in *A DEEP PIT.* . . ."

Kathy herself has already made some associations with being "caught in a deep pit." Let's elaborate on those with a few associations of our own. *Caught*. What do you associate with being caught? Words and images that come to me are *trapped, on a hook, possessed, powerless, held, not free, on a trapeze, caught in mid-air, risk, flying, caught in the wind, caught up within myself, with someone else, with others*. Now, imagine yourself in *a deep pit*. What images and words emerge? *Dark, down, narrow, endless, bottomless, alone, afraid, unable to move, unable to escape, unable to see the light, unfree*. A deep pit could be *a well, a hole, a crater, a cell, a jail, a tunnel, black, dark, damp, dry, empty. . . .*

Kathy also speaks of "many forces" coming down on her. With what do you associate many "forces"? What might they represent? *Weight, heavy, burdensome, holding you down, pinning you down, enemies, powerful, armed forces, weapons, soldiers, war. . . .* What inner dynamics might Kathy associate with her images? Questions we might ask are, "What traits do I have in common with this image?" Or, "What is going on inside of me?" For example: Where am I in a deep pit? What is the deep pit within me? How am I caught? Who is holding me? What is trapping me? etc.

In her journeying with our group and with counseling and spiritual direction, Kathy identified one major dynamic going on within her, represented by her image. *It was her powerless in the "deep pit" that helped her to realize that she was depressed.* She gradually recognized that she was cutting herself off more and more from others, closing herself in, allowing herself to dig deeper and deeper into that "pit," becoming more and more depressed, alone, angry, frustrated. The deeper she dug her hole, the less able she was to move, becoming less and less free, not knowing which way to turn. It was getting lonely and dark.

Trapped, Kathy felt like a fragile animal: at first hurting, withdrawn, afraid, then becoming more and more angry, aggressively lashing out at anyone near. She was feeling utterly helpless, powerless at the bottom of that pit, as she says, "unable to function . . . almost paralyzed, and there seems to be no way out." Again, Kathy recognized her depression through *attending to the image.* She later shared that she had finally found "the courage to enter the pit and find myself there, to feel again and to recognize the forces that I felt were keeping me powerless and in the dark." At some point in relating some of this transitional experience, Kathy said, "God did not seem helpful to me during this time because the only image I had was Jesus, sympathetic, but also powerless with me in the face of all these forces."

Our inner dynamics also have to do with our belief systems, attitudes, and values, our positions toward life and others. What might this image be telling us about these? If we think back to Kathy's experience with the woman from her *favella*, we might sense that in some way her own beliefs and values were being smothered or compromised in the way she was living. She was paralyzed, and remained so, without a clue as to how to break loose from the system she was stuck in.

We can approach the image by asking deep spiritual or existential questions: What is existence like *within* the image? What is *broken and sorrowing* in the image? What is dying, being born, or healed?" (See Killen and de Beer, 88.) Different questions and explorations of the images will depend on where each person is in their transition. The important thing is to allow the image to lead us deeper into ourselves through our experience. "By entering the space of the image, we open ourselves to new insight, to new learning, to being changed, and potentially to revelation" (Killen and de Beer, 41).

## 2. Beginning with a Cultural Text: Unpacking Silence[53]

Another good source or place to begin theological reflection is with culture.[54] A "cultural text" could be a work of art, music, film, literature, or similar sorts of communication media. Other expressions of cultural texts might include artifacts: objects of art, clothing, jewelry–or simply objects possessing symbolic value; e.g., a stone, a photograph, etc. Virtually anything that expresses any aspect of a given culture can be considered a "cultural text."[55] Then, as with images, the reflection proceeds to explore experiences, feelings, and images associated with that text. I've often used films and novels that represent a cross-cultural context of mission experience. The position of the author or narrator, the setting, the characters, the theme, etc., which express various cultural and/or religious points of view, these can be a particularly good way of helping missioners vicariously get in touch with their experiences and feelings. The images in a novel, short story, or film sometimes express better than we can, our own feelings from our past mission experience, as well as our frequent ambivalence in the midst of transition.[56]

One powerful example of this kind of reflection comes to us from Shusako Endo's haunting novel, *Silence*.[57] We read *Silence* in several of the transition and re-entry groups of which I've been a part, and it never fails to both "move and disturb" with its probing theological questions and its, at times, overwhelming images. Quite a number of missioners have found it a rich source for an even deeper reflection on their own missionary journey and their understanding of mission.

The novel is based on the 17th century persecution of Christians in Japan, during which there was a brutal effort to exterminate Christianity–and every Christian–from the country. Many Christians, including some missionaries, went underground. Many were cruelly tortured and executed. Some apostatized and lived. *Silence* is about a Jesuit named Sebastian Rodrigues, who left Portugal for Japan to carry on the underground ministry. Perhaps he went especially with the hope of refuting the apostasy of his former teacher and provincial, Christovao Ferreira. If not, perhaps by going, Rodrigues himself would atone for it. David Bosch summarizes:

> **Eventually Rodrigues, too, was captured and tortured. And much of Endo's novel deals with his ordeal and his refusal to renounce the faith. For many months he refused. All along he prayed fervently, prayed to God for guidance, for a clear direction to go. But there was only silence, as though God did not hear him, or was dead and did not exist. Then, one evening, the interpreter said confidently, "Tonight you will certainly apostatize." To Rodrigues this sounded like the words addressed to Peter: "Tonight, before the cock crows, you will deny me thrice"(Endo, 263). . . . Then Ferreira explained why he himself had apostatized. It was not because of being suspended in the pit, he said, but**

**because "I was put in here and hear the voices of those people for whom God did nothing. God did not do a single thing. I prayed with all my strength; but God did nothing." (Endo 265). . . . It was this silence of God that has given Endo's novel its title–the silence of a God, a Christ, who did not respond to prayers or to torture. Still, in the end, the silence was broken. Christ did speak to Rodrigues–not, however, the beautiful, haloed, and serene Christ of his devotions, but the Christ of the twisted and dented *fumie*,[58] the Christ whose face had been distorted by many feet, the concave, ugly Christ, the trampled-upon and suffering Christ (Bosch "The Vulnerability of Mission," 74).**

Endo's *Silence* is itself a reflection on images, not only the image of the trampled, crucified Christ, but of countless other images which fill the pages of the novel, images of God, faith, suffering, and death: persecuted Christians "hanging in the pit"; Ferreira, the former Jesuit provincial, now "the honorable Sawano," clean-shaven, pig-tailed, and dressed in a black Japanese kimono; the apostate and traitor, Kichijiro, "thin and dirty like the tattered rags he wore" (Endo, 189); the moaning of the peasants of Tomogi, Mokichi and Ichizo, hanging from their stakes at the edge of the dark, pounding sea (Endo, 100-102), and so many more.

As an example of how a cultural text can be the beginning of the process of theological reflection, following are excerpts from two missioners' reflections on *Silence*:

> *During my mission in Kenya, there were times when I came in contact with tremendous suffering, the suffering of the poor, and the seeming silence of God.*

> *I recall the day when I watched helplessly, with fear
> and dismay, as uniformed men trampled on the veg-
> etables of the poor street vendors in Nairobi. These
> vendors, who had no other means of livelihood, had
> taken their produce to the streets. This was illegal,
> and they paid for it. Those who were caught were
> thrown into prison, and all of them—hundreds of
> them—lost all of their belongings. . . .*
>
> *The novel by Endo paints once again for me a
> vivid picture of human pain and the reality of
> evil. . . . When I recall the image of those two men,
> Mokichi and Ichizo, hanging there on the beach to
> be overpowered by the stormy waters, I marvel at
> the human capacity to inflict pain on others. . . . It
> is this haunting sense of apparent abandonment
> by God which gives the novel its powerful and eerie
> atmosphere. I sometimes saw the "silence of God"
> as something I could not fathom. . . I wondered,
> "What does one do?"*
>
> *In Endo's novel, the dilemma is evident. "What is
> the purpose of being a missionary among suffer-
> ing people?". . . . I am reminded that when the
> situation is charged with human suffering, there
> is a greater opportunity to relinquish false power
> and a false sense of security. . . . We are called to
> accompany the suffering Christ in his brothers and
> sisters. While immersed in the adversity and hard-
> ships that can be an inescapable part of life, we are
> challenged to remain hopeful, trusting that God's
> is the final victory (Kate, 1995).*

Another missioner, using *Silence* as a starting point, finds himself connecting three "protagonists": Rodrigues (*Silence*), the "Rich
Fool" (Luke 12:16-21), and himself:

*In Luke's passage, God zaps the "rich man" right between the eyes: "You fool, this night your life will be demanded of you; and the things you have prepared, to whom will they belong?" (Luke 12:20). And who is the a "fool"? Because he only thought of himself and what he wanted to keep for himself. He had his own expectations. And Shusaku Endo tries to pierce the bubble of his protagonist's expectations just as directly. One moment Rodrigues is filled with feelings of happiness and self-worth; the next moment he's running for his life. . . . I find his reaction very understandable, because I was doing the same thing in my life. I was becoming discouraged with myself, with what I was not accomplishing, with others who were not meeting my expectations, with life in general. . . . Though the life situation was changing all around me, I still wanted to hang on to my own expectations, and to what little sense of peace and security I had left. So does Rodrigues. . . . So did the "rich fool". . . . But foolish, too, Rodrigues, and foolish me! The signs that our worlds are about to fall apart are all there. Yet we fail to recognize them. . . .*

*As I write this now, the temptation is just to forget the whole thing. I've been stuck in the same groove for so long that it has become a kind of rut. But it's my rut and I know it well. . . . I can hear God calling me, "You fool!," trying to get through to me. . . . Part of me wants to pretend I'm deaf, and another part of me knows that I can't. I thought I had life figured out reasonably well, but I know I was "fooling" myself. It's time for me to listen. I have to listen and respond if I want to live more fully (Terry, 1993).*

### *3. Beginning with Tradition:*
   *Unpacking Exodus 40:34-38*

Sometimes a scriptural text itself or a particular aspect of one's religious *tradition* generates images, and this begins the theological
reflection on our experience.59 My own transition bears this out.
Just as Anne's experience, which we will describe in more detail later,
speaks of her re-discovery of freedom through her long trek across
the desert, I also spent several years wandering in a sort of "desert
experience." In particular, during my first year back from Zaire, I
was wrestling with the obstacles of my own resistance. It was indeed
a liminal time, a space of confusion, murmuring, and tears. It was
a period of waiting and wondering where God was leading me. But
through it all, I somehow did not doubt that *the Divine was leading
me somewhere–though I did not know where and I did not know the
way.* As hard as it was, there were also many consoling "signs" of the
Divine's presence guiding me at that time. I am aware, however, and
I would caution, that this consolation is not necessarily experienced
during times of transition. Recall that Kathy seemed to lose all hope
in God during her first two years of transition. Not unlike the Jesuit,
Ferreira, in Endo's novel, Kathy was so angry at this God who seemed
as powerless as she felt in her deep pit.

   For me, however, although it did not take away the painfulness or
confusion, I believed that God was with me in that journey through
the desert. This became explicit for me one day through a particular
passage from Exodus. It was simply part of some reading I was doing
for a class at the time. But as I read this excerpt, it was as though
I had never heard or read it before. I believe that my own *explicitly
theological* reflection upon my experience in transition began with
this passage from Exodus.

> *Then the cloud covered the meeting tent, and the
> glory of the Lord filled the Dwelling... Whenever
> the cloud rose from the Dwelling, the Israelites
> would set out on their journey. But if the cloud did*

*not lift, they would not go forward; only when it lifted did they go forward. In the daytime the cloud of the Lord was seen over the Dwelling; whereas at night, fire was seen in the cloud by the whole house of Israel in all the stages of their journey* (Exod 40:34-38).

It was not the historicity nor the theology which struck me.[60] Rather *it was the image* it contained that later would sustain me "in all the stages" of my own journey. It seemed clear that in the midst of my own "desert wilderness," God was present in the cloud that seemed to hover over me. In this sense, it was an ambiguous image for me. It seemed that as long as "the cloud did not lift," I could not go forward. I had to remain in this state of liminality, of discernment, waiting–until the time when I could move on in my journey. On the other hand, humbled, I felt that *God was in that cloud*, at times *overshadowing me* as it did God's Dwelling Tent in the desert.[61]

There were times when I seemed to be making "progress," and other times I seemed to be moving in circles, or just not moving at all. I learned, in the desert, to be patient and wait for God to show me the way. This passage seemed to make explicit for me what I was experiencing in faith. There were even rare moments when I seemed to be privileged to be in "the Meeting Tent," in dialogue with God. In its "homely character it was more like 'a chat' but without the 'dramatic frills' and 'emotional thrills' of the theophanies of Mt. Sinai. (Terrien, 178). As for myself, I too was sometimes "complaining," sometimes asking, "Your ways, O Lord, make known to me, teach me your paths" (Ps 25:4). Mostly I kept hearing God ask me to be patient and learn to wait: "Be still, and know that I am **God**" (Ps 46:11). Not only that "I am God," but especially that "**I** am God."

Finally, as I mentioned earlier, after being in this wilderness for about a year, the moment came when "the cloud lifted" and I knew which route I had to take. It was actually a hard revelation, not one I had expected or wanted. But only then, I recognized, would I continue into another stage of my journey. It was this scriptural image which enabled me to take some distance from my own experience, reflect upon it, while at the same time live through it, and gain wisdom and insight from the lived experience of others before me.

## Part III: Images in Dialogue with Tradition

> *I came having crossed over the Red Sea into the wilderness, the desert of having almost nothing left–no path, just endless shifting sands (Anne, 1997).*

I am convinced that all authentic spiritual reflection grows out of life "Experience," in that broad sense with which we have defined it (i.e., with a capital "E"). "Experience" is the "raw material" of one's life: the interaction and influence of *one's lived narrative*–(experiences with a small "e"), with one's *culture, religious tradition*, and *standpoints* in life. This why a theological reflection on the world of Experience may have different starting points, "taking off," as it were, from different runways.[62] All of these reflections nevertheless contain the same basic elements which are part of the process of theological reflection (i.e., narration of a situation or event, attending to feelings, exploring images, discovering the heart of the matter, seeking insight)–and all of this in the context of a dialogue with Tradition (see Fig. 3.1). Our reflection becomes theological when we use questions arising from themes in our heritage to explore an image that emerges from our experience" (Killen and de Beer, 42).

One's Lived Narrative        <--------->        A People's Lived Narrative
(personal experiences)        <--------->        (collective experiences)
One's Culture(s)        <--------->        Cultural Context

EXPERIENCE -> IMAGE->    <- DIALOGUE -> <-IMAGE <- TRADITION

One's Tradition(s)        <--------->        Traditional Context
One's Horizon        <--------->        A People's Horizon
(personal stance, beliefs, positions) <-------> (common stance, beliefs, positions)

**Figure 3.1. Dialogue: experience, images, and tradition (see Killen and de Beer)**

Throughout the process, we are always conscious of permeable walls along the way, through which flow a continuous dialogue between our Experience and the tradition. This religious tradition, while an element within one's individual life Experience, is also far greater than that, embodying the experience of God's people through time and history. It is vital to *consciously and explicitly* invite our spiritual tradition into our process, seeking its wisdom, even as we bring to the dialogue the wisdom of our own personal Experience.

Although we might draw on any number of sources from our tradition for this valuable aspect of our theological reflection (e.g., art, music, poetry, literature[63]), our focus here is primarily on sacred scripture. In my experience, and that of most of the people with whom I have worked, a scriptural image often tends to be a significant and dominant metaphor during times of crisis, grief, or other kinds of life-changing transitions. In addition to the examples above, another missioner wrote:

> *After a nervous breakdown (some today might call it a severe case of "burn-out") and needing to come home, I took time off for rest, counseling, and healing. . . . As the end of that year was approaching, I needed to make a DECISION: Either to stay home or to go back. The decision came one day unexpectedly, like a volcanic eruption!*

> *After months of hesitation, now suddenly there was no doubt. I wanted to go back! It was a surprise. It was a gift. What came to my mind was the image of Abraham being willing to sacrifice his only son Isaac (Gen 22:1-19). It seemed to me that I was called to sacrifice my "Isaac"–to throw reason to the winds and to trust God. . . . Abraham named the place, "The Lord provides"* (Ed, 1997).

## *Scripture as a "Classic Text"*

Perhaps spiritual images arise spontaneously for missioners because often they are persons of prayer, steeped in a religious tradition and other forms of spirituality. Many a missionary kid or an aspiring religious or priest has grown up with biblical images. They have often been assimilated and have found a place in the unconscious, if not conscious memory. As I consider the second edition of this book, I am aware that for some today, other sources may be personally rich and meaningful, such as classic or modern poetry, or perhaps musical lyrics. That said, sacred scripture (from any of the great religions) is generally regarded as the "classic text" of that particular tradition. As such, it has intrinsic authority.

> **The fundamental model was first worked out and decisively appropriated in the Old Testament. That model was reaffirmed, restated, and reintegrated in Jesus. Christian faith is faith which relates itself to this classic model. The God in whom Christians believe is the God who was known in the Bible; the Jesus in whom they believe is the Jesus of the New Testament (see McFague, 54-61).**

At the same time in speaking of the Bible as a classic text, McFague also demonstrates that it is "the *poetic* classic of Christianity," by which she means to emphasize that "the essence of a great poetic text is that through its particular images it does speak universally, but in a way that is open to diverse rather than fixed interpretations" (McFague, 60-61). In this regard, it is interesting to note that Robert Johnson, in *Inner Work*, suggests that one of the ways for finding associations to dream images is what he calls "*archetypal amplification . . .* a process of gathering information about the archetypes that appear in our dreams by going to sources such as myths, fairy tales, and ancient religious traditions" (59-60).

Part of our dialogue with the tradition follows a similar process; i.e., gathering more information about our own images by going to the Bible as a source and model for interpreting our experience as "theological"–that is, in some way, directly or indirectly, related to the Divine. We turn to scripture in order to seek out *prototypes*, as it were, for our own mission and transition experiences and feelings, trying to interpret, gain insight, and deepen our understanding in the light of the experiences of our ancestors, and the biblical interpretation of them. The Bible, as a "Christian classic," gives shape to many dimensions of Christian experience and understanding of God; and as a "poetic classic," it has, as does any great work of art or literature, an enduring and universal power to move and even transform the hearer or reader (McFague, 61).

## Scripture and Metaphor

Another reason why sacred scriptures are a primary source of dialogue with our tradition is that it is so *rich in metaphor*. For all the religious traditions, such as Hinduism or Islam, I would suggest that it is much the same. According to McFague, if the Bible has a "reforming and revolutionary power" (McFague, 63), much of that power comes from its metaphorical nature. It is not difficult for those who are familiar with the Bible to think readily of dozens of examples of metaphorical language. The parables found primarily in the New Testament gospel accounts are classic examples of different types of metaphor: "The kingdom of heaven is like . . ." (Matt 13:24, 31, 33). "A sower went out to sow . . ." (Matt 13:3-9). Then there is the gospel according to John, with its rich symbolism and metaphor: "The light shines in the darkness, and the darkness has not overcome it." (John 1:5); "I am the Good Shepherd . . ." (John 10:11); "I am the way, and the truth, and the life . . ." (John 14:6), and so on. The Old (or First) Testament is also rich in metaphor:

> *Woe to the shepherds who mislead and scatter the*
> *flock of my pasture, says the Lord. . . . You have*
> *scattered my sheep and driven them away. . . . I*
> *myself will gather the remnant of my flock from all*
> *the lands. . . . I will raise up a righteous shoot to*
> *David; as king he shall reign and govern wisely. . . .*
> *This is the name they give him: "The Lord our*
> *justice" (Jer 23:1-6).*

Peter W. Macky's theory is that biblical writers used much metaphor because it is the language form that best enabled them to communicate their "central purposes":

> **It is likely that the ultimate purpose the**
> **biblical writers had was usually relational,**
> **to serve as mediators enhancing the rela-**
> **tionship between God and their hearers.**
> **As a means to that end, the writers often**
> **used dynamic speech, seeking to illumi-**
> **nate hearers' minds (pedagogical), to move**
> **hearers' hearts (affective), and so bring**
> **them to commit themselves to becoming**
> **God's children, servants and friends (trans-**
> **forming). And as a further means, one that**
> **could draw hearers on a journey of dis-**
> **covery, the writers often used exploratory**
> **speech, evoking wonder and a desire to**
> **know better, thereby stimulating readers to**
> **take the narrow path that leads down into**
> **the depths (Macky, 248).**

Macky maintains that "metaphors, especially concrete ones," are very often the most effective way to practice these three types of "speech-acts"; i.e., relational, dynamic, and exploratory, "which are the most profound of all the biblical writers' purposes for speaking"

(Macky, 17). This is why, for our part in this process of reflection, we are interested in biblical metaphor. It goes far beyond the cognitive and informative purposes of speech, or even its affective purposes; e.g., the arousal of the emotions. Metaphor has the power to reach deep into the human heart and "to illuminate darkness, solving puzzles so the hearer responds, 'Oh, now I see!' . . . to change hearers' attitudes, values, and commitments" (Macky, 16).

## *Creative Imagining and Scriptural Metaphors*

Probably the most relevant dimension of metaphor for our purposes is its "exploratory" potential. This "mental exploring" is done by "presenting an experience of some kind and inviting hearers (usually implicitly) to explore imaginatively how their own experience may be illuminated by the one presented" (Macky, 16-17). This is the invitation to which I hope those in transition will respond: to use their imagination and seek the kinds of experiences and images that may illuminate their own experiences, interior movements, and images. This can be done through a form of participant knowing, which Macky calls "re-creative [or creative] imagining"; i.e., "the process of hearing a word or phrase or description and re-creating what probably was being imagined by the speaker" (Macky, 11).[64] For example, when Matthew has Jesus saying, "Come to me, all you who labor and are burdened, and I will give you rest" (Matt 11:28), Matthew was inviting his hearers to take their experience of bearing a heavy load, of being weary from hard work, and re-create for themselves what he was picturing (see Macky, 11-12).

Macky's insight into the metaphorical nature of biblical language sheds some helpful light on our process. I have found it helpful for us to enter into a sort of "encounter" with scriptural images, experiences, personages, or themes, which somehow connect with our own transitional process. (It doesn't matter whether the image is related to a moment in the past, present, or imagined future; to organize or "categorize" our associations in this way would be too analytical at this stage. That kind of organization will happen naturally, when we begin to interpret our experiences, feelings, and images in search of "the heart of the matter," or an organizing principle or theme for our personal journey.)

All we want to do at this point is allow free-flowing associations between our lives and the lives of our ancestors in faith; i.e., both the characters and the writers of the text. I hope that those in the midst of transition can enter simply into a "conversation" with the text, a creative dialogue between the writer (in his or her personal, historical context), the text (in its context), and the reader (in their personal, historical, liminal context). With the help of modern biblical criticism,[65] a simple process of biblical theological reflection might be readily accessible to those struggling within the mysterious context of a certain "rite of passage"; i.e., their own transition.

## Part IV: Dialogue Initiated by Personal Images

As noted earlier, one may begin our reflection from different *starting points or sources*; i.e., beginning with a personal narrative, a text from tradition (e.g., Exodus) or from culture (e.g., *Silence*). My main purpose in this chapter is to illustrate how *we may explore personal images in dialogue with scriptural images*. This, of course, will vary according to individual ways of thinking and processing experience. However, in my experience with those in transition, I've found their *narrated life situation* to be the most common and effective starting point for reflection. I offer here an example of an in-depth reflection that begins with that narrated experience. It unfolds in two movements: first, a free association from one's personal image to biblical images; second, a focusing in on one particular biblical image which seems to *generate the most energy*.

**The exploration which follows does not necessarily represent Kathy's exact *actual* exploration, but I have tried to preserve the essence and integrity of her experience and insights. Our deepest reflections should**

**always be held sacred and reserved for those we trust: a support group, counselor, spiritual director, soul friend, or for oneself alone. "It has to be clear that only *you* will ever read these pages [that you write]; otherwise it will be very difficult to be honest in what you record" (Johnson, 164).**

## Kathy's Images and Scriptural Associations

We turn again, then, to Kathy's image and begin to "brainstorm," as it were. Allow yourself to freely explore whatever scriptural associations come to mind when *you* think of *"being caught in THE PIT, trapped and powerless."* What scriptural images come to you? What scriptural personages have experienced "the pit" in one way or another? Are there any images which come to mind from other images in Kathy's experience: being "trapped and powerless," "almost paralyzed," "there seems to be no way out."

For example, we can recall Joseph, who was thrown into a cistern by his brothers (Genesis 37-50). "So when Joseph came up to them, they stripped him of the long tunic he had on; then they took him and threw him into the cistern, which was empty and dry" (Gen 37:23-24). Then there's Jeremiah, who was also thrown into a well, where he "sank into the mud" (Jer 38:6). We can think of John the Baptizer in the depths of his prison cell (compare Matt 11:2-6), or Lazarus buried in a tomb for four days (John 11:1-44). Maybe you relate more to being paralyzed, calling to mind the paralytic being lowered through the roof by his friends (Mark 2:1-12). Or maybe the word "powerless" calls to mind the image of the woman who had been afflicted with hemorrhages for twelve years (Mark 5:25-34), or the man who had been afflicted for thirty-eight years, and had no one to put him into the healing waters (John 5:1-18), or again, Luke's woman who was "bent over, completely incapable of standing erect (Luke 13:10-17).

After we have taken some time for these images to freely and spontaneously come into our consciousness, we then observe which image seems to give us *the most energy,* the one that seems to capture our feelings and draw our attention. As someone put it, the image that is saying, "Choose *me, me, me!*" Allow yourself to sit with that image and just let it lead you where it will, and this time try to get inside the experience of the subject(s) in the biblical text. We can do this first of all by imagining ourselves in *their* position, by asking ourselves the same kinds of questions that we did with our original image, by making associations. Depending upon the situations of transition in which we find ourselves, this scriptural image might invite some serious reflection, prayer, and even study, in order to better make connections between our own lives and experiences, and those that come to us from others before us.

Of the different scriptural associations that I make with Kathy's images, I want to spend a moment on the image of the prophet Jeremiah. The purpose of a scriptural study or reflection in our context of transition is for the sake of deepening our understanding of our own experience, gaining insight and wisdom from the connections made between our lives and our tradition, and ultimately, deepening our faith, hope, and love. This kind of in-depth study might not be the best method for all, and *each of us might discover our unique way of making that vital spiritual connection.* This reflection on the prophet Jeremiah's experience is an example of how missioners might develop an in-depth reflection on a scriptural text to which they feel drawn.

### Kathy's Image and Jeremiah: A Prophet Who Found Himself "In the Pits"

> *"This man ought to be put to death. . . ." King Zedekiah answered: "He is in your power"; for the king could do nothing with them. And so they took Jeremiah and threw him into the cistern of Prince Malchiah, which was in the quarters of the guard,*

*letting him down with ropes. There was no water in*
*the cistern, only mud, and Jeremiah sank into the*
*mud (Jer 38:5-6).*

At first, it is the *image* which is the point of connection here. The very words, "and Jeremiah sank into the mud," seem to capture for me what Kathy was feeling during this time, as though she were in the bottom of an empty cistern, sinking deeper and deeper "into the mud." When we approach this part of our reflection with an attitude of prayer, we want to be attentive to the Spirit's lead. I don't believe it is by chance that one or the other scriptural text will seem to stand out for us as significant. The image is the apparent connection with one's life and transition, and there are usually other, sometimes more significant, connections when we reflect upon an image within its context.

Jeremiah's vocation as prophet, especially the second period of his life after the death of the young and zealous King Josiah, presents one of the most challenging of the pre-Exilic era. Brother John of Taizé, in *The Pilgrim God*, calls his chapter on this prophet, "Jeremiah and the Inner Exile" (95-113), and Fr. Carroll Stuhlmueller refers to this period as "that long, long trek across the dreary plateau of failures" (*Pilgrim*, 48). If "misery loves company," then Kathy, who experienced misunderstanding, frustration, and failure in her vocation and mission, can certainly turn to Jeremiah for company and consolation. Jeremiah's life and suffering–(the suffering particularly "affirms his message as authentic" (see CSB: RG, 309))–is revealed both in the more biographical prose accounts of the prophet's ministry as well as in the more poetic "confessions."[66]

Believed to be written down by Jeremiah's faithful disciple and "secretary," Baruch, the book of Jeremiah reveals a sensitive man, "the most personal of prophets . . . a man of gentleness and peace, forced in spite of himself to preach a message of condemnation and ruin, a man whose innocence is cruelly wounded by the incomprehension and aggression he encounters" (Br. John, 105). Stuhlmueller calls him "*par excellence* the person of prayer" (52). Although

Jeremiah spent most of his life searching for "the meaning of his vocation" (Stuhlmueller, 45), he was able "to be at peace in the midst of
darkness and mystery . . . the surest indication that one is following the
intuition of God's will" (Stuhlmueller, 52). This was no small challenge
for Jeremiah, nor is it for anyone going through the "darkness and mystery" of a life-changing event, such as a major transition.

Jeremiah began his prophetic ministry in 627 BC (Jer 1:1).[67] The
same year marked the death of the Assyrian king, which was followed
by civil war and the ensuing collapse of that great empire. About
the same time, the young King Josiah at Jerusalem denounced the
Assyrian gods, and would shortly launch his vigorous "Deuteronomic
reform" (2 Kgs 22:1-23:27). The beginning years of Jeremiah's ministry were not unlike Kathy's in Brazil, indeed not unlike those of many
a missioner eager with "first fervor."

> **The first six years of Jeremiah's preaching
> career (627/6-621) were years of excite-
> ment over hopes, ideals, and undreamed-of
> possibilities. Achievement came quickly.
> This success, thought Jeremiah, must
> certainly demonstrate the genuineness of
> God's call and the nature of his vocation
> (Stuhlmueller, 47-48).**

"Then came a series of reversals" (Stuhlmueller 48). Although
Jeremiah agreed with its goals, he didn't agree with the *way* in
which Josiah and his immediate entourage were ruthlessly im-
posing the reform. It seems that he was more or less a silent and
somewhat credulous observer during those years.[68] Shortly after
that, however, at the death of Josiah in 609 BC (2 Kgs:23-29),
things indeed turned from bad to worse. In accounts like the one
cited above, where he was left to die in a cistern, we are told that
he was often accused of inciting the people, arrested, beaten,
and jailed more than once (37:21; 38:13, 28); he spent a night "in

stocks"(20:2) and, suspected of treason, in a dungeon (37:16); he was threatened with death (26:1-9), sometimes fleeing for his life (36:19), and finally exiled to Egypt (43:6) "where we lose his trail" (Br. John, 105).

Jeremiah, indeed, is no stranger to incomprehension in suffering. It is easy to identify and connect Kathy's inner turmoil with his "interior crisis." We can imagine Jeremiah voicing his solidarity with his compatriots caught in corruption, just as Kathy, in a different time and place, expressed her solidarity with the people of her neighborhood. I'm not suggesting that the social, political, religious, or economic circumstances in these two contexts, in which both the missioner and prophet find themselves, are necessarily the same. Rather, I want to point out a similarity in the experience of suffering in solidarity with the people, in the feeling of powerlessness and anger at the surrounding situation.

> *My grief is incurable, my heart with me is faint.*
> *Listen! The cry of the daughter of my people, far*
> *and wide in the land! Is the Lord no longer in Zion,*
> *is her King no longer in her midst? "The harvest*
> *has passed, the summer is at an end, and yet we*
> *are not safe!" I am broken by the ruin of the daugh-*
> *ter of my people. I am disconsolate: horror has*
> *seized me. Is there no balm in Gilead, no physician*
> *there? Why grows not new flesh over the wound of*
> *the daughter of my people? Oh that my head were*
> *a spring of water, my eyes a fountain of tears, that*
> *I might weep day and night over the slain from the*
> *daughter of my people (Jer 8:18-23).*

Stuhlmueller, in an exegesis on Jeremiah's confessions, gives us insight into the darkness of Jeremiah's own "deep pit": *You, O Lord, know me, you see me, you have found that at heart I am with you* (Jer 12:3a).

**The Hebrew implies, "You explore, walk-
ing with my footsteps. As I plunge into the
darkness of my heart, you God, are there
with me." Jeremiah must search into darkness to be where God is to be found. God's
answer to Jeremiah, written indeed by
Jeremiah after long, silent prayer, says literally in the Hebrew: "If you have run with
legs (that is, with other human beings) and
have fallen exhausted, how are you going
to get along galloping against horses? If
in the land of peace, you seek to find your
confidence, how are you going to fare in the
jungle of the Jordan?" (Jer 12:5). We can
think and ponder and pray long over that
verse of Jeremiah. Basically, what it says
is: "Jeremiah, things will get worse before
they will get better" (Stuhlmueller, 49-50).**

During a class, which I was privileged to take with Carroll
Stuhlmueller, he paraphrased the verse in this way: "Jerry, you think
this is bad?! You ain't seen nothin' yet!"[69] God asks Jeremiah to "hang
in there," to hold onto faith in that deep darkness, no matter what. Is
this not the ultimate demand in every Christian vocation, certainly
in every missioner's? Throughout one's ministry, and perhaps even
more so when one's mission is abruptly changed or apparently ended,
the "mission" is not doing what one thinks God wants, but doing that
which *God has known even before one is formed in the womb* (compare Jer 1:5). Stuhlmueller develops this thought in terms of every
apostolic vocation:

> **A vocation, then, according to Jeremiah,
> is not doing what one thinks God wants
> of a person. It is doing that which God
> has known even before one's conception.**

**A vocation can, in fact it must, begin by responding to apostolic opportunities. Yet, such a response is only the occasion, not the deepest meaning, of a vocation. In the most profound level of the heart, a vocation is a personal union with a God who seeks everyone in peace and love. A vocation must not degenerate into personal ambition. Rather, it means losing one's self totally in God, there to find one's self again in the union of all persons with God. How is such an interior conviction to be established? In Jeremiah's case, it demanded that his apostolic dreams crumble like paper houses. Somehow he had to sustain repeated failures and difficulties. Only then would he confess deep within his heart: My desire for God must be none other than God's desire for me (Stuhlmueller, 51).**

Jeremiah was personally overwhelmed by the misunderstanding, and even contempt, of those around him. He was plagued by personal discouragement and a sense of failure in his life's dream and mission. Nevertheless, because of an interior conversion, he was able to sustain and communicate hope. We will look more closely at this notion of interior "conversion" in the next chapter.[70]

## Part V: Dialogue Initiated by Scripture and Other Texts

One final and very valuable way of proceeding in spiritual reflection is by starting with a theme.[71] In this case, I'm choosing a scriptural theme, but the theme could come from any source.[72] Having looked at one missioner's images and scriptural associations from different perspectives, I like the recurring biblical theme of "journey" as a model, or sustaining metaphor, for the life of a missioner–a life that is always, in one sense, in "transition," conscious of moving toward the Divine, the ultimate fulfillment for the cosmos.

## The Biblical Journey

Brother John of Taizé, in his book, *The Pilgrim God*, does in a profound and amplified way what we are encouraging transitioners to do in their journey; i.e., "search through the Bible for ways the image [of journey] could illuminate our understanding of faith" (3).

> **The image of the journey as a key to the Bible has one great advantage: its dynamic, open-ended character. In addition to corresponding well to the mentality of our time, it enables us to grasp the progressive quality of God's self-revelation, and the dimension of risk, of adventure, which is so fundamental to the life of faith. . . . As for Abraham, the journey and the risk only begin when one says yes to God's call and sets out on the road of the promise (Br. John, 4).**

Brother John explains that he worked with "pilgrims" in the literal sense, doing Bible studies with young adults who came to spend some time in Taizé in France. He describes pilgrims "in the widest and in fact original sense . . . as people on the road, sojourners, passing strangers moving on to other horizons" (3). He developed his work around the theme of "faith as a pilgrimage," describing pilgrimage not "as the movement *toward* faith, conceived of as a static certainty, but on the contrary, an aspect of believing itself. . . ." (4). When I refer to "pilgrimage" in this book, it is also in this sense that we use the word: *the journey is an aspect of believing in itself.*

Brother John organized his work around the central image or model of "journey" as a way of understanding the biblical message:

> *This may well be one of the oldest metaphors for*
> *human experience, but it is deeply rooted in the*
> *Pentateuch itself. Abraham is called to a new land;*
> *Jacob must find God far from home. Joseph must*
> *go to Egypt, and Israel must cross the desert to*
> *find a promised Land. Not only does the journey*
> *motif stress the future to which we go, but also em-*
> *phasizes our way of life as a walking with God and*
> *under divine guidance (CSB: RG, 53).*

Certainly every Christian, having said "yes" to God's call, has embarked on a journey of faith. But missioners, perhaps more than most, embody in their lifestyle "the dimension of risk, of adventure" which we associate with our mothers and fathers in faith, and with our ancestors who journeyed out of Egypt in search of a promised land. The image of journey, as suggested above, provides a variety of dynamic metaphors within it, offering many possibilities of comparison with the life of a missioner who is continually moving *from→through→to→from→through→to→* . . . Journey implies the call and/or decision to go somewhere, the preparation (the "packing"), the setting out, the difficulties and delights along the route, long days and long nights, exciting adventure and exhausting fatigue, arriving, "unpacking" and "repacking" to set off again.

The missioner's life, not unlike that of our ancestors, is one full of the unexpected. This should come as no surprise to us–but it always does–since the God who has called us is full of surprises! The God who called Abraham and Sarah (Gen 12:1-4) is the God who invites us to uproot our lives from wherever they are settled and move on "to a land that I will show you" (12:1). It is God who takes the initiative with our ancestors, and with us. And God can take it again and again, in ways we may not always recognize (Exod 3:6-8; Is 43:19, John 14:9).

Sometimes in life we are treated in ways we would least expect, like Jeremiah and Jesus, unwelcome prophets when we try to speak our truth. At other times, we are ready to settle in and fold up our tent, tired of wandering in a land of liminality, ready to "ask for a king" (I Sam 8:4). Brother John reminds us that keeping a "pilgrim heart" (53) and a sense of ourselves as always on a journey, is a challenge demanding that radical "desert faith," the faith that assures us that the God who has called us, and calls us again and again, will be with us in our journey: "I will show you. . . ." (Exod 3:12);"I will be with you . . . (Jer 1:8); I will bless you . . . and you will be a blessing. . . ." (Gen 12:2-3; Exod 3:10; Is 6:7; Jer 1:10).

As I reflect on my own life, it has been a continued journey *from→through→to→from→through→to→* . . . Looking back to my past, when I perceived my initial call to mission, I could have never predicted where and how God would direct me, by what routes the Divine would lead me. In every "present" moment, there has been the temptation to compromise, to nestle in, to settle for a more "established" lifestyle. Then the Spirit would come along and disturb me again, prodding me to continue the journey into the promise of a future even fuller than the present.

## The Exodus-Event

To consistently believe that the Divine is in the journey, even in those disturbing transitions that uproot and upset us, demands a kind of radical faith, such as we find expressed in the story of the Exodus.

> **To find the core of Israel's faith, the events which more than any other gave an identity to the people of the Bible, it is to the books following Genesis we must turn, and especially to the book of Exodus. . . . We are dealing essentially with the story of an exodus, a liberation from bondage followed**

**by a long march across the desert under the
leadership of a man named Moses, toward
a land of promise "flowing with milk and
honey." Once again we meet a tale of pilgrimage, and this pilgrimage, together with
the traditions of the patriarchs and even
more than these, will provide the central
framework for the expression of the faith
of the Hebrew people in the course of their
centuries-long journey through history (Br.
John, 29-30).**

The biblical journey mirrors each of our journeys. The exodus
event symbolizes each of our struggles to be free. If we try to understand how this event became the "central framework" (or model) in
the expression of faith of the Hebrew people, we might ask ourselves
the question that "second generation" believers asked themselves
about their own history: "How did we get here?" Their answer was
clearly one of faith: "God brought us here!":

> *Later on, when your children ask you what these
> ordinances ... mean ... you shall say to your chil-
> dren, "We were once slaves of Pharaoh in Egypt,
> but the Lord brought us out of Egypt ... brought
> us from there to lead us into the land promised on
> oath to our ancestors, and to give it to us (Deut
> 6:20-23).*[73]

Many of us who have been on mission are aware that for a primarily "oral" culture there is no dichotomy between myth and history. What "facts" are altered, transformed, or simply forgotten in
the telling depends on their significance–or lack of it–in the mind
of the transmitters and the hearers. In this kind of culture, as was
that of the Hebrew people at this time in their history, the past

and the present merge into one, because there is no past apart from its being continually actualized in the present. For us today, if we can insert ourselves into the "oral" mentality, we can better grasp what was the experience of our ancestors in faith, and the important messages contained within the images and story of the exodus event: God is with us! God is for us! God delivers us! "And the Lord said, 'I have witnessed the affliction of my people in Egypt'" (Exod 3:6-10).

## *In the Wilderness*

But in order to pass from Egypt to the promised land, the Israelites had to pass through the desert of Sinai. They had to wander "forty years," in what is generally called a "wilderness," before reaching the land of the promise.[74] Scholars who have studied this wilderness narrative show that many aspects of this part of Israel's pre-Canaan journey provide us with a biblical lens through which we might understand our own missionary transition. Robert Cohn, using Victor Turner's categories, does a comparative study of the wilderness tradition as a liminal time and space for three distinct groups in Israel's history: the refugees fleeing Egypt, the Babylonian exiles, and the community in exile at Qumran. He writes:

> **The exilic writers preserved and reworked the wilderness tradition, especially, because it provided a paradigm with which to understand their own experience. . . . Into the story of the wilderness march, the exiles projected their own fears and hopes. Like generations before them, they viewed the wilderness as a chaotic place and the march as a terrifying journey, yet as the space-time coordinates in which a new community was created out of the chaos of**

> despair. Thus they saw themselves in the
> "wilderness" of exile being purged of the
> old and primed for the new. Similarly, the
> exiles at Qumran, several centuries later,
> understood themselves to be the wilderness
> generation...and read their own story out
> of the Pentateuchal account. . . . All three
> groups–the wilderness generation, the
> Babylonian exiles, the Qumranians–were,
> or saw themselves to be, societies in transi-
> tion, not settled in time or space, but on the
> move and awaiting the fulfillment of divine
> promises (Cohn, 7-9).

Both Cohn and Brother John point out characteristics of this liminal wilderness period in Israel's history, at least in the narrated account of it,[75] which can be helpful to us in a reflection on our own experience. "First of all," says Brother John, "the desert is a place of transition, 'a land where . . . no one lives' (Jer 2:6)" (35). Further, Cohn points out:

> When viewed as a whole, the Pentateuchal
> picture of Israel in the wilderness is anal-
> ogous to several of the phenomena which
> Turner describes. Like the initiates in a rite
> of passage, for instance, the Israelites pass
> through three distinct phases: (1) separa-
> tion, the exodus from Egypt in which the
> crossing of the Red Sea marks the final
> break . . .; 2) limen, the transitional period
> of wandering for forty years; (3) reincor-
> poration, the crossing of the Jordan river,
> conquest, and settlement in the new land
> (Cohn, 12-13).

## A Time of Trial

Wilderness or desert indicates, above all, a land without order–chaotic, uncultivated, undomesticated. Cohn points out that the attention given to this wilderness narrative by the Pentateuch authors indicates that "wilderness" signifies more than a geographical space. It is a symbol of that liminal transitional period in their history.

> **The wilderness is "betwixt and between,"neither here nor there, neither Egypt nor Canaan . . .," a moment in and out of time." The past is wholly cut off, and the future but faintly envisioned. Slavery is over but freedom is not yet. There, God punishes but also protects. The Israelites are in a quarantine chamber, able neither to return to the "house of bondage" nor to proceed directly to the "land of milk and honey" . . . The wilderness forms the setting for a trek through a time and space apart, ambiguous, liminal (Cohn, 15).**

It was a place of difficulties, hardships, cruel desert winds and sun. "By the harsh conditions it entails, the desert offers *an experience of human fragility.* . . . We learn humility, our fundamental poverty before God: walking under a burning sun "through a land of deserts and rifts, a land of drought and darkness" (Jer 2:6), "that thirsty and waterless land, with its venomous snakes and scorpions" (Deut 8:15) (Br. John, 36). Wandering in the wilderness is a time of trial. Sometimes misunderstood when translated into English or other languages, the test is not a "temptation" aimed at making us fail, but rather a challenge, representing *an interior struggle to either trust God entirely, or not.*

> **In the Bible, a trial is fundamentally an event that reveals what lies hidden in the**

**human heart, and it does so through the encounter with a resistance. In the face of this resistance we are obliged to respond, to act. And so what was merely implicit and unreflective becomes explicit, visible; our priorities are made evident and thus become more pronounced. . . . In this respect the trial is a reenactment, under the sigh of adversity, of our basic vocation, the call to "leave everything behind" in order to walk with God towards the land of promise. It offers us the opportunity to say "yes" to God once again, a yes stripped of all imaginary consolations. It proves to us, in the midst of tears and sorrow, that we are still pilgrims on the road of the Promise (Br. John, 37).**

Paraphrasing Brother John, I think that the time of transition for missioners offers *us* the opportunity to say "yes" again to our missionary vocation; this time perhaps, a "yes" more authentic, stripped of many of our illusions about our mission, and more in touch with what it truly means to be a missioner, a sojourner, an alien in a strange land (compare Exod 2:22; 22:21; 23:9; Deut 23:7). And that land may not only be in the past but also the very "homeland" on which we plant our feet now. One missioner wrote: *I came with the image of having crossed over the Red Sea into the wilderness, the desert of having almost nothing left—no path, shifting sands. . . . That image is still with me—however the mountains on the horizon are much closer now* (Anne, 1997).

## A Time of Death

This wilderness period of forty years is indeed a time of dying, not unlike a rite of passage, from one stage to another. Cohn develops this idea, pointing out that there are continual references to dying in the wilderness narratives, especially in the "murmuring" episodes. ("Murmuring" is the common translation of this term in Biblical scholarship, and it could best be understood as "complaining.")

> *Were there no burial places in Egypt that you had to bring us out here to die in the desert? Why did you do this to us. . . . Far better for us to be the slaves of the Egyptians than to die in the desert"* (Exod 14:11-12). *Would that we had died in the land of Egypt, or that here in the desert we were dead! Why is the Lord bringing us into this land only to have us fall by the sword* (Num 14:2-3).

Historically this "forty years" was a period of death during which one entire generation died out before another could take up life again in the land of Canaan. There is no record of births during this time, almost as though even birthing came to a halt.

> **Especially after the emphasis on the amaz-
> ing fertility of the enslaved Hebrews in
> Egypt, the silence is striking. The natural
> process of generation is halted in this time
> and space apart, when Israel is ground
> down, not built up. Yet as soon as the people
> cross the Jordan, all those who had been
> born in the wilderness are circumcised;
> the natural life cycle resumes (Josh 5:5-7)
> (Cohn, 16).**

For those in transition or reentry, this period also often demands a kind of dying: dying to dreams that will never be realized; to illusions about missionary life; to relationships that will be difficult, if not impossible, to sustain; dying to one's identity, to a certain extent, the dying of one's very self. Anne (mentioned above), shares with us a part of her experience of "dying" and the images which helped her begin to understand it. She refers to a moment in her life as her "Red Sea Experience":

> *Everything in my life seemed to fall apart at once: my parents died within a short space from one another. My best friend left our religious community. And we were more or less "thrown out" of our ministry—which meant everything to me—by the apparent conspiracy and mutual consent of the local bishop and my congregation's superior. At that time I felt that I had literally lost everything, including my self-confidence.*
>
> *At some moment within that period. . . . I pictured myself with a big bag, like a knapsack, thrown over my shoulder. The bag had the initials of my religious congregation on it. I had just "crossed the Red Sea," and was standing before the tombstones of my parents. Behind me was the Red Sea. Before me stretched a desert of endless sand. No plants. No life. Just sand as far as I could see into the horizon. . . . My life went on like that for a long time, trying to get where there was some life. The image was always very present to me.*
>
> *Then, I don't know when, at some point during the next year or two, I began to see the faintest glimpse of mountains far ahead. . . . Gradually, as I worked my way across the desert, the mountains began to get bigger and closer, until at some point I found myself at the foot of them, smack dab up against a sheer straight cliff of hard solid stone. . . . The MOUNTAIN loomed straight up before me, like a huge stone wall. It seemed insurmountable. I didn't know what to do, or where to turn. I was through the desert now, but I didn't know how to face that*

> *mountain. . . . I knew I couldn't go back, but there*
> *seemed no way to go forward (Anne, 1997).*

## *A Time of Consolation*

It took Anne several months before she could begin to even think
about that mountain and what it might mean in her life. She re-
members dreaming once during that period about a huge, thick,
stone wall, and it seemed that there was something ominous on
the other side. It is only in recent months, and after having worked
in spiritual direction with her images, that she is beginning to gain
insight into what the mountain, the insurmountable stone wall, is
about. Finally arriving at the point where she could ask herself
what it had to do with her life, with what she had experienced and
what she was carrying around in that bag, that wall is "beginning
to crumble":

> *It's only now, three years later, that the mountain*
> *is beginning to crumble, little by little, as I'm*
> *finding healthy ways to express all of my anger*
> *and grief . . . anger at the injustices that were*
> *done . . . my grief at the death of my parents, and*
> *my friend Mary's leaving, and our departure from*
> *St. Jude's.*
>
> *I'm also beginning to have a new image. . . . I think*
> *it may have grown out of my reading Harriett*
> *Lerner's* The Dance of Anger*) . . . and I am*
> *beginning to dance! Oh, sometimes I just bumble*
> *around. . . . Sometimes all of my other images are*
> *with me in the dance. . . . But, having crossed the*
> *Red Sea, and the desert, I am finally beginning to*
> *understand what freedom is all about . . .and that*
> *it is within me (Anne, 1997).*

## *A Time of Ambiguity*

A "wilderness period" of betwixt and between is almost always a difficult time and space, but for pre-Canaan Israel, it was also a time of unusual divine intervention and protection. Brother John calls this "a place of unparalleled intimacy with God":

> **Almost nowhere else in the Hebrew scrip-
> tures do we see such a concentration of
> signs and wonders: The water from the
> rock, the quails and the manna, the puri-
> fication of the waters, and so on: the wil-
> derness road is punctuated by attentive
> gestures of God's loving kindness, as [God]
> gives the people to eat and to drink (42).**

The negative "murmuring" traditions are secondary. God's presence among them at this time was almost tangible. One of the differences between the gods of most ancient peoples and the God of Israel was precisely this itinerant character of God, *who journeyed with them every step of the way.*

> *The Lord preceded them, in the daytime by means
> of a column of cloud to show them the way, and
> at night by means of a column of fire to give them
> light. And so they could travel both day and night.
> Neither the column of cloud by day nor the column
> of fire by night ever left its place in front of the
> people (Exod 13:21-22).*

It is this precise aspect of "consolation," intermingled with the "desolation" of trials and death, which makes this period of Israel's transition a time and place of *ambiguity*, which, as we have seen, is characteristic of all transition. This ambiguity was one of the

strongest experiences of my own transition. In this way too, as with
the trial episodes, the wilderness teaches us an important lesson
about the nature of freedom.

> **En route from one social role to another,**
> **from being held by a land to holding a land,**
> **the Israelites occupy a precarious status**
> **of landlessness. They are free, but root-**
> **less. . . . Only those who learn that freedom**
> **means nothing left to lose, are ground down**
> **sufficiently to experience the other side of**
> **freedom, the promised land (Cohn, 17).**[76]

It seems to me that, in the midst of our transition—or, for that
matter, at any other time in our life—we need to be especially attentive to the ways God might privilege us with the Divine Presence.
The desert is a privileged place. God may surprise us in "fire flaming
out of a bush" (Exod 3:2), or in "a cloud by day and a pillar of fire by
night," (compare Exod 13:21), or, like Elijah on Horeb, in the entrance
of our cave of refuge, in "a tiny whispering sound" (1 Kings, 19:12).
However mysterious or obscure, let us be careful not to neglect or
ignore the signs of that Presence, but be willing to let it guide us in
our journey, however long or difficult the way.

Indeed it is important to say that the images of transition need
not be all dark. When we cross over that threshold, we do find ourselves in a sort of "promised land," not without its own problems
and challenges. Two missioners I talked to spontaneously and inde-
pendently of one another, used the following metaphor to describe a
certain new movement in their transition. I paraphrase: *It's like being
in a new room with new furniture: things are arranged differently
and it takes some getting used to, but there are also new windows and
doors, bringing new light and different opportunities.* Often, before
we can truly be at home in our own journey, we must pass through
a necessary time and space of "chaotic wilderness." It is part of our
rite of passage, just as it was for our ancestors in faith. Often we too

murmur and grumble while crossing this desert, which ultimately gives us the occasion to deepen our trust in the Divine who is with us in our journey.

## Moving On: Some Concluding Comments

As we turn to Chapter Four, we will still be reflecting upon images, but with more attention to their *interpretation* and to that of our experience as a whole, seeking to identify, in our transition process, what Killen and de Beer have called "the heart of the matter" (61f). *It can be discovered in the energy of our feelings and in the power of our images.* While the authors do not indicate "identifying the heart of the matter" as a singular step or phase, I do. Not only is it important in the process of theological reflection, but I believe it is vital in coming to integration. *This discovery of one's unique heart of the matter is the crossroads of the journey of transition. It is the key for opening the new door that awaits us as we cross the threshold of liminality.*

In the next chapter we will continue to dialogue with tradition, but our conversation will be nuanced by a new theme, that of *conversion that leads to transformation.* We will look at what "conversion" means in the context of scripture, spiritual literature, and in missioners' lives. I believe that *openness to this often-painful process is the "heart" of every successful transition.* As we cross the desert, we begin to find life on the other side. It is in walking new paths, with renewed vision, that we will eventually become "at home in the journey."

Chapter Four

# Examining the Heart of the Matter: "Conversion"

*Helpless, insecure, and frustrated, I feel like
a bloody stump, a broken mask, a blind man.
"Behold the man!" Me (Jim, 1993).*

We have come now to the crossroads of our reflection. Having
explored our feelings and images in dialogue with tradition, it
is the moment of identifying and articulating "the heart of the matter."[77] This, simply put, is what emerges as *the underlying significant
issue in our experience*. In our process of understanding and integration, "the heart of the matter" becomes the primary focus of our
reflection. According to the model–and in my experience–missioners
will have already, on some intuitive level, identified their "heart of the
matter" through the articulation of their feelings and the exploration
of their images. It is through these images that we can usually find
at least one, if not many, important issues or focal points for reflection. In fact, in many cases, *the image has already articulated it.*
The advantage of an image is that in capturing the significant issue,
it retains the emotional or affective energy expressed through our
feelings. *That energy is an important indicator of where to look for
the heart of the matter.*

## Part I: Getting to It

> *A clay pot sitting in the sun will always be a clay pot. It has to go through the white heat of the furnace to become porcelain. Actually, there's nothing wrong with being a clay pot. It's just that some of us are called to become porcelain. And it's not just a question of being fired or not. Some of us explode in the kiln, some collapse before we reach the kiln, and some develop cracks that refuse to heal. Yet probably the saddest response of all is to successfully survive the firing and refuse to become porcelain. All of us have furnaces in our lives. It's up to us to glean the learning from the firings* (Mildred Witte Stouven (www.lifequoteslib.com)).

Some years ago a friend handed me the above lines from her daily calendar. They struck me at the time, and seem like appropriate lines with which to begin this chapter's reflection on "conversion." As we enter into that refining fire to reach whatever the "heart of the matter" is for each of us, it's important to know that approaching it, exploring it, and reaching it will inevitably demand change on our part–one for which we are rarely prepared. Perhaps it is easier to remain "clay pots" when, in truth, we are being called to become porcelain.

We have already seen the revealing nature of images in missioners' narratives from the previous chapters. Anne, for example, drew an image of herself carrying a big duffel bag over her shoulder. Only after months of processing in group and spiritual direction was she able to begin to ask herself such questions as: *"What does that bag represent? Why am I carrying it? What is in it? Why don't I put it down?"* As she made her way "across the desert" she realized that something was weighing her down, "hindering me from getting to where there was life." Anne's heart of the matter was symbolized in that heavy bag. Another missioner expressed herself this way:

*When I first arrived home, I felt like a huge rock,*
*immovable. For four weeks I sat and did almost*
*nothing. I didn't want to be involved in anything.*
*I just wanted to sit. Sometimes I didn't even think,*
*other times I sat questioning why I decided to*
*return home. I was asked several times to help out*
*with summer work. I said no. I felt too immobilized*
*to do anything and I didn't even feel guilty. I felt*
*lost and without energy. I felt disintegrated. . . .*
*The scripture story that stayed with me for many*
*weeks was the woman at the well. The water jar*
*was an essential part of life in Kenya. . . . I had left*
*behind my water jar in order to come home, and*
*to leave it behind was to leave behind my life there*
(Sue, 1997).

For Sue, that last sentence summarized in a clear image what she
eventually recognized to be her heart of the matter. She *felt* like she
had left her life behind in Kenya. She had no energy, no motivation,
no reason to go on. It was with this issue that she had to grapple
during many months of transition. We all find different ways of exploring our issues. Some with words, such as journaling or poetry;
others through various art forms, such as dance or drawing. Some
work in clay. One group acted out an issue in a role play. One veteran
missioner expresses his heart of the matter in a few words, as an
authentic "crossing over." It is both his challenge and his conviction;
as he puts it, "a reliable entry point every time I enter–or re-enter–a
new culture."

*First off, you have to see what is there TODAY,*
*which is always quite different than it was ten or*
*even five years ago. . . . I have re-entered the USA*
*five times, and each time, in a certain way, it was*
*like entering a new country. . . . You have to cross*
*over to another place and come back to yourself,*

*knowing that you too are a changed person. . . . It*
*can be painful, but less painful than crossing over*
*to what you thought it would be like, as it was ten*
*years ago, and less painful than not crossing over*
*at all* (John, 1997).

Learning to identify the heart of the matter is not easy. It is perhaps the most challenging skill one must learn when doing theological reflection (Killen and de Beer, 80). As we saw in Chapter One, just remembering and retelling events using *nonjudgmental narration* is, in itself, an art. Now what is most important is to locate within our narrative those images and feelings which seem to generate the most *energy* in us at this moment. That energy is an indication that it is *this* space that we are being called to explore more deeply. Somewhere within this space will be found the most significant issue in this particular experience. Finally we must *articulate* the heart of the matter clearly enough, at least initially for ourselves, so that our personal reflection be *focused*.

Sometimes one may have to examine several issues in order to discover that which holds the most significance at the time. Using an analogy, if you've had pain in your upper back, or maybe in your leg, you may have discovered that the *cause* of the problem actually lies somewhere in the lower back or spinal column. Oftentimes our bodies have been absorbing the trauma and adapting themselves to the problem, but eventually there will be signs that something is not right, that something needs healing. In the same way that much of our physical pain often signals displaced symptoms of a problem residing elsewhere in our bodies, so too *the feelings generated by an event are like "symptoms" of an unresolved issue which needs attention.* Ideally, this can be done with others, in the context of a supportive family or faith community.

Often returned missioners and veterans may not believe themselves to be in need of any help. You have probably encountered those for whom everything is "just fine"–who don't need any "touchy-feely" group to talk to! Although the personalities and the degrees of need may differ, most of us benefit, sooner or later, by intentionally reflecting upon our experience in the light of our faith. This is one of the ways we will continue growing as missioners, and as *persons*. Those who quickly plunge into new work or a new community, claiming no time or space to process what they have left behind, are often in denial or still in re-entry shock. Eventually, symptoms will indicate that they too need "a reliable entry point" if they are to carry on fruitfully in their new situation. The jolt or the ambiguity of a transition are sometimes the "kiln" of conversion through which we are invited to become porcelain.

## Part II: Conversion: A First Look

> **No one sets out deliberately upon a journey of conversion: we are always called to it . . . launched upon it, by circumstances outside our control (Searle, 38).**

Exploring the heart of the matter will often lead to a form of "conversion." Conversion is "a highly confusing and controversial issue today, largely because the term 'conversion' refers not to one reality but to an enormously wide range of very different human realities" (Conn, *Christian Conversion*, 7). While some authors maintain that conversion is essentially a religious phenomenon, I consider it a *human* phenomenon (often set within a *religious context*).[78] What's more, any authentic study of conversion ought to be *holistic*, including, at the very least, four components: "cultural, social, personal, and religious systems" (Rambo, 7).

In the midst of the many and varied factors that make each transition unique–like each missioner–there is often a common phenomenon. Something within is often in need of healing. Maybe some part of us has been bruised or broken and badly in need of "resetting." Perhaps something is festering like a sore, filled with infection. Like a bone that needs to be re-broken before it can be set straight, or like alcohol applied to a wound, so too the resolving of our issues can often be quite painful. Sometimes it may be that we have simply arrived at a new crossroads in our life, and we must leave one path behind and turn to another. But in each case, what is demanded of us is some sort of conversion, a "turning around," which may sometimes require a radical "change of heart" (*metanoia*), if indeed we are ever going to get around to really healing the heart of the matter.

A major guide for our reflection on conversion is a classic article by Mark Searle entitled, "The Journey of Conversion"(1980). I was introduced to it only a few months after my return from Zaire, but I have yet to find a better paradigm for the particular process we are talking about. Searle focuses on features which seem to be characteristic of all periods of transition in human life, offering those features as fundamental to the "pilgrimage of faith or the journey of conversion":

> **"Conversion" consists of the successful negotiation of crisis or change; that conversion is a form of "passage" or "transition," whereby a person may pass through to a new lease on life and enter into a new set of relationships with [themselves], the world around them, and with life itself. The journey of conversion, then, would be a journey through crisis, using the term "crisis" here to refer not only to moments of alarm and anxiety but in the broader sense of any turning point or moment of change (Searle, 36).**

In this description, we find three elements which are especially important for our particular understanding of it: (1) the sense of *journey*, which is itself passage or transition, a process rather than a fixed moment; (2) the negotiation of *crisis*, being understood in its broad sense as a moment of opportunity–a turning point or crossroads; and

(3) the sense of **new relationships**, which will mark the completion of this particular passage as part of the longer journey, which is life itself.

### Conversion as Essential in the Process of Transformation

One of the major discussions about conversion in the literature is whether or not it is something that is gradual and ongoing, or whether it is a sudden, one-time event. Almost any serious discussion of conversion in the literature will refer back to William James, who offered one of its earliest definitions in his classic *Varieties of Religious Experience* (1902). He describes conversion as "a psychological process, gradual or sudden, of unifying a divided self."[79]

With James's psychological study as a foundation, the topic of conversion *as a process* has since been explored by many authors. David O'Rourke emphasizes that, as much as it is a decisive activity, it is also a complex process involving long periods of time and interrelated causes and effects, significant people and relationships, inaction and repression, postponements and sufferings. Ultimately it involves all of these elements "*woven together* into the whole that is the person's life" (O'Rourke in Eigo, 9).

Lewis Rambo provides a very comprehensive definition:

> **Conversion is a process of religious change that takes place in a dynamic force field of people, events, ideologies, institutions, expectations, and orientations . . . (a) conversion is a process over time, not a single event; (b) conversion is contextual and thereby influences and is influenced by a matrix of relationships, expectations, and situations; and (c) factors in the conversion process are multiple, interactive, and cumulative (Rambo, 5).**

While more recent scholars in the field do not discount the fact that sometimes there may be a moment within the process that stands out as a "moment of grace," there seems to be a consensus that conversion is indeed "an ongoing process, at once personal, communal, and historical (Lonergan in Conn, *Conversion*, 14). Someone at the crossroads of transition is, I believe, invited to enter into that process. A life of fidelity involves a sort of continual transformation, a journey of "turning" and "re-turning" to one's true self, wherein dwells the One who created us in the beginning, and who never ceases creating us.

*To live a life of mission is essentially a transformative spiritual process.* We are being called to "mission," no matter where we find ourselves, but sometimes it takes a radical change of heart to recognize that call. In fact, anyone who wishes to make a successful transition from one culture to another, from one mission to another, *must be willing to change*—not only on the outside, but more radically, on the inside! And this process of "turning oneself around,"[80] examining in the light of faith one's unique journey—this is, perhaps, the "heart of the matter."

## Part III: Stages within the Process

Many authors, including Griffin, O'Rourke, Rambo, [81]and Searle, find it helpful to articulate the process of conversion in terms of stages, while acknowledging that the process is necessarily a continuous one, and that the stages may interact and overlap. Since the process involves a complexity of factors, the description of "stages" varies from author to author. Searle speaks of the stages as three main parts of a story, or "as a drama in three acts": the beginning, the middle, and the end. He calls these "The Setting Out," The Adventure," and the "Return." He describes the unfolding simply:

> **The beginning of a story tells of the**
> **way things were and of how the seed of**

**circumstance was sown, from which the
ensuing events then sprang. The story goes
on to tell of how that original state of things
came to be altered or put in jeopardy, and
it concludes by relating how these events
were resolved in a new state of affairs
(Searle, 36-37).**

Searle himself acknowledges that his paradigm is nothing new. The reader will quickly recognize van Gennep's description of *separation, liminality, and reincorporation*, which I referred to in Chapter One, as well as Larry Lewis's theme: "*from→through→to→-from→through→to→ . . .*"[82] Searle's descriptive model may be helpful to missioners as they wade through the sometimes murky waters of their own transitional "rites of passage."

—> The Setting Out  —> The Adventure  —> The Return  —>

—> Separation  —> Liminality  —> Reincorporation  —>

—> From  —> Through  —> To —> From  —> Through  —>To  —>

**Figure 4.1**

## *Stage One: "The Setting Out"*[83]

Essentially, then, this first stage of a conversion process involves both the "setting out," and the "setting." Setting is important for any story. Rambo calls this the "context." Usually one can recognize a particular moment or event, a turning point of sorts, which we often identify with the beginning of a conversion process. This is usually the *onset* of the "crisis" (crisis usually considered an essential element of the process). But neither the crisis nor the transformation happens in a vacuum. There will have been previous events or circumstances, perhaps unnoticed—or if noticed, unnamed—which announce the arrival of a turning point in much the same way that nature announces the arrival of a storm.

> **Conversion begins with longing or desire, a heart's ache for something. . . . This longing may come in the form of a nostalgia, when things seemed happier . . . or . . . of world weariness, a disenchantment and disappointment with the world around us (Griffin, 36).**

For missioners in transition, this process may have begun in the past, the overall situation which we are transitioning *from*. Or our present time of transition *through* may also be the context which invites transformation. It could be the people, community, relationships, an institution, a system, an event or series of events–political, religious, or economic, local or national. It could be an environment of overt violence or more subtle oppression. "Context embraces . . . people, events, experiences, and institutions . . . the total environment" (Rambo, 20).

> **Conversion takes place within a dynamic context. This context encompasses a vast panorama of conflicting, confluent, and dialectical factors that both facilitate and repress the process of conversion. . . . Context embraces an overall matrix in which the force field of people, events, experiences, and institutions operate on conversion. Context is more than a first stage that is passed through; rather, it is the total environment in which conversion transpires (Rambo, 20).**

Whatever the circumstances which led to it, those in transition find themselves in a new environment, being forced to relate to it, sometimes reluctantly. They are challenged to take a new direction, to think in a new way, and to form new sets of relationships: with others, with self, and ultimately, with the Divine. Something has already begun to change, if not externally, then internally–usually both.

How does this invitation present itself–to turn transition into transformation? This "context" is not readily detected, much less easily articulated, when one is in the midst of it. Searle maintains that this onset of a "conversion crisis" is "necessarily perceived in images and expressed in symbolic language" (39). I have seen it most often spoken of in descriptive terms, such as we saw in the narratives: I'm "at a low ebb," "out of rhythm," "lost," "floating in air," "swaying in the wind," "in a deep pit," "in a wilderness," "burned-out," or "having a nervous breakdown." One missioner, Terry, whom we met earlier in Chapter Three, describes the context or onset of his own turning point this way:

> *I found myself swinging between daydreaming as*
> *escape on the one hand, and redoubled effort on the*
> *other. But almost every time I tried to work harder,*
> *it did not last very long. I was just getting more*
> *and more tired and frustrated. And I kept wonder-*
> *ing why. I was becoming discouraged with myself,*
> *with what I was not accomplishing, with others*
> *who were not meeting my expectations, and with*
> *life in general. What was happening to me? ... My*
> *confusion was nearly total: physical, emotional,*
> *mental, and spiritual. When I tried to pray, after a*
> *few days of extraordinary effort, I would fall right*
> *back into lethargy. And that lethargy in prayer*
> *spread into most areas of my life. My personal*
> *energy was running out. I didn't realize it then, but*
> *trouble was well on the way (Terry, 1993).*

## Marker Events

This crossroads of our transition will often be associated with some sort of external event or happening in our lives. This is not usually the crux of the crisis (although it may be), but rather what Searle (and Levinson before him) calls a "marker event" (Searle, 39). This event can be thought of as a catalyst which will bring about–or bring to awareness–a series of other "events" and realizations, usually more internal than external. It often signals the onset of the transformation process.

How might a missioner in transition experience this marker event? It could be in the words of a church community suggesting that it is time to move on and surrender the leadership to a local member. It may be the onset of sickness or the death of a family member or other loved one. Perhaps it is the voice of a superior saying that one is needed elsewhere. Then too, it may be less evident. Sometimes a seemingly insignificant happening turns out to be the "straw that broke the camel's back." In whatever fashion we may experience or express it, this marker event will often throw us into a new phase of our transition, into a crisis which some might experience as the "heart of darkness" or perhaps others as the "winds of a tornado." *When one is in this phase, it seems like it will never end. But it will. It can be survived.*

→ Marker Event → The Setting Out → The Adventure → The Return →

→ Separation → Liminality → Re-Incorporation →

→ From → Through → To → From → Through → To →

**Figure 4.2**

## *One Marker Event: A Personal Story*

They say every good story has to have a beginning, a middle, and an end. But in one's own story "one is always somewhat at a loss to know quite where to begin" (Searle, 37). Missioners too are often at a loss in trying to capture the essence of a complex personal experience, especially in the context of several years in the making. In my story, I recognize, in retrospect, a growing predisposition or internal restlessness, which was leading into crisis. This crisis would eventually lead me to make life-changing decisions. There was, however, amid this period of dis-ease, a definite "marker event," which now seems to have marked the beginning of the crisis, tumbling me into a period of darkness and disorientation:

> *My marker event occurred in the Spring of 1992. I had been working in the equatorial region of Zaire for eleven years. I had spent the last three of those years in the village of Iboko, in the rainforest just north of the equator. I was coordinating a program of Literacy, Development, and Evangelization, based on Paulo Freire's classic,* Pedagogy of the Oppressed *(1971). One of the several aspects of the program was that participants were able to purchase necessities at retail value, and on a sort of interest-free "lay-away" plan. During the process, their items were stored in a small two-room library until fully paid for.*

> *On a particular Monday in March, I went to the library and found it unlocked. Surprised, I assumed my young co-worker, who had cleaned up last, had been careless about locking it when he left the day before. Rather unusual for him, but these things happen. Then in the dimly lit space I noticed that the inner storeroom door was also ajar. This seemed very strange, as I was sure to have locked it, and no one else had a key for that room. Still unsuspecting, as I entered I saw used papers scattered all over the floor. I confusedly tried to recollect if there had been some storm in the last few days that could have blown loose papers about.*

> *Then suddenly my heart sank. I recognized the papers on the floor as those that had served as*

*packaging for the pieces of cloth that had been on
lay-away. Frantically I opened the large cardboard
carton where I had packed them. Empty. Feeling
genuinely sick to my stomach, I slowly began to
examine the other boxes and the footlocker where
the other items were stored. Everything was gone:
the bolt of sheet material for burials, the bicycle
parts, the machetes and hoes, the "special orders"–
all were missing. The only things left undisturbed
were the literacy materials: books, pencils, chalk,
etc. Another item missing was a spare padlock that
I had placed in reserve on a back shelf. Few people, except those I worked with, could have known
about that padlock.*

*I checked the doors and windows. Apparently none
of the locks had been tampered with. The reading
room was in its usual order, and neither room had
the appearance of having been "searched." It was
as though the thief or thieves had known exactly
where to go and what to look for.*

*I slowly went outside, wondering how to break the
news to those who were lined up, eagerly awaiting
their purchases. I must have showed my shock and
disbelief, because they quickly seemed to understand what had happened, without my even saying
it. When I explained, their immediate reaction
was concern for ME. "Who could have done such a
thing to you?" they asked indignantly. They were
shocked and angry. I, acutely aware that these
stolen goods were theirs, not mine, was at a loss
for what to say. When they gradually began to
realize the implications of such a loss, their faces
fell. They became strangely silent. But they still
continued to try to console me and assure me that*

*the goods would be found–that everything would
be all right. I sensed that their trust in me assured
them that somehow I would "make good" on their
investments.*

*The news quickly spread in and around Iboko–a
small village where everyone knows everyone, and
nothing is private. All sorts of friends–and even a
few traditional enemies–came offering advice as
to how to pursue the affair. I tried to maintain my
calm–and my integrity. I resisted the constant re-
frain that the two young men who regularly helped
me, John and Rigo, had "obviously" been involved
in the theft. I resisted believing that my young
friends–or any of my collaborators–could have
betrayed me. I was still in a state of shock.*

*The two came around the next day, declaring their
innocence. John swore he had locked the door, and
that someone must have made a duplicate key.
They were insistent on undergoing a search for
some trace of the robbers. They left. I didn't see
them for quite a few weeks after that.*

*I became physically ill for several days after this
theft. And psychologically speaking, I couldn't go
to the library and storeroom for weeks. I tried to
tell myself that this was just a theft; it happened
all the time and to everyone. And yet this particular break-in had affected me on some deeper
psychological level: I felt betrayed, deceived, used,
abused, misunderstood. I was deflated, discouraged, de-energized.*

*Everything I was and had done seemed to be called
into question: my ministry, my relationships, my*

*presence among the people—even our commu-
nal presence as missionaries, as part of the local
Church. I questioned our purpose, our strategy,
our methodology, and even our reason for being
there at all. All the doubts and questions that had
occasionally surfaced in my life as a religious and
missionary, and in particular during my ministry
in Zaire over the past eleven years: these questions
suddenly seemed to engulf me.*

*My relationships seemed to change. I found it hard
to trust as before, to have confidence in those with
whom I worked. I found myself more conscious
than ever of not wanting to become cynical—an
attitude I had often perceived in some veteran
missionaries.*

*Over the next months and year, I gradually began
to resume my ordinary routine, to again visit the
people in their homes and in the villages, to give
myself again to my ministry. But things were
never quite the same. I lacked the enthusiasm and
conviction that had motivated me before. The same
questions continued to plague me: Who had really
been involved in this theft? Had the two young
men been pawns in the hands of some local gang?
Had they sold out their loyalty for money? Was
the other lay collaborator involved, to whom I had
confided much responsibility and had designated
as Director of the program.*

*I never learned the answers to these questions, and
probably never will. The theft was never solved nor
the goods discovered. I kept wondering why this
affected me so much. I remember asking myself, "Is
this what they call "burn-out"? In fact, it probably*

> *was. And it was this incident more than any other*
> *factor, which prompted me, a year later, to ask for*
> *a sabbatical. The theft's devastating effect on me*
> *seemed to suggest that maybe I needed some space,*
> *some distance from Zaire and from my work: a*
> *time to study, to rest, and then to return–renewed.*
>
> *I did not like the idea of leaving Zaire, even tem-*
> *porarily. This meant separation from the people*
> *and culture I loved, the country I had come to call*
> *"home." But following the theft, a series of circum-*
> *stances also seemed to tell me that I needed to*
> *leave. I left somewhat reluctantly in July, 1992,*
> *almost a year and a half later. And at that time,*
> *I thought that I would be returning to Zaire the*
> *following year. I could not have imagined the kind*
> *of tumultuous transition I was entering. And this*
> *seemingly isolated theft became a catalyst, set-*
> *ting off a whole new process of discernment that*
> *would, in fact, change the direction of my life and*
> *ministry.*

The theft at our little storeroom threw me into serious questioning and doubt about the very meaning of my life, my vocation, my
ministry. It had been a shock to my system, to my world of values,
to my idealized, self-created reality. This produced in me all sorts of
physical and emotional responses. It wounded my pride, my dignity,
my sense of safety. I felt a loss of trust in others, especially the feeling of having been betrayed by those I loved like my children, and
even by "the very people I was trying to help!" I was hurt, offended,
angry. I was confused. I felt resentment and indignation. I became
physically sick; I found myself moving into a generalized mood of
discouragement. It eventually led me into a dark time of desolation,
and an internal "dying" process. Robert Kegan maintains that all
disequilibrium is a crisis of **meaning**; a crisis of *identity*, which puts
the self at risk (Kegan, 240). And Solomon notes:

> **Emotions are the life force of the soul, the source of most of our values. . . . Emotions are said to distort our reality; I argue that they are responsible for it. Emotions are said to divide us from our interests and lead us astray; I argue that emotions create our interests and our purposes (Solomon, 14-15).**

Yes, this marker event, this encounter with "reality," had thrown me very off-balance. It forced me to understand that the world was truly not as I would like it to be, or as I perceived it to be. It is filled with injustices and inequalities not only on global levels, but in relationships, on a personal level. "The rich get richer and the poor get poorer." I had, more than once in my life, been prodded to this disequilibrium by the challenges of those we call "poor," or by a person whose eyes would call to me out of a deep well of dignity and pride: "Who do you think you are, anyway? I don't need your pity. I don't want your charity."

For some mysterious reason, however, this experience of the theft had jolted me into a deeper conflict. I was challenged to relativize what, until now, I had taken as ultimate. Viewed from the old perspective, in which I had long been invested, I experienced this crisis as a loss of self, disorientation, and as an experience of not knowing what was happening to me, of felt "meaninglessness" (Kegan, 231). I felt suddenly stripped of my pretenses and defenses. I experienced a kind of rupture or incongruity in my way of knowing and understanding everything around me. In some way, one might say, my "world" was falling apart, and a new one was not yet clear on the horizon.

## Stage Two: "The Adventure"

Searle calls the second stage of conversion "the adventure" (39), but many would probably not think of crisis as an "adventure." Terry (see

above), refers to crisis as "trouble," and that is probably the way most
of us experience it. Griffin refers to this crisis stage as the "struggle"
(102-147); O'Rourke calls it the "noisy" stage (Eigo, 10); and Rambo
refers to it simply as "crisis" (44-65). *This struggle for survival of the
old self, as we know it, is the most difficult time of all*. It requires of us
a kind of introspection and self-examination that we have not under-
taken before. It may be, if not the first, the deepest encounter with the
self that we have made, a confrontation with our own weakness and
failures and inadequacies. It is both a struggle to hold on to beliefs
and a struggle for new ones emerging–accompanied with a sense of
uneasiness, of being cut loose from familiar emotional moorings,
not knowing when, if ever, one will touch land again (Griffin, 91-92).
Perhaps when we look back upon the time, we can recognize each of
these elements (adventure, struggle, noise, "the pits") as part of our
own wrestling with the heart of the matter. Like Jacob in the book of
Genesis, we often come away from that struggle limping–but somehow mysteriously blessed (Gen 32:23-33).

Crisis represents an *essential element* of conversion. Although
not the most important, it's usually the most *characteristic* part of
the process, often the most noticeable moment. This path to transformation consists in "the *successful negotiation*" of a particular
crisis (Searle, 36). It's evident that death, suffering, loss, or trauma
can challenge one's interpretation of life, or one's fundamental direction–calling everything into question. There are also other kinds of
events which, on the surface, may appear to be relatively insignificant, which may also eventually provoke a crisis. In fact, *cumulative*
events, seemingly innocuous, often play a crucial role on the path of
transition evolving into transformation.

## *The Heart of Conversion: Surrender*

Crisis *alone* is not clearly enough to explain this call to conversion.
*At the heart of true transformation is an essential act of letting
go, or surrender*. Why is it, then, that crisis has such an impact in
leading to–or at least potentially leading to–surrender? Because

crisis—certainly a crisis of transition—leads us to "the heart of the matter," by placing us in the *"heart" of our humanness*. It brings us smack up against our weakness, our vulnerability, our brokenness as human beings, and we are forced to surrender our masks and pretensions. We are challenged to let go of false expectations, both for ourselves and others. Authentic crisis challenges all of our false conceptions and illusions about mission, ministry, community, others, God, and especially perhaps, ourselves.

> *Every time you make a choice you are turning the*
> *central part of you, the part that chooses, into*
> *something a little different from what it was before*
> (C. S. Lewis, in *Griffin*, 30).

In reflecting upon this essential aspect of conversion as an "act of surrender," we look in particular to the work of Walter Conn, who in turn based his developmental study of conscience and conversion primarily on Bernard Lonergan's understanding of conversion as *essential to self-transcendence*. For Lonergan conversion is a human phenomenon occurring on three distinct yet interrelated dimensions: *intellectual*, *moral* and *religious*. Conversion simultaneously occurs: *cognitively*, through critical understanding and realistic knowing; *morally*, through responsible choices and decision-making; and spiritually, through free and generous love in service of the other.

Most significant for us in Lonergan is his understanding of human conversion as *a process of self-transcendence*. For Lonergan, conversion, like the drive for self-transcendence, must be an intelligent, responsible and free act of surrender.

**The Gospel demand calling us to intelligent, responsible, loving service of the neighbor requires no more and no less than the fulfillment of this fundamental personal drive for self-transcendence. As the criterion of personal authenticity,**

> self-transcending love is also the norm by
> which every other personal concern, inter-
> est, need or desire must be judged–and, if
> necessary, sacrificed. Fidelity to this law
> of the human spirit, this radical dynamism
> for self-transcending love, sums up the
> demand of the Christian life because it is a
> response to the divine within us–God's gift
> of love (Conn, *Christian Conversion*, 24).

Lonergan's definition of conversion as part of self-transcendence provides us with an important insight. Self-transcendence is the authentic self-realization which occurs when one actively moves *beyond one's own self*. It occurs when persons respond to the radical drive within themselves, the always deepening search for meaning, truth, value and love. Sometimes a conversion is being demanded of us which has little to do with the externals: the "projects" or mission assignments we are given. Paradoxically, self-*realization* is not an end in itself, but occurs as a by-product of authentic self-*transcendence* (see Conn, *Christian Conversion*, 22-25).[84] Conversion, then, is demanded by the human spirit's radical drive for "meaning, truth, value, and love" (see Conn, Christian Conversion, 24).

And this experience of moving beyond one's own self *is* conversion, it is the turning toward something other. It is as much an act of freedom as it is an act of surrender. The point is that conversion does not consist in "simply surrendering," but rather "*surrendering to someone or something*"...in some mysterious way one is aware that something new has been born (Searle 42). I like to think of this process as *transition . . . transformation . . . transfiguration*.

## *Surrender and Transition*

> If every crisis, every conversion, is a kind
> of dying to one's previous life and world; if

> **every crisis provokes what Levinson calls
> "de-illusionment," "a recognition that long-
> held assumptions and beliefs about self
> and world are not true"; then the moment of
> conversion, the turning point, is that mo-
> ment of surrender (Searle 41-42).**

How might we characterize the kind of conversion that is demanded of someone in transition? We may sometimes be those who go quietly along leading good lives, virtuous lives, perhaps never feeling quite radical enough to lead "holy" lives. Christian "holiness" is "transformation in Christ" and this is intimately connected to conversion and freedom. To become holy means being open, being willing to change, not once, but over and over again. In the words of Thomas Merton,

> **We are not converted only once in our lives,
> but many times; and this endless series of
> large and small conversions, inner rev-
> olutions, leads to our transformation in
> Christ. . . . But while we may have the gener-
> osity to undergo one or two such upheavals,
> we cannot face the necessity of further and
> greater rendings of our inner self, with-
> out which we cannot finally become free
> (Merton in Searle, 48-49, 55).**

Many of us are good, just like that clay pot. But some of us are called to become better than good . . . to become porcelain. For a missioner who has spent two or twenty years doing good for others, and, in fact, being a good person, sometimes it is a moment of transition or re-entry which provides the fire which leads to genuine holiness. This is the "stuff" of which saints and martyrs are made: a surrender which knows how to "drink the cup," how to say—and live—"Not my will, but thine be done." As we saw earlier (Ch. 3), Ed described his own surrendering to the "heart of the matter" as being willing to sacrifice his Isaac: "*to throw reason to the winds and to trust in the God who provides*".

It may be that as missioners, we have to think of "mission" in new ways, yet still built on the foundation of our previous understanding and praxis. In this case, as Lonergan says, the new horizon is consonant with the old, a development out of its potentialities. On the other hand, it may be a total "about-face" and new beginning. A missioner may be asked to conceive of life and mission in terms of *a totally new paradigm*, demanding new mental and psychological structures–not to mention the physical and geographical changes that a particular transition may demand.

Someone may have spent fifteen years in "the missions" of another continent, and is now being challenged to be "in mission" to the provincial administration of their religious order, or to the street people in the city where she or he grew up. I know an experienced missioner who was very involved in a project in a remote part of Asia. He felt that his contribution there was significant and necessary. He was asked to leave that project in the midst of its development in order to work in formation in the United States with seminarians doing theological studies. When he got to the house of formation, he became part of a formation team where there was a ratio of one "formator" for each seminarian. He found himself asking the question, "Is this mission? Is this what I became a missionary to do? There are lots of people around who can do this . . . and do it better than me!"

In returning to my own story, I had left "my father's and mother's house" years before I had gone off to Africa, not knowing where or what it would be like. I had considered these acts of faith–and in fact, they were. But it had seemed so clear then that the Divine was calling me. This was my vocation! But years later, leaving a country and my religious community, both of which were "home" for many years; this was truly *embarking on a new path, in the dark, having no idea where it was leading me*. And even trusting that *the Divine* was leading me was perhaps the greatest challenge. How could I really believe that I was still following my vocation, when it appeared that I was being led to abandon it?! In some way, I too felt that I was being asked to sacrifice my "Isaac." This surrendering into the arms of a providential God was the greatest act of faith I had made so far, and it was painful and scary.

## Stage Three: "The Return"

**The return begins . . . when in a hidden and imperceptible way our perception of the situation begins to alter (Searle, 43).**

As one surrenders, as it were, to a *new* kind of call, as represented through this transition, the time of turbulence, resistance, or mourning eventually subsides. Rambo notes two reactions to having surrendered. First of all, with the initial "enormous burst of both energy and relief," one feels a sense of liberation–"*the energy that was consigned to maintain the conflict is now channeled into the new life. . . .*" (Rambo, 135). The second phase involves maintaining or sustaining the surrender, being able to consolidate the new life into a firmer, growing commitment" (Rambo, 136). Thus, after the conflict has subsided, and one has "made the turn," there comes the need for owning what has happened, for making it a part of one's new reality.

Now, more than ever, there is a need for a certain withdrawal, for a time of prayerful reflection on what has happened. A receiving community or support group needs to be aware of the importance of this time of interiorization. This is the *actualization* of the surrender in one's life. *We have begun the return home.* "A new life has begun to quicken, a quiet joy, deep-seated and intangible, a more deeply rooted peace begin to make themselves felt beneath and beyond the continuing darkness and disorder" (Searle, 42).

**It is not that external circumstances
change–simply waiting for things to get
better is one of the ways of avoiding conversion–but our vision changes. We see things
in a new light. . . . This new vision cannot
be defined any more than the moment of its
coming can be exactly identified. But the
knowledge that one has somehow been rec-
onciled with Ultimate Reality, that one has
been in contact for once with all that finally
matters, is revealed in a nascent mood of
optimism, a feeling of deep integration, of
wholeness and renewal (Searle, 43).**

Signs of conversion, like little shoots of green, begin to break
through the dark soil: sprigs of hope, peace, and joy are barely visible.
In the process of surrendering, we sense at last that we have taken a
significant turn and started out in a new direction.

> *As I walked around the farmland in Door County,
> I identified with the greening of nature that was
> happening around me and felt new sap flowing in
> me, new life, and a healing perspective in relation
> to some of the painful experiences I had had in El
> Salvador. . . . I am like a tree whose leaves are be-
> ginning to open at the beginning of Spring.* "See, I
> am doing something new! Now it springs forth,
> do you not perceive it?" (Is 43:19) (Pam, 1996).

## Part IV: Biblical Conversion and Transition

> *"Oh, that today you would hear God's voice:
> Harden not your hearts"* (Ps 95:7-8)

Throughout this process, I have encouraged the dialogue between *our own experience* and our spiritual tradition. Now we will reverse the process in a sense, and take a look at some experiences of conversion found in scripture. Much as we did with images, we will allow our own unique experience to lead us to the scriptural experiences or passages which resonate, in some mysterious way or other, with our own. Turning to biblical commentaries on the subject of conversion in scripture as reference points,[85] we will briefly review the most common biblical understandings of "conversion" as found in the First and New Testaments. Then I will suggest some possible "conversion stories" as models for deepening experiences of hope in the midst of transition and one's journey. A main source for our reflection here will be my and other missioners' allusions to scriptural texts while in the midst of their own transition.

## Conversion: Some Common Understandings

### THE FIRST TESTAMENT:[86] *SHUB*

In the First Testament the Hebrew word *shub* is the most common term for any form of conversion. Michael Crosby tells us that, according to William Holladay, *shub* is the twelfth most frequently used verb in the First Testament, appearing 1,059 times (see Eigo, 31-74). There are two basic meanings implied in the word *shub*. One involves physical motion, the act of turning from or turning to something or someone. The other meaning adds to the act of "turning" a dimension of relationship, especially covenant faithfulness or faithlessness, as in turning back, toward, or away from Yahweh (Crosby in Eigo, 31-32). One simple translation of *shub* is simply "returning home"(Conn, *Christian Conversion*, 200).

But *shub* in its different forms can help us understand better the many dimensions and meanings of radical change. A passage from Jeremiah (8:4-5) illustrates this well:

> **When they fall, do they not rise again? If**
> **one turns away (*yashub*), does he not return**
> **(*yashub*)? Why then has this people turned**

> away (*shub bah*) in perpetual backsliding (*m
> shubah*)? They hold fast to deceit, they refuse
> to return (*lashub*) (Crosby in Eigo, 31).

In the First Testament, Jeremiah perhaps best reveals the essence of conversion. It is not so much a matter of external observances of the law or ritual that matters to God. Rather, our values and priorities need reordering, thus "circumcision of the heart" (Crosby in Eigo, 44). "Circumcise yourselves to the Lord, remove the foreskin of your hearts, O men of Judah and inhabitants of Jerusalem" (Jer 4:4). Dom Marc-François Lacan summarizes that, in the First Testament, "to be converted is to become faithful," and he adds, "To succeed in this, a person must rely on God in perfect trust" (Conn, 87). This theme of unconditional trust in God will be reinforced in the New Testament understanding of faith.

## THE NEW TESTAMENT: *METANOIA*

In the New Testament, *shub* was usually translated into the Greek root *strepho*, meaning "to turn." While *strepho* has a covenantal sense in some of the writings of Paul, the gospels use a new series of words to indicate conversion, all having *meta* as their prepositional prefix. (*Noia* derives from *nous* (Greek), or mind; related to thought.) *Metanoia*, then, implies both repenting and *reordering* one's life.

> To be converted (*metanoein*) is not only
> to repent for one's sins, but also to bring
> about an interior transformation which
> blossoms out in a change of conduct, in a
> new orientation of life; a spiritual or moral
> "about face" . . . To be converted is first
> of all to believe in the Good News which
> Jesus proclaims. And what is this news?
> The presence of the Kingdom of God. This

> **is indeed news capable of causing whoever
> hears it to "turn around," on the condition
> of believing in the one who proclaims it
> (Lacan in Conn, *Conversion*, 100-101).**

Conversion, far from being simply a once-and-for-all act of repentance, is intimately connected with the ever evolving presence of the Divine in the world: "Repent, the reign of God is at hand" (Matt 5:17). In the synoptic gospels, faith implies seeking the reign of God, and accepting Jesus as the inauguration of its presence. Conversion is a condition for entering this new divine order, not only for "sinners" but also for the just. It would seem that a permanent state of metanoia is a necessary condition for a living and active faith that witnesses the justice and peace of God's reign, or what the Reverend Dr. Martin Luther King Jr. referred to as the "Beloved Community."[87] Crosby confirms Lacan's observation:

> **The axis of Matthew's gospel is the
> proclamation of Christian justice which
> is the fruit of conversion and the re-
> quirement of faith. Now, this justice is
> nothing other than a permanent conver-
> sion; Jesus defines the just person in a
> word . . . the one who "seeks," who has
> never stopped "seeking the reign of God
> and his justice" (Matt 6:33) (Lacan in
> Conn, *Conversion*, 109).**

It is precisely to this sense of "permanent turning" that we are invited: to never stop seeking God and God's justice. *It is my belief that the "crisis" of transition is, in God's own mysterious way, a personal invitation to greater wholeness–and holiness.* Whether with a whisper, a gentle nudge–or a jolting shove–God is saying: "Seek me with all your heart, and you will find me. (compare: Jer 29:112-13).

## BIBLICAL EXPERIENCES: SOME HELPFUL PARADIGMS

> *O you of little faith. . . . Do not worry and say,*
> *"What are we to eat?" or "What are we to drink?"*
> *or "What are we to wear?" . . . Your heavenly*
> *Father knows that you need them all. But seek*
> *first the reign of God and its righteousness, and*
> *all these things will be given you besides (Matt*
> *6:31-33).*

Transformed living demands that we be always ready for the unexpected, ready to make another turn in the road or an "about face"; willing to sacrifice our "Isaac," (compare: Gen 22), to become like little children (compare: Mark 10:14-15), to seek God in all things, to never cease striving to "be holy as your heavenly Father is holy" (Matt 5:48). We know, however, how easy it is, over time, to just gradually accommodate the "new normal," to slip into a comfortable life, becoming accustomed to the norms of society and maintaining the status quo, in whatever society or culture we find ourselves. This is why the call to transformation is not reserved only for a few, but for all of us. We now look at two classic examples of this call, one from the First Testament and the other from the New.

## AFTER GOD'S HEART

David's conversion, recounted in the Second Book of Samuel, is one of the best known conversion stories in the Bible. As a paradigm, it allows us to discern "the essentials of an authentic conversion": God initiates it; it is a grace; it is necessary to receive it as a grace and to become a witness to this grace (see Lacan in Conn, *Conversion,* 76-79).[88]

David is a man with a vocation and a mission: to be faithful to Yahweh by observing the law and the prophets, and by governing God's people with justice. He is a good and a humble man. David carries out his mission with fidelity and zeal. We can witness this from his youth, in his devotion to King Saul and Saul's son Jonathan (compare 1 Sam 16:14-23; 17:32-58; and 24:1-23). Later, as Lacan puts it, David, "A wise, valiant, and devout king, remains humble in success, as indicated by his behavior at the time of the entrance of the Ark into Zion (2 Sam 6)" (In Conn, *Conversion*, 76). This is one of my personal favorite images of David, leading the procession before the Ark of the Lord, dancing "with abandon."

Yet gradually David becomes complacent and eventually begins down a slippery slope. He allows his lust for life and beauty to lead him into a succession of serious transgressions, both of his own conscience and of the Law. When David fell, he fell hard, as was typical of his life pattern. It took a harsh encounter with the truth, through the prophet Nathan, to bring David, literally, to his knees before his God (2 Sam 11-12). And again, when David came to awareness and repented of his sin, he likewise did it with humility and his whole heart.

Michael Crosby suggests that the stages in David's conversion "can serve as a model in all personal conversion." He outlines them as they are recounted in 2 Samuel:

> *The sinner remains in sin and justifies it (2 Sam 11:1-26).*
>
> *The sinner is confronted with a realization of the sinful situation (2 Sam 12:1-12).*
>
> *The sinner admits/confesses the sin (2 Sam 12-13).*
>
> *The sinner, guilt-ridden, repents of the sin and atones for it (2 Sam 12:14-25).*[89]

I take the liberty below of paraphrasing these stages in a slightly different way, as they might correspond to Lonergan's dimensions of conversion, and to someone in transition. Following is an example of how this conversion might resemble a "rite of passage" *from→through→to→from→through→to→* ... This includes brief excerpts from one missioner (Spring 1993), as he describes his experience and makes scriptural associations with it.

**1. "From . . ."** We still hold on to "illusions" in our situation, and yet gradually become vaguely dissatisfied with it.

> *When I had come to the island, I had known there*
> *would be difficulties, but I thought that I could*
> *handle them well enough. I seemed to be able to*
> *adjust to new situations. . . . The weather would be*
> *hot, but I could adjust to that too. After all, I came*
> *from a land of very cold winters. . . . I knew that*
> *I could learn about new ways, new customs. . . .*
> *Sure I was a "proud" person from time to time, but*
> *usually I felt that I tried to be genuinely "humble"*
> *toward others. . . . How is it that now, island of my*
> *missionary dreams, you have become my night-*
> *mare? Why have you become so impossibly humid,*
> *so unbearably hot. . . . I cannot rest. I am weak,*
> *irritable, impatient, tired. . . . Suddenly the former*
> *pastor is gone, and I am pastor of 20,000 people!*
> *I cannot even speak to them. After all those years*
> *of study, all I can do is say Hello and smile. . . . I*
> *feel so frustrated. . . . With myself, with others, with*
> *God. I know that many of my "images" are false,*
> *but I hold on to them for security. . . .*
>
> *Peter said to him, "Even though all should have*
> *their faith shaken, mine will not be." Then Jesus*
> *said to him, "Amen, I say to you this very night*
> *before the cock crows twice you will deny me three*
> *times." But he vehemently replied, "Even though I*
> *should have to die with you, I will not deny you."*
> *And they all spoke similarly* (Mk 14:29-31).

Then something occurs (marker event, sudden change) which confronts us with the human condition, radically clarifying "stubborn and misleading myths concerning reality, objectivity, and human knowledge"; e.g., self-sufficiency, complacency, false expectations, false sense of security, illusions, lack of compassion, etc. (compare: intellectual conversion, Lonergan, *Method*, 238).

> *Suddenly, everything had collapsed. Like some strange quirk of fate, everything had turned upside down. I felt disowned, a failure. The only choice I could make was to leave the mission. I had no choice. . . . Yet leaving was like cutting away half of my heart, half of my life. . . . Just to return to the States was shock enough. . . . Helpless, I sought to find walls of protection to shelter me from further storms. It seemed to be the only way to stay alive. Often though, I found myself almost "buried alive."*
>
> *Jesus said to them in reply, "Have you come out as against a robber, with swords and clubs, to seize me? Day after day I was with you teaching in the temple area, yet you did not arrest me; but that scriptures may be fulfilled." And they all left him and fled* (Mk 14:48-50).

**2. "Through . . ."** We reluctantly accept the change and enter into transition, reevaluating the criteria of our decisions and choices (compare: moral conversion; Lonergan, *Method*, 240).

> *This was my frame of mind when I was asked to write about something from my mission experience, as part of a course for returning missionaries. . . . I chose a "nice" story, innocuous enough, I hoped, to prevent further injury to a heart already adrift in a sea of confusion, doubts and fears, sorrow, and a lot of hurt. . . . As we progressed in the course, bit by bit, my walls of protection started to come down. As we delved deeper into the many*

*levels of our "simple" stories, I felt free enough to
start asking myself some very important questions. . . . I began to see a gift of hope appear.*

*Now that very day, two of them were going to a vil-
lage seven miles from Jerusalem called Emmaus,
and they were conversing about all the things that
had occurred. And it happened that while they
were conversing and debating, Jesus himself drew
near and walked with them, but their eyes were
prevented from recognizing him* (Lk 24:13-16).

**3. "To . . ."** We struggle with the new demands of faith, but finally allow ourselves to be "grasped" by that which is greater than
self, surrendering "without conditions, qualifications, reservations"
to the God who continues to call and challenge (compare: religious
conversion, beginning of self-transcendence and insight; *Lonergan,*
Method, 240-243).

*I finally turn toward God . . . and ask for help. Why
is it that I turn to God "last"? After all of my other
choices fail me. . . . This is "holy ground" . . . the
"meeting place of God" where just one condition is
mandatory: total honesty between myself and God.
At last, I allow no more excuses, no more escapes
in this holy place. It is time to search for the Truth.
I must wait before God for answers. . . . God must
bring light to my darkness. . . . How long must I
wait? Does it really matter? . . . I have finally come
to realize that my views are no longer sufficient for
"life." I must see it in a new way . . . no matter how
long it takes. . . . There is no half-way in "overcom-
ing myself" to become like Christ. I either make the
choice, or not. . . .*

*And he said to them, "Oh, how foolish you are! How*
*slow of heart to believe all that the prophets spoke!*
*Was it not necessary that the Messiah should*
*suffer these things and enter into his glory?" Then*
*beginning with Moses and all the prophets, he*
*interpreted to them what referred to him in all the*
*scriptures* (Lk 24: 25-26).

The invitation to "rend our hearts" (Joel 2:13) comes to us in strange packages, under unusual conditions, and when we least expect it. Neither do we *choose* it. Rather, like crisis, "it is thrust upon us" (Searle, 38), sometimes by circumstances that hardly seem conducive to any preconceived notion of conversion, much less with "God's will." (Recall how Marty spoke of his "nervous breakdown," which eventually precipitated an authentic transformation, exploding in his life like a "volcanic eruption.") Ultimately, conversion is a call to "Rend your hearts, not your garments, and return to the Lord, your God" (Joel 2:13). And transformation is the consequence of God's enormous gift of love (compare: Lonergan, *Method*, 237-243).

## *"The Road Not Taken"* (Robert Frost)

Let us turn now to a New Testament model of a transformation process. Michael Crosby presents Matthew's theme of "seeking-finding-selling-buying" as a paradigm for such a process. We have already seen the intimate connection between "seeking the reign of God" and conversion. We are continually called to be seekers after the gifts and fruits of the Spirit, which puts us in a continual state of transformation. Or might I say a continual *dance*–of turning, turning . . . "til we come 'round right."[90] The Synoptics present to us the case of a "seeker" who does not have the courage–or whatever he is lacking–to bring his call to completion. I am speaking of "the rich man" who approaches Jesus with the question: "Good teacher, what must I do to inherit eternal life?" (Mk 10:17-31; Lk 18:18-23; Matt 19:16-22).[91]

The main character in this gospel account is obviously a good person, a "just" man. He comes to Jesus seeking how to become *better*, how to live his life more fully. In other terms, he is asking how to "be perfect" as his heavenly Father is perfect (compare Matt 5:48). Jesus answers by reminding him of the commandments. Perhaps still kneeling before Jesus, he replies: "Teacher, all these things I have observed from my youth." And Jesus, looking at him with love, said to him,

> *"You are lacking in one thing. Go, sell what you have, and give to the poor and you will have treasure in heaven; then come, follow me." At that statement his face fell, and he went away sad, for he had many possessions (Mk 10:21-22).*

This person had evidently entered into a process of conversion. He had found himself restless, in some way looking for "something more." This good person, propelled, as it were, toward self-transcendence by a pursuit of truth and goodness, is seeking the ground of all goodness: "Good Teacher. . . . " And Jesus' response makes this clearer: "Why do you call me good? No one is good but God alone" (Mk 10:18).

What was it that caused this man to come to Jesus in search of that "ultimate good"? Was there a "marker event" that symbolized something of which he had been only vaguely aware until then? Had he suffered a loss? Had there been some death in his family that had caused him to consider more seriously his own quest for "eternal life"? Or had he been listening to Jesus for some length of time and had long been wanting to talk to him. Was it Jesus "setting out on a journey" from that district that made the rich man want to seize the opportunity to ask his burning question? We can only speculate. What does seem clear however, is that when it came to the moment of surrender, the man could not let go. Both Matthew and Mark report that when he heard Jesus' proposal: "'Go and sell what you have, and give to the poor . . ., his face fell, and he went away sad, for he had many possessions" (Mk 10:21-22).

Imagine this person to be a "missioner," one of us who has "kept the commandments from our youth," spent many years in the mission field, and are now being asked to make a change, to be stretched beyond our comfort zone, to become "porcelain." Sometimes we may pride ourselves–if even unconsciously–on our lack of possessions. We make visits to our "homeland" (especially if it's the so-called first world), and are overwhelmed, sometimes genuinely distressed, at the enormous quantity of "things" that people have. We are sometimes hostile to the capitalist consumerism that seems to tolerate, if not perpetuate, the systemic poverty of over two-thirds of the world's population–the people we have been serving. All of this may well be an authentic response from one who has spent a number of years away from the "first world."

But is it not also true that we too have our own possessions, our "Isaacs." Often we have built our own "kingdoms," losing sight of that which is the Source and End of all our being–and our coming and going. We have our achievements: churches, schools, programs, hospitals, and clinics. We speak about "our" catechists, parishioners, base communities; our workers and farmers, our girls and boys, nurses and midwives–as though *we own* them or made them who they are. (Remember Kathy, who was so convinced that *she would* change things! She burned herself out in her over-ambitious zeal.)

Also there are our interior idols: our pride; our need for affirmation, security, or control; our jealousies and rivalries–existing sometimes among our churches,parishes, or organizations, even among ourselves as colleagues or companions. We have our hurts and wounds that we often protect and nurse more carefully than the patients in our clinics. I look at my own experience. Had I not exaggerated the importance of *my* literacy program or *my* little "lay-away" project? One of the reasons I was so devastated by the theft in the storeroom was that I took it so *personally*. I who was so dedicated, so appreciated, respected, accepted, loved by the people. How could this have happened to *me*?!

Transition brings an opportunity to start over, to begin again the process of "leaving everything." One of the greatest challenges is putting *all* of our trust in the One we follow:

*"Master, master, we are perishing!" He awakened,
rebuked the wind and the waves, and they subsided, and there was a great calm. Then he asked
them, "Where is your faith"* (Lk 8:24-25).

*Look at the birds in the air; they do not sow or
reap, they gather nothing into barns, yet your
heavenly father feeds them. Are you not more important than they* (Mk 6:26).

*Do not store up for yourselves treasures on earth,
where moth and decay destroy, and thieves break
in and steal. But store up treasures in heaven,
where neither moth nor decay destroy, nor thieves
break in and steal. For where your treasure is,
there also will your heart be* (Mk 6:19-21).

Jesus invites us again and again to let go of our possessions, to
stop clinging to our settled nests of security, to let go of our fears and
doubts, as well as our accomplishments and failures. *Allowing our
transition to renew us is to enter into a conversion, to get our priorities straight, our relationships in order.* We did it once perhaps, but
over the months and years, we gradually began to take it all back–everything we thought we had left behind in our early missionary fervor
and enthusiasm. Often, little by little, we have been accumulating
again. And our hearts have become so heavy that there is no way for
God's Spirit to move them anymore! What a striking contrast in the
gospel between the one whose "face fell, and . . . went away sad" (Mk
10:22), and the one who "out of joy goes and sells all . . . and buys
that field" (Mt 13:44). Maybe we are being called to swallow our pride
and see ourselves anew, to see ourselves in the woman who, "left her
water jar behind and went into the town and said to the people, 'Come
see a man who told me everything I have done. Could he possibly be
the Messiah?!'" (Jn 4:28-29).

## Moving On: Some Concluding Comments

As we began the process of "setting out" and were thrust headlong into "the adventure" of our transition, we recognized at some moment the invitation to surrender our "heart of the matter" to the One who has called us, and continues to journey with us. The "transformation" is not yet over; it may have just begun. In the past when, full of enthusiasm, we set off for our first mission assignment, the time probably arrived when we felt the urge to "look back," even though we had "put our hand to the plough." So it may be with us now. At first, perhaps with renewed courage and energy, we are ready to put our hands to new ploughs. But we find ourselves in new and strangely different fields. *We must trust*. It will take time to learn the new terrain and to cull the wisdom of our past in order to help us live our new call to life.

> **Order is not at once restored, still less is the old order reestablished: to that there can be no going back. Yet gradually, one is led to a new set of relationships, more genuine and more realistic, with one's world. The sense of futile restlessness gives way perhaps to a growing sense of new direction and meaningfulness. One's defeats and failures are not taken away, but forgiven. Physical and material losses are not necessarily made good, but perhaps the sense of loss is transformed into that detachment which is the condition of genuine freedom. The disintegration of so much that one had clung to, fades before the hope of a richness and wholeness one had not previously guessed possible (Searle, 42).**

There remains now one final invitation: that of *integration*. How do we integrate new insight into our lives? This is the challenge to be explored in the next and final chapter. In some ways we are still "betwixt and between." But now, having probed the "heart of the matter," having surrendered, we are in a different space. We have taken the risk of letting go of those idols: of false hopes and unrealistic expectations, of a false sense of self-reliance and security, and of having to be in control our life and destiny. Having offered our "Isaacs" to the Holy One who led us up this mountain from the beginning, we have crossed over the threshold and are one step closer to home.

## AT HOME

I
sit by
Mother Ganga
as She crashes over stone,
freeing Herself from the dark forest
where I walk early mornings past a naked Naga
smeared in ash tending his dhuni fire at the mouth of his cave.
I feel at home.
The sound of chattering birds, the peacocks crossing path,
the elephant dung piled high, the sound of
streams propelled to the body of
Mother Ganga
by my side—
these    bring
me    home.
But in every
country    I
feel  home.
Every place
I    touch
the earth
is home.

Rishikesh, India

Chapter Five

# Insight and Integration: "Coming Home"

> At every turning point in our journey, we
> can hope, reasons of the heart will come to
> light (Dunne, *Reasons*, xi).

In this chapter, we reflect on "homecoming," reflecting upon John Dunne's insights from his own journey of "passing over" and "coming back," and drawing inspiration from Henri Nouwen's meditation on *The Return of the Prodigal Son* (1992).[92] With an understanding of the "true self" as our authentic "home" within,[93] I trust we will arrive at some new insight for truly being "at home" in the constantly changing context of our journey.

## Part I: Marginality: From Surviving to Thriving

> *Now we look for a new place to pitch our tent for*
> *awhile, until it be time to move on again. We feel,*
> *above all we worry, that we'll be overpowered by*
> *the desire to move from the tent into a house and*
> *so lose our missionary freedom, our missionary*

> *values. We don't want to leave either our tents or*
> *the tents of the poor with whom we share a corner*
> *of this earth (Ron, 1996).*[94]

## Cultural Marginality

In Chapter One we considered the challenge of the changing identity of the missioner, and what mission means in our global church
today. We have been exploring, in the context of our Christian tradition, the transition of moving *from* our mission experience, wading
*through* feelings and images of the past and present, which lead us
*to* the heart of the matter. Let us now explore our current and future
identity through the concept of "cultural marginality" (see Bennett,
109-135).[95] According to this concept, individuals find themselves
marginalized from their own cultural frames of reference.

> **An individual who has internalized two
> or more cultural frames of reference fre-
> quently faces an internal culture shock.
> This intrapersonal response is not due so
> much to external interaction with a single
> different culture, but rather to the recog-
> nition of conflicts between two cultural
> voices competing for attention within one-
> self (Bennett, 112).**

When this situation occurs, the subject could get "stuck" in a
state of encapsulated marginality, or walk toward a dynamic situation of constructive marginality. I believe that the veteran returning
home or the missioner being sent to another culture, will certainly
experience this phenomenon, and face this kind of choice.

## "Encapsulated" Marginality

This is an ambiguous state in which one's choices are muddled by
conflicting perspectives, combined with a lack of inner responsibility

to think and decide autonomously.[96] The "encapsulated marginal" represents that which is the worst or most unsettling about "reverse culture shock." As we pointed out in previous chapters, missioners *will* experience culture shock upon reentry or in a process of changing missions. This is the nature of being "betwixt and between." The problem, however, as Bennett suggests, is when one gets ***stuck*** there; i.e., "encapsulated." Those who are *stuck* in their transition are not unlike individuals who get "stuck" in adolescence. They are very self-conscious, preoccupied with their sense of marginality, never "at home" with themselves nor with others, because they don't know where they belong. They squirm, uncomfortable with themselves, and neither are others comfortable with them.

Such sojourners may have a wealth of wisdom and experience to communicate, but they are trapped in a perceived state of "terminal uniqueness," feeling estranged and alienated from the culture from which they've come, from the culture that they are currently in, and consequently, from themselves (see Bennett, 115). This state of cultural and self-estrangement could lead a missioner to experience an estrangement from God, thus producing the kind of anxiety and sense of meaninglessness and hopelessness that I have sometimes encountered in returning missioners. The characteristics of encapsulated marginality are shown in Figure 5.1.

## CHARACTERISTICS OF ENCAPSULATED MARGINALITY

- Loose boundary control
- Difficulty in decision making
- Alienation
- Self-absorption
- No recognized reference group
- Multiplistic (i.e., more complex than duplistic)
- Conscious of self
- Disintegration in shifting cultures
- Troubled by ambiguity
- Never "at home"

**Figure 5.1 Adapted from Bennett, 113.**

## *"Constructive" Marginality*

This describes a person who has come–usually through doing their inner work, and sometimes with others who are also in transition–to experience marginal status as *constructive* rather than destructive. We begin to evaluate life around us in terms of the *context*, thus "intentionally and consciously . . . creating our own [new] identity" (Bennett, 113). A constructive marginal is not immune to the throes of culture shock, however. To the contrary, this missioner also has to deal with what Bennett calls "disintegration" (see 112-119). In terms of transformation, this might be considered a process of "dying" in order to be reborn again. "There must be a finding and a losing, and then a losing and a finding" (Dunne, *Reasons*, xi). The situation of constructive marginality includes the characteristics shown in Figure 5.2.

### CHARACTERISTICS OF CONSTRUCTIVE MARGINALITY

- Self-differentiation
- Well-developed boundary control
- Self as choice-maker
- Dynamic in-betweenness
- Authenticity
- Marginal reference group (recognizing oneself as part of a marginal group; not the mainstream)
- Commitment within relativism
- Conscious of choice
- Intrigued by complexity
- Never *not* "at home"

**Figure 5.2. Adapted from Bennett, 113.**

As people of faith, we know that the cultural context has influenced our way of knowing and being; i.e., our values and standpoints on political or religious issues, our way of thinking and of viewing life, our spirituality–our way of praying and being in the world with God and others. If we have been faithful to our vocation, we will have been continually forging our identity, allowing our "evolving self" to be influenced by, even as we influence, the vitality around us. Just as we have learned from the people and cultures where we have been in the past, we can be confident that we have something new to learn from the people and culture that surround us now, in the *present*. The *constructive* marginal recognizes that the future is "full of hope," and has come to be at home, realizing that "one is never *not* at home in the world" (Bennett, 113, 118). This realization will carry us gently into a new future full of hope. *For I know well the plans I have in mind for you, says the Lord, plans for your welfare, not for woe! plans to give you a future full of hope* (Jer 29:11).

I've emphasized here certain aspects of what it means to be an "encapsulated marginal" (which Maryknoller, Larry Lewis, might call a "maladjusted misfit") and a "constructive marginal" (a "well-adjusted misfit.") I suggest that the process explored throughout this book might be considered as a sort of "rite of passage," which would facilitate the movement *from* encapsulating marginality *to* constructive marginality. This shift within cultural marginality is expressed in Figure 5.3. Living in cultural marginality implies both active waiting and subtle movement toward insight.

## TRANSITION IN CULTURAL MARGINALITY

**ENCAPSULATED MARGINALITY** → → → **CONSTRUCTIVE MARGINALITY**

| | | |
|---|---|---|
| Disintegration in shifting cultures | → | Self-differentiation |
| Loose boundary control | → | Well-developed boundary control |
| Difficulty in decision making | → | Self as choice-maker |
| Alienation | → | Dynamic in-betweenness |
| Self-absorption | → | Authenticity |
| No recognized reference group | → | Marginal reference group |
| Multiplistic | → | Commitment within relativism |
| Conscious of self | → | Conscious of choice |
| Troubled by ambiguity | → | Intrigued by complexity |
| Never "at home" | → | Never not "at home" |

**Figure 5.3 Adapted from Bennett, 113.**

# Part II: Insight: Passing Over and Coming Back

> The movement toward insight is like a
> journey. We travel from experience through

**feeling to image to new ideas and awareness
that can change and enrich our lives. At
our most intuitive moments, we may not be
aware of the flow of the movement. Bringing
it to awareness allows our reflection to
become more conscious and critical. . . . It
opens us to being more discerning of God's
presence and action in our lives (Killen and
de Beer, 45).**

Theologian John Dunne has written much about a rather unique
process of finding one's true self. Paradoxically, his discovery takes
place in the context of "the other": other people, times, places, cultures, religions. While not a missioner in the ordinary sense of the
term, Dunne has, I believe, given us a model for missionary life in
his method of doing theology. "My method is my journey," he tells
us (*Reasons*, 151). And for those who know Dunne's works, his nov-
el-like autobiographical writings reveal that his personal journey *is*
his theological method.[97]

     This method and journey are one of "passing over" and of "com-
ing back," which can be traced through all of the books he has written
since he wrote *The City of the Gods* (1965),[98] in which he first made
his method explicit. Dunne articulates this method, as he attempts to
live it, in his written "spiritual adventures" (*The Way of All the Earth*,
ix), each of which attempts to describe an ultimate search for God
through sympathetic understanding of the other. One example of
this "passing over" occurs on a riverboat, a journey that was to lead
Dunne not only up the Amazon River, but also from his standpoint
of "personal religion" to "the religion of the poor," (Dunne *Church of
the Poor Devil*, vii-x).

**When you are willing to be on a personal
journey, you step into your own aloneness,
say Yes to it, become one with it. "You
find a way a lone a last a loved a long the**

**riverrun." At the same time, you find that the way "a long the riverrun" is a way for everyone, that you have companions on the journey, that we are on a voyage together. A time like that came for me on the riverboat, a moment of vision, a moment of conversion. I saw in that moment how our voyage on the riverboat was an image of the human journey in time. . . . It was a glimpse of the human essence. Passing over to others reveals how we are sources of life to one another; coming back to yourself reveals how we have the source life within ourselves (Dunne, *Church*, 20 (quoting James Joyce, *Finnegan's Wake*)).**

## *Passing Over and Coming Back*

Dunne's theological method unfolds in six moments,[99] which correspond almost directly to Killen and de Beer's movements for theological reflection.[100] Each leg of Dunne's spiritual–and usually geographical–journey, like each book, begins from a different starting point; i.e., his personal standpoint or horizon at that given time and place. He then attempts to "pass over," through a process which he calls "sympathetic understanding," to a different standpoint–that of another person, culture, place, time, religion, etc. He then, in turn, "comes back" to his own original standpoint–which is, however, no longer the same as it was before. He describes each "passing over" and "coming back" as a "step of the journey which begins as a kindling of the heart and ends as an illumining of the mind" (Dunne, *Reasons*, 152). The fifth and six moments are: waiting for insight, and once received, allowing the new or renewed insight to become a guide for life. *This "illumination of the mind" through the heart's way of knowing is what Dunne calls the "insight."*

*"It is when reasons of the heart become known to the mind, I believe, that insight occurs"* (Reasons, xii).

> **Passing over to others and coming back to oneself, when it does occur, changes one's relationship with others and with oneself, and when it occurs among a group of people . . . it is an image of change in society. . . . It is the image of a society based on passing over and coming back, on sharing the human essence. It is a changing image, much as time is a changing image of eternity (Dunne, *Church*, ix).**

What missioner has not entered "sympathetically into the feelings of another person?" For most of us, one would hope, if we have discovered anything in our years of cross-cultural ministry, it's that, in attempting to teach others, it is *we* who have been taught; in healing others, it is *we* who have been healed; in attempting to help others, it is *we* who needed help; in giving to others, it is *we* who received much more in return. "Passing over" may be expressed and nuanced in different ways; e.g., acculturation, empathetic presence, compassion, etc. Regardless of what we choose to call it or however we may understand it, this process is, I think, the essence of ministry.

But there is the second half of the process. We come to understanding by "coming back to that of our own lives and times." *Often this "coming back" is the most difficult leg of the journey, which provides an equal or possibly greater challenge.* It is, however, this cyclical process that makes the journey complete, leading to a new understanding which Dunne refers to as "insight." Isn't this precisely what most of us are seeking as a result of a transition: a new or "renewed" understanding of our life? New insight will be like "a guide" as we continue on our journey into a new context.

Dunne has articulated an intentional way of doing theology based on his experience; i.e., he learns and speaks of God by passing over into the lives of others and then returning to his own. Missioners–perhaps less consciously–have also been doing this throughout our missionary lives. Perhaps we might say that many of us have been living "practical theology" without knowing it, the only difference being intentionality.

Initially, Dunne entered into this process spontaneously, simply because he was *attentive to his feelings*. It was in reading the epic of *Gilgamesh*, that he found his own deep concern and uneasy feelings reflected in the hero. Through the *image* of Gilgamesh and his own journey, Dunne was able to recognize his "*heart of the matter*," which he calls his "real gut problem" (Nilson, 48).

> **The story of a man who had been so trou-bled by death that he had embarked on a quest for unending life could be his [Dunne's] own story too. He found him-self reading the epic not to find data to support a thesis but to gain insight on an issue engaging his whole existence. Having "found that my real gut problem was death, not political theology," Dunne was now at a crossroads. He could continue his work on political theology and relegate his real issue, death, to the private realm of medi-tation, or evade it altogether. Or he could, like Gilgamesh, set out on his own quest by letting his "gut problem" occupy his mind as well as his heart. He could go on his own journey in search of insight into this prob-lem, which he had come to see occupying the hearts and minds of humankind across all ages and cultures (Nilson, 68).**

His writings clearly evidence which path Dunne took at his "crossroads," and that, as the poet might say, "made all the difference."[101] As returning or transitioning missioners, we too are at a crossroads. We have a unique opportunity for renewed growth and discovery. Transition can be a privileged time for re-discovering "the other" with whom and to whom we have been ministering, and the ultimate "Other," without whom our life would not make sense. Most especially, we have a time and space in our liminal moment to rediscover with renewed understanding, *ourselves*, as persons, ministers, and missioners. We have become, in the words of Maryknoller, Larry Lewis, "misfits."[102] Paradoxically, it is this very "misfitness" at a transitional crossroads of our journey, which places us on a threshold of possibility; i.e., the integration of a new and transformed self.

> **Missioners who have worked and lived many years in either host or home culture and return to the "other" find it one of the most wrenching of experiences. Returning to the "other," of host or home cultures, is a paradigm of the missioner returning to The Other, The More Than, which alone can give humanity its distinguishing characteristic as human. . . . This analogy of the homelessness, the misfitness of the foreign missioner and the returning again and again to The Other, is what roots the missionary vocation in the fundamental structure of human formation (Lewis, unpublished paper, 8-9).**

## Integrating the Misfit

But "straddling" two or more cultures does not *automatically* make the missioner a "sacrament" for others, a "beacon" to the "misfit" in all of us. This kind of straddling could, in fact, make us nothing more than disjointed! Threshold living can only be sustained by a *deep rootedness* in the transcendent and immanent Other, the Divine

Presence. And this kind of rootedness grows in the soil of our own solitude, where we discover, accept, and own the "truth" about who we are, and who God is. It is the fruit of prayerful, sometimes painful, reflection on one's experience of being transitional.

It is in this experience of knowing ourselves deeply rooted, in spite of the continuous, sometimes stormy movement of our lives and everything around us, that we "come home" to ourselves. We are able to hear that "tiny whispering sound" that says, "Be still, and know that I am God" (Ps 46:11). Home is that inner "place" where we meet our "truth,"where we know who we are, and *Whose* we are. And then no matter *where* we are, *at home* we are safe and whole. Paradoxically, it is in understanding, accepting, and embracing our marginality and vulnerability–our very restless "homelessness" as human beings–that we gradually begin to find ourselves strangely at home in our journey.

Larry Lewis names *his* truth. He calls it "the void" that he tried to ignore for much of his life. Traveling to China and beyond, like Luke's prodigal son, he tried to run away from himself. He found his "home" by remembering where he had met his truth, in "the rear, right-hand side pew of St. Mary's." There he had embraced his misfitness, yet knew he was safe. He felt "not laughed at," because he knew that "God didn't laugh at people," even at a fat, little eight- or nine-year-old kid (Lewis, 61).

> **As I look back over the three years in China and see how much came together interiorly for me, I realize it was because circumstances outside of me erupted into disorder and provided the occasion for interior disintegration as well. The exterior disintegration occasioned a felt social misfitness, and the interior disintegration revealed long-held memories of childhood social misfitness. The social misfitness of my childhood had brought me to God Who doesn't laugh.**

> **Everything that happened during my time
> in Wuhan had served to draw me closer to
> the truth that had originally brought me to
> that God. The cultural/geographical dislo-
> cations of my foreign missionary vocation,
> going to and from Wuhan, Hong Kong, and
> my home in the States all served to bring
> me back to the gateway to the void (Lewis,
> *The Misfit*, 162).**

A new and important dimension of our lives as missioners will be in owning and sharing this "otherness," especially with those *who have also experienced it*–but who are as yet *unable* or *unwilling* to name it or claim it. In this way, we will be able to strengthen others who, often unknowingly, remain alienated from themselves and others. But for this to happen, it is necessary to have not only "passed over" into others' lives and cultures, but also to have in some way successfully come back into our own. This is the process of genuine integration.

This does not mean that we will now "fit in." Nor should we–*part of constructive marginality is never really wanting to fully fit in*. But in finding a home within ourselves, in that deepest soul of our being, we will find peace in our experience of being other. "Peace I leave with you; my peace I give to you. Not as the world gives do I give it to you. Do not let your hearts be troubled or afraid" (John 14:27).

This peace of soul will not be mistaken nor go unnoticed, for it is a rare commodity in today's world. It is for this reason that I invite all who are in transition to claim as their own, to whatever extent they can, and in whatever way is helpful, the spirituality and lifestyle of "passing over" and "coming back." To enter sympathetically into the feelings of another person, become receptive to the images which give expression to those feelings, attain insight into those images, and then come back enriched by the insight to an understanding of one's own life, which can guide one into the future (Dunne, *Way*, 53).

It is difficult to synthesize Dunne's thought without oversimplify-ing it, which would be an injustice to the profound insight of this in-novative theologian. As we have seen in earlier chapters, sometimes we just don't know what to do with the images and feelings that we take with us from our ministry. The "baggage" that we carry weighs us down. Or sometimes, as another friend in transition recently put it, "I feel like a rubber band ready to break." If we don't handle that "rubber band" carefully, it just might stretch too far, and break. Likewise, if we allow our feelings to fester or form hard scabs to hide infection, we remain wounded without healing. *Human beings connect in our woundedness.* But if we cannot address our own wounds, we will never be able to fully understand or to help heal wounded others. We will both be in too much pain. To enter into the sufferings and joys of others on our new path, will need to be able to pass over into their lives of family and friends, or into new cultures and times of ministry. But healing takes time, and we must wait with patience for insight, for the "reasons of the heart" to become known, listening for that true inner voice leading us in our journey.

## *Waiting for Insight: Waiting on God*

Dunne's notion of passing over and coming back leads to new insight. *The ultimate insight, I believe, is coming to know one's true self, the self that is God's beloved, the dwelling place of God's Spirit.* For Dunne, the experience of waiting for insight is also a "waiting on God." As he puts it, "The waiting is the praying, and the coming of God is the answer to the prayer, and the coming takes the form of a kindling of light in the darkness. This kindling of light I shall call 'insight'" (Dunne, "Insight," 3). And he adds, "Waiting for insight . . . is waiting for one's heart to speak" (5). Dunne considers insight not primarily as an intellectual experience (Lonergan.)[103] Rather it belongs "both to the realm of mind and to that of the heart" (Dunne, "Insight," 3).

> **That . . . may be the unifying factor . . .**
> **listening . . . waiting for insight. In fact that**

> **waiting . . . is the willing of one thing . . .**
> **in so far as [it] is waiting for one thing:**
> **the one thing is like the x in an algebraic**
> **equation. It is an unknown quantity, the**
> **unknown path one must walk, and willing it**
> **is really a willingness to walk it. . . . Purity**
> **of heart . . . consists in waiting for insight,**
> **in waiting for [the] unknown path to be**
> **revealed. Yet . . . in the darkness; the path is**
> **still unknown. . . . That seeing of the way . . .**
> **will be the seeing of God, a seeing of the**
> **will of God. . . . If God leads by the heart,**
> **then God's leading should come to light, as**
> **it seems to be doing, when the heart be-**
> **comes pure, when the heart begins to will**
> **one thing ("Insight," 4-7).**

When in transition or re-entry, we really *must* wait. We are, as we have seen earlier, on the "waiting threshold" of neither there nor here. *No matter how busy we make ourselves, no matter how much we try to avoid it or rush it: transformation, like birth, will happen in its own time. And so we must wait in the darkness of the womb until the time of birthing is over.*

The question is: *Are we willing to wait for God?* And if so, *how* are we going to wait? Are we simply going to resign ourselves to it? Or are we going to *freely choose* to enter into it through *active, yet contemplative*, waiting. Surely we know by now that God's timing is not our timing (compare, II Peter 3-10). *Are we able to allow the time for our new selves to be born out of the transition?* The spirituality of Thomas Merton maintains that "the whole of the spiritual life finds its fulfillment in bringing our entire life into a transforming, loving communion with the ineffable God," and that this communion is both "the raison d'être and fruition of our deepest self" (Finley, 19).

## Part III: Homecoming: Where the Heart Is

> *Home is where one starts from. As we grow older*
>
> *The world becomes stranger, the pattern more complicated*
>
> *Of dead and living. Not the intense moment*
>
> *Isolated, with no before and after,*
>
> *But a lifetime burning in every moment*
>
> *And not the lifetime of one . . . only*
>
> *But of old stones that cannot be deciphered.*
>
> *There is a time for the evening under starlight,*
>
> *A time for the evening under lamplight*
>
> *(The evening with the photograph album).*
>
> *Love is most nearly itself*
>
> *When here and now cease to matter.*
>
> *[The] old . . . ought to be explorers*
>
> *Here and there does not matter*
>
> *We must be still and still moving*
>
> *Into another intensity*
>
> *For a further union, a deeper communion*
>
> *Through the dark cold and the empty desolation,*
>
> *The wave cry, the wind cry, the vast waters*
>
> *Of the petrel and the porpoise. In my end is my beginning.*
>
> ELIOT, "EAST COKER" V (190-209)

## *Upon Arriving*

Most of you reading this have been on many journeys: planes and boats and trains have taken many of you across oceans and continents. As "mountain climbers," we have trekked across deserts, reached high peaks, and ventured into deep tropical rain forests. We are "nomads" living on the edge of two or more lands. We are "marginals," and it is difficult to know where we belong, where to call "home." In fact, we sometimes wonder if we will ever be "at home" again.

These reflections have led us on another kind of journey. We have moved *from* our past and present experiences, *through* our feelings and images, and *into* the "heart of the matter," with its demand for surrender to an interior conversion. What I now want to emphasize is that the "waiting" in transition (like being in transit between planes) is *a necessary step toward the integration of our experiences, toward* "homecoming." If we are ever to truly come home, whatever or wherever it be, we must expect to live in a certain cultural marginality, and in fact, welcome the kind of healthy tension that comes with it. In this new context, we will be invited to embrace the Divine *living within a transformed and enriched self.*

Perhaps we have never been on any journey so challenging, so heart-rending, as this inner journey which calls us to become more whole and holy. Before us is the invitation we have been waiting for, *the invitation of a lifetime.* It's like coming to a new bend in the road. In the midst of a transition, perhaps not of our choosing, perhaps freely chosen, we need to attend carefully those experiences, feelings, images, and insights along the way. And if we carefully heed those signposts, our insights, and intuitions, we can hear ourselves being called to a new-found freedom and to a more fully integrated life. The voice comes from deep within and invites us to "come home."

For some of us, we were ready to leave our assignment. Still, it takes time before we are really ready to begin again in new surroundings. We must recognize that we are again in new and unknown territory (even when it—and we—appear to be the same.) Perhaps more than ever, it's necessary to unpack carefully and heed the voices guiding us on our way. For others, if we're not ready, it's even harder to "come home." We feel uprooted, especially if we've planted our heart there. I have often heard missioners—perhaps not unlike veterans, teachers, nurses, and others who render direct service—say, "I left my heart in Tanzania ... Brazil ... China ... Algeria. ..." Oftentimes, this is more than an expression–it is a perceived reality! How does one survive "without a heart?" How do we begin a new chapter if we can't "put our heart" into it? Is it better then, as some would believe, not to invest oneself anywhere, because it hurts too much to uproot it when the journey calls us on? I think not. Maybe these sound like silly or romantic questions. But in fact, I believe they are quite real and relevant–and certainly for missioners, in today's increasingly dynamic and mobile world of global mission.

In one From Mission To Mission workshop, a returning missioner asked the group what they thought about letter-writing. She explained that she had been a year away from her mission in South America, and still continued to receive many letters. There was genuine angst in her voice as she said, "I don't know what to do. I feel like each letter really needs a response, but then I wonder, *am I still holding on?* Should I stop answering their letters? Should I cut it off and let go?" Then she added, almost in tears, "The thing is, well, what I mean is, I feel like half of me is still there!"

Half of her *was* still there. As I've said earlier, "Once a missioner, always a missioner." In a sense, missioners don't really ever "hang up our hat"–much less our heart. We just perhaps hang them *differently*, in different places. Mission is not a question of geographical place and linear time. Rather, *mission is the passionate commitment that burns and grows, no matter where we are or what we do.* It is born in *kairos* time, that critical moment of awareness that, perhaps, changes everything–the critical moment–and is part of the dynamic and ever-changing "reign of God," which is both "here and now," and also "not yet." At the same time, sojourners on this earth also need to be rooted, need a space within ourselves that we can, in a very real way, call *home*. But as we have seen, arriving at this space is easier said than done.

## *"There's No Place Like It?"*

For many, especially those who have been away for many years, even the word "home" may evoke a "yucky feeling" in the pit of the stomach. Home is fine when you're just on furlough or a holiday visit. But the thought of going home *for good* can be frightening, revolting, depressing, even devastating to some–especially when it is coupled with the false idea of having to "leave the mission behind." I remember clearly when I would come to the US on my home visits from Zaire. I would go from my parents to other family members and friends in different parts of the country: vacationing, eating out, swimming, relaxing, etc. In general all of this was tolerable–most of it even enjoyable–because I knew that *this wasn't "home" for me anymore*. I remember feeling as though I were on a fast train ride during those few months in the US, with everything and everyone kind of whizzing by me in a surreal way. I knew that this lifestyle was only temporary, and in a few months I would be back in "reality," in "my world," the place I had come to call *home*. My family and friends couldn't understand this, and it hurt them if I tried to explain. So I kept it pretty much to myself.

At the same time, back in Zaire, after over a decade there, I was increasingly aware that it was not really my *home* either. In fact, today it is more important than ever that we recognize from the outset that we are guests in the countries where we serve–even "strangers," as Gittins puts it.[104] The irony is that oftentimes the longer we stay somewhere, the more we love the people and want to make this place "home." All the more, we also realize, as missioners, that we need to "work ourselves out of a job," eventually leaving this adopted home where, ultimately, we know we don't belong. On the occasion of his ordination as a bishop, the beloved Maryknoll missioner Bishop Walsh said, "The task of a missioner is to go to a place where he is not wanted, but needed, and to remain until he is not needed, but wanted."[105] A wise missioner knows it's time to leave when the people begin inviting her/him to stay forever!

This is, then, the dilemma: "loving and leaving." And indeed, we do leave parts of ourselves behind us as we go, living on in the lives of those whom we've loved. And in some ways, we *will* always feel like a stranger, not knowing where to call home. At the same time, this is the missioner's call, both a challenge and gift: to be a symbol for others in this world, attesting to the fact that here there is no "lasting dwelling place" (Hebrews 13:14). We are *all* nomads, pitching our tents and then taking them up again, like the One who was willing to "pitch his tent among us" (John 1:14). So then, none of us, at least as Christian believers, is *really* at home anywhere here on this earth. We are all on a journey, and since all human beings–(and maybe even extra-terrestrials like ET!)–need a home, we must find our home *in the journey*.

## The True Dwelling Place

> *Whoever loves me will keep my word, and my*
> *Father will love them, and we will come to them*
> *and make our dwelling with them (John 14:23).*

A friend of mine was born in Cuba, lives in Miami, studied in Chicago, and does missionary work in Haiti and the Dominican Republic. I once asked her where she felt most at home. She answered, laughing, "On the plane!" So how do we, who have traveled the globe, come to be at home in our missionary journey, no matter where we are? In reality, we missioners have begun that long journey home a long time ago, "passing over and coming back" perhaps many times. If we have been faithful to this voyage, carefully attending to all of our unpacked bags, listening to the voice within that has been leading us, then we have already arrived at the threshold, at the door of our true dwelling place:

> **Home is the center of my being where I**
> **can hear the voice that says: "You are my**
> **Beloved, on you my favor rests." Jesus has**
> **made it clear to me that the same voice**
> **that he heard at the River Jordan and on**
> **Mount Tabor can also be heard by me. He**
> **has made it clear to me that just as he has**
> **his home with the Father, so do I. . . . Faith is**

**the radical trust that home has always been
there and always will be there (Nouwen,
35-36).**

This book has been all about that journey of coming home: telling our story, acknowledging our feelings, seeking the heart of the matter through our images, while listening to the wisdom of our heart and our tradition, naming our "Isaacs," and offering them to our God. Nouwen's semi-autobiographical meditation (inspired by Rembrandt's painting of the parable often called "The Prodigal Son" (Luke 15: 11-32)), assures us that *this journey to the center of our being is indeed the most challenging we ever make.* Perhaps Nouwen's beautiful writing makes it sound easy to accept this truth, that each of us is "the Beloved," but if we're honest with ourselves we know better. Dunne reminds us that this process goes on throughout our lifetime (*Search,* 219). He says that if we have been sincerely seeking *understanding,* and not certainty, then the quest would verify the saying, "Seek and you shall find, knock and it shall be opened to you" (219).

What is it that we seek and shall find when that door is opened to us? Dag Hammarskjold said, "We all have within us a center of stillness surrounded by silence."[106] Thomas Moore (*Care of the Soul*), among others, would probably call this center the "soul." Merton refers to it as "the true self," and Dunne has spoken of this "center" in a variety of ways. In The Church of the Poor Devil, he refers to it as the "heart of light," "religious essence," "human essence," and "source of inexhaustible life" (21). Five years later, in *The Homing Spirit* (1987), Dunne notes that his authentic "coming back" is not to his self, but to *the God dwelling within himself.* "I am! Here is the home of the spirit, where we can hear and say *I am,* a kingdom of persons, a life larger than life" (*The Homing Spirit,* 103).

Those who find themselves "alone" in their transition might take consolation from the image of Jesus in a critical moment of his own transition. Even his most faithful followers didn't understand what he was going through. When he needed them most they were overcome by sleep. "They could not keep their eyes open and they did not know what to answer him" (Mk 14:40). He too felt himself alone–but not totally. "Abba . . . all things are possible to You. Take this cup away from me, but not what I will, but what You will" (Mk 14:36). "The prime turning point in a life is the point where one goes over, if and when one does, from God as the unknown and uncontrollable, to God as Abba" (Dunne, *Search*, 222). "Our weakness remains, but it is a handed-over weakness, made strong in its openness and abandonment to God's mercy (Finley, 87).

## Trust and Gratitude

The essential attitude of being "at home" in our journey is one of **radical trust**. Dunne refers to it below as "unconditional relation." Merton refers to it more as "faith." No matter what we call it, this attitude is not really achieved by working hard at it. It will come, however, in prayer, if we sincerely listen to the Spirit dwelling within, if we really *want* to trust in "Abba" or the Divine Mother enfolding the earth (however or whomever we name it) and enter into that "stillness surrounded by silence."

> **We should not look for a "method" or "system," but cultivate an "attitude," an "outlook": faith, openness, attention, reverence, expectation, supplication, trust, joy. All these finally permeate our being with love in so far as our living faith tells us we are in the presence of God, that we live in Christ, that in the Spirit of God we "see" God our Father without "seeing." We know God in "unknowing." Faith is the bond that unites us to God in the Spirit who gives us light and love (Merton, *Contemplative Prayer*, 34).**

Faith, as we have seen in previous chapters, requires a continual letting go: letting go of control, letting go of all of our illusions and expectations for our lives. Going over to a trust relationship with God involves a change that is quite radical. It means relinquishing control of our life in the central area, where we care and where we also are able to exercise control (see Dunne, *Search*, 222). Roger Schroeder, member of the Society of the Divine Word and professor at Chicago's Catholic Theological Union, explained his own "letting go" in this way:

> *Since returning to the States. . . . I have come to name, value, and "let go of" my missionary experience of the past, so that I can move on to name, value, and embrace my new missionary situation of the present. The "best of days" and the "worst of days" of my earlier cross-cultural missionary life have had a tremendous impact in shaping me into the person I am today. I and those I now teach–and learn from–continue to struggle to be a part of God's mission–to cross over to and be transformed by not only the poor and other cultures, races, religions, and Christian denominations, but also those of my own culture and nationality. In many ways, I continue to feel like a "stranger" in "my" own land, but now I do not associate feeling "at home" with a particular place, but rather with being "at home" in the missionary journey itself.*

This kind of radical trust means living with uncertainty, with the ambiguity that is characteristic of living on the edge. It means living in the "dynamic in-betweenness" which will always be the lifestyle of missioners, no matter where we find ourselves, and no matter how unclear the future may be. Perhaps it was Hammarskjold who best put this radical trust and gratitude into simple words that have become well known to many: "For all that has been, Thanks! To all that shall be, Yes!"[107]

## Part IV: At Home with One's Self

What I have been doing in this chapter, and actually throughout these reflections, is to invite you, dear reader, and all who are in "re-entry" or in a "transition" stage of their journey, *to find a home within yourselves. This coming home means radically encountering one's true self.* We now take a final brief look at what this implies.

### *The False Self*

To say I was born in sin is to say I came into the world with a false self. I was born in a mask (Merton, *New Seeds*, 33). Merton reminds us that our personality; i.e., the empirical identity, which we often call our self, is often mistakenly taken to be our "entire self." In this way, that identity that we cling to and protect as our "self," really becomes a *false self*, an obstacle to realizing our *true self*, our "whole self before God," the self we were created to become (see Finley, 18-19).[108]

There are so many idols surrounding us and voices of "false prophets" building up a negative image of both ourselves and our God, making us afraid to encounter either one, telling us *not* to go home. Merton calls this "the false self," the creation of our egotistical illusions and desires. For Merton, this "I" is not the real "I" but an "illusory person," a "non-existence" that perpetuates a state of alienation from God (and our true self), a state of sin.

> **Every one of us is shadowed by an illu-sory person: a false self. . . . My false and private self is the one who wants to exist outside the reach of God's will and God's love. . . . And such a self cannot help but be**

**an illusion. . . . A life devoted to the cult of
this shadow is what is called a life of sin. . . .
All sin starts from the assumption that my
false self, the self that exists only in my ego-
centric desires, is the fundamental reality
of life to which everything else in the universe is ordered (Merton, *New Seeds*, 34).**

The "prodigal son" had to deal with the illusion of this false self.
He went through a long and difficult time to "come to his senses."

> *I shall get up and go to my father and I shall say
> to him, "Father, I have sinned against heaven and
> against you. I no longer deserve to be called your
> son; treat me as you would treat one of your hired
> workers"* (Luke 15:18-19).

Like him, so many of us—and missioners are probably among
the best at it—imagine that we have to *earn* God's love. Often we too
don't dare to go "home" just as we are. We feel lost, unworthy, useless, confused, a failure, hurt, tired, angry, rejected, guilty, abused—or
abusive—and the list could go on. Finley suggests that Merton's basic
dynamic of the spiritual life could be summarized in the experience
of the alienated prodigal son journeying back home (Finley, 37-38).
And Nouwen reminds us also of the alienation of the "elder son" who,
while remaining in his father's house, never really feels at home there.
Rather than feeling trust, gratitude, and joy in his life in the service of
his father, he is filled with anger, resentment, and envy.

> *He became angry, and when he refused to enter
> the house, his father came out and pleaded with
> him. He said to his father in reply, "Look, all these
> years I served you and not once did I disobey
> your orders; yet you never gave me even a young
> goat to feast on with my friends. But when your*

*son returns who swallowed up your property with*
*prostitutes, for him you slaughter the fattened calf"*
(Luke 15:29-30).

But the father gently and lovingly reminds the elder son that
his love, his "home" has always been there for him: *My son, you are*
*here with me always; everything I have is yours* (v. 31). "What is so
clear is that God is always there.... Whether I am the younger or the
elder, God's only desire is to bring me home (Nouwen, 74). We who
have often been caught up in our projects and projections sometimes
still configure God in our image, rather than ourselves in God's. We
continue–though often unconsciously–to think of God's love as con-
ditional, and about home as a place we are not yet sure of. While
walking home, or rediscovering it beneath our feet all along, we keep
entertaining doubts about whether or not we are truly welcome there
(Nouwen, 47).

## The True Self

> **There is only one problem on which all my**
> **existence, my peace, and my happiness**
> **depend: to discover myself in discovering**
> **God. If I find [God] I will find myself, and if**
> **I find my true self I will find [God] (Merton,**
> ***New Seeds*, 5).**

In an authentic "passing over and coming back" we will discover that
the Other, and the "others" into whose lives we have entered, are to
be found within ourselves, that is, within our true selves. "By our love
and our need for love, we become for one another midwives of the
true self" (Finley, 97). As Merton says,

> **The inner self is precisely that self which**
> **cannot be tricked or manipulated by any-**
> **one, even the devil. The true self is like a**

**very shy, wild animal that never appears at
all whenever an alien presence is at hand,
and comes out only when all is peaceful, in
silence, when it is untroubled and alone. It
cannot be lured by anyone or anything, because it responds to no lure except that of
the divine freedom (Merton in Finley, 91).**

And in birthing our "true selves" for one another, we find love,
and in this home we will find a deep and lasting peace. In entering into
the inner dwelling of our heart and soul, we come into the Presence of
the One in whose image we all are made. "Once a missioner, always
a missioner." We are, in a metaphorical sense, an "ark of Yahweh,"
carrying the Divine within us on our nomadic journey. "Now, if I have
found favor with You, do let me know Your ways so that, in knowing
You, I may continue to find favor with You. . . . *I myself*, the Lord answered, *will go along with you, to give you rest*" (Exod 33:13-14).[109]

It is our hope that, no matter where we are, "en route" or "on
mission," we will, at one and the same time, always be "at home."

**To say I am made in the image of God is to
say that love is the reason for my existence,
for God is love. . . . Love is my true identity.
Selflessness is my true self. Love is my true
character. Love is my name (Merton, *New
Seeds*, 60).**

## Moving On: Some Concluding Comments

We are no longer who we were before being sent on mission (or into
combat or assignment). Nor are we the same as we were during
our time of service. To the extent that we have "passed over" into
other lives, cultures, thoughts, feelings, sufferings, and joys, we have
changed, and we will never be the same again. To the extent that
we have "come back" into our own life, culture, thoughts, feelings,

sufferings, and joys, we will sense that we have somehow found a "home" here, yet with new and renewed horizons. In *The House of Wisdom*, Dunne speaks of this new-found sense of being "home" as "being in the hands of God." He writes:

> **Now I understand what it is "to be in the hands of God." It is this double relation, this to and fro, on the one side the relation of past and present and future to me, the encompassing peace I have felt again and again, that becomes inward peace as it enters my heart and soul, and on the other, my own relation to past and present and future, my response to the peace of God, that becomes self-realization in God in my "Yes" . . . As I stand in the present with the past behind me and the future ahead of me, I can feel time's arrow as a longing, and I can see it as the tangent of a great circle of love that comes from God and goes to God. "Unconditional relation" means being heart and soul in the longing, and my heart's speaking is calling ever more fully into the great circle of love (Dunne, *House*, 112).**

As for myself personally, it is only because I believe that I am "at home"–at least to a great extent–with *myself*, with *others*, and with *the Divine*, that I have been able to put this "journey" into writing. I would not have been ready to do it within the first few years after my return from the DRC, and my eventual departure from my religious congregation. I recognize, with much gratitude, that *I am still on an amazing journey*. I don't really know where it is leading, but I do believe that I am held and carried in the loving embrace of an ineffable and provident Presence in this universe. With that confidence, I am truly "*at home in the journey*."

# Moving On: Some Final Remarks

## THE SHARING

*We told our stories—that's all.*

*We sat and listened to each other, and heard the journeys of each soul.*

*We sat in silence, entering each one's pain and sharing each one's joy.*

*We heard love's longing and the lonely reachings-out for love and affirmation.*

*We heard of dreams—shattered—and visions fled,*

*of hopes and laughter turned stale and dark.*

*We felt the pain of isolation and the bitterness of death.*

*But in each brave and lonely story*

*God's gentle life broke through.*

*And we heard music in the darkness and smelt flowers in the void.*

*We felt the budding of creation in the searchings of each soul.*

*We discerned the beauty of God's hand in each*
*muddy, twisted path.*

*And God's voice sang in each story.*

*God's life sprang from each death.*

*And our sharing became One story of a simple*
*lonely search*

*For life and hope and Oneness in a world which*
*sobs for love.*

*And we knew that in our sharing God's voice with*
*mighty breath was saying...*

*Love each other and take each other's hand.*

*For you are one though many and in each of you I*
*live.*

*So listen to my story and share my pain and death.*

*Oh, listen to my story and rise and live with me.*

EDWINA GATELEY[110]

And so our "mountain-climbing" adventure is over: our journey of
reflection comes to an end. But then again, not really. There will undoubtedly be more mountains to climb. Borrowing from T. S. Eliot,
"In our end is our beginning." One's life is in some ways a continual
process of passing over to others and a coming back to self, and to the
spiritual adventure that carries us beyond ourselves—a recovering of
heart and soul; in Dunne's words, "when one is heart-free and heart-
whole in the journey with God" (Dunne, *Reasons*, 151). Coming *home*
for missioners, as for *both* sons in Luke's parable (Luke 15:11-32), is
not always easy. Perhaps the task is more complex, because we often
confuse our "home" (our identity, our self), with a geographical place,
a culture, a country, a role, a function, a title, etc. While it may be
true that every culture and person we have encountered along the
way *has become a part of us* and enriches the *whole* of who we are, it
is so easy to make of these people, places, or accomplishments false

selves, false images, false expectations, perhaps even false gods. And any one of these false homes in some way compartmentalizes and minimizes our true self and makes us less whole.

The *from→through→to→from→through→to→* . . . of a transition, the passing over and coming back, and the sharing of insights gained in that crossing, are a part of the human journey that can lead to greater wholeness, integration, and integrity of heart and soul. But this inner journey, as we have seen, is very demanding. It requires no less than *all* of ourselves. It asks of us a vigilant attitude of prayer and discernment, of openness, exploration, patience, perseverance, and perhaps above all, hope. It is, as Larry Lewis taught, an "active waiting." Dunne puts it this way:

> **The waiting is the praying, and the com-
> ing of God is the answer to the prayer, and
> God's coming takes the form of a kindling of
> light in the darkness. This kindling of light
> I shall call "insight" (Dunne, "Insight," 3).**

There is movement in the waiting, but not movement toward certainty and decisions. It is rather a movement toward insight, toward understanding with a kind of "certitude of the heart," which brings with it a new clarity, courage, and peace. "At every turning point in our journey, we can hope, reasons of the heart will come to light" (Dunne, *Reasons*, xii). It is the incorporation or integration of these reasons of the heart into our lives that enables us to move on with authentic freedom and renewed hope, precisely because we have found a place of peace within. We have, in some fashion or another, *come home to ourselves*, where the Divine–and others–dwell *within* us in the journey.

Yes, our adventure continues. If we have managed to climb mountains and pass through valleys, to withstand the firing kiln and the drenching rain, we will have, after all, arrived at a new vision. We will recognize that, while we *have* come home, at the same time, we know, more than ever, that *we are still on the way*.

I want to close with a prayer written by Fr. Ken Untener, who later was named Bishop of Saginaw, Michigan. Often called "The Romero Prayer," it honors one who knew all about transformation. He knew what it meant to *pass over* into other lives, and to *come back* to himself reborn, renewed. For Oscar Romero, I believe it is safe to say, the waiting *was* a praying, and his life was one of hope.

*It helps, now and then, to step back and take the long view.*

*The Kingdom is not only beyond our efforts, it is even beyond our vision.*

*We accomplish in our lifetime only a tiny fraction*

*Of the magnificent enterprise that is God's work.*

*Nothing we do is complete, which is another way of saying the Kingdom of God lies beyond us.*

*No statement says all that should be said.*

*No prayer fully expresses our faith.*

*No confession brings perfection, no pastoral visit brings wholeness.*

*No program accomplishes the Church's mission.*

*No set of goal and objectives includes everything.*

*That is what we are about.*

*We plant seeds that one day will grow.*

*We water seeds already planted, knowing that they hold future promise.*

*We lay foundations that will need further development.*

*We provide yeast that produces effects far beyond our capabilities.*

*We cannot do everything, and there is sense of liberation in realizing that this enables us to do something, and to do it very well.*

*It may be incomplete, but it is a beginning, a step along the way,*

*an opportunity for the Lord's grace to enter and do the rest.*

*We may never see the end results,*

*but that is the difference between the master builder and the worker.*

*We are workers, not master builders, ministers, not messiahs.*

*We are prophets of a future that is not our own. Amen.*[111]

KENNETH UNTENER

# A Process of Naming and Narrating Our Experience[112]

**Introduction to the Process**: We are invited to think of our cross-cultural, life-changing experience as a story, or as a sort of novel. And we examine that story within the context of our traditions–the literary, visual, auditory, and felt experiences of our community.

The shaping of one's own "story" is the study of the Divine's presence (however you individually understand that) in one's life; i.e., the reflection on one's life is a way of doing a practical and personal study of beliefs, expectations, and theories.

## I. Prologue or Introduction ("The Setting Out")

A. You are invited to write 1-2 pages describing or explaining in some way the situation, steps, significant people, etc., that caused your life's journey to abruptly change course. Was it a decision you made, or was it a life event happened to you? In other words, *what or who brought or led you to this change*? Include a description of what preceded the change.

B. Do you recall an *image* or *symbol*, a significant song, book, person, quote, etc., that seemed to capture the context of your "setting out" on this new journey?

## II. Divisions ("The Adventure")

A. Divide your "novel" into several (3-4) main parts or divisions. This may be by theme, chronology, places, events, people, etc. Think in terms of titles or subheadings for the main parts of your story. For example, *Part 1 – Osaka: Language School*; *Part 2 – 1st Assignment*; *Part 3 – The Incident with Kim*, etc.

B. For some, it may be helpful or necessary to divide the main parts into sub-parts or chapters. This may depend on the length of time involved or the variety of experiences encountered.

## III. People

A. For each of your divisions, identify at least *1 or 2 significant persons* who stand out in your memory of that time. Briefly describe the persons and why they are significant. The memory of these persons may be positive or negative, or your feelings toward them may be ambivalent. The fact that a person comes to mind indicates they may be significant to your experience.

## IV. Marker Events (Moving toward the "Heart of the Matter")

A. For each division, identify one or two particularly *significant moments or experiences*. These "marker events" or moments may have been happy, sad, painful, joyful, hard, easy, a "first," etc.

B. Is there an *image, song, symbol, etc.*, which seems to capture these experiences for you? Name or express it in some way. Have you had a dream which might seem to represent these particular experiences? If so, what would you "entitle" that dream? Write out the dream if you care to do so.

C. In reflecting upon these marker events or moments, can you identify any *significant issues, conflicts, concerns, etc.*, which seem to recur or stand out in these moments or happenings? Another way of asking this question is to look for any *common threads* running through these moments in each chapter; does anything seem to stand out or strike you as a *recurring theme or themes*? Try to identify and briefly name these themes.

D. Reflecting upon each of the above-named issues or themes, consider the following six aspects: which seem to bring the most focus or attention to the theme? Which aspect is most at play within the theme? (Some of your issues or themes may be a combination of several or all of these aspects.)

| 1) individual | 4) spiritual/religious |
|---|---|
| 2) communal | 5) psychological |
| 3) cultural | 6) other ... |

## V. One Experience (Probing the "Heart of the Matter")

From the significant people and experiences you have identified thus far, *choose one particular experience* and *describe it in as much clear detail as possible*.

A. Is there an *image, song, symbol, etc.*, which seems to capture this experience for you? Name or creatively express it in some way. Have you had a dream that might seem to represent this particular experience or theme? If so, what would you "entitle" that dream? Write out or draw the dream if you care to do so. Provide as much detail as possible.

B. Identify the *particular theme or themes* that mark this particular experience. Describe this theme in more detail than above, trying to indicate what significant movement it might indicate in your own life. If you have not already done so, indicate which *kind* of an issue or theme it seems to be for you; i.e., individual, communal, cultural, spiritual, etc.

## VI. Fiction, Movie, or Scriptural Association

A. Identify a theme or person from another story that is vivid in your mind. This may arise from a book, movie, or scriptural passage, which seems to express, capture, or in some way connect with the experience you chose to describe in detail.

B. Then identify a particular passage that expresses your theme or focuses on a person described in detail. Cite this passage, quote it, or write it out in your own words (or the most significant part of it, if it is long).

C. Then briefly describe in what way the text, theme, or person relates to your experience. You may choose to express this passage in some artful way; in addition to writing or drawing, you might role play, sing, mime, or present it dramatically.

## VII. Epilogue or Future Script ("The Return")

Having reflected upon your recent or past experience, *what insights have you gained* for the present and the future?

A. Explain how you see your past affecting or relating to your present.

B. What are your dreams for the future? If you could plan your future, what and where would it be?

C. *Is there an image* that seems to capture your "dream"? A scriptural passage or other theme from your tradition, which particularly relates to it?

D. In brief, describe (act out, dance, symbolize, sing, etc.) how you might imagine the unfolding of your future, in the light of your past and present.

## Appendix II

# Suggested Resources in Fiction, Non-Fiction, and Film[113]

## A SELECTION OF NOVELS and SHORT STORIES (in chronological order)

| | |
|---|---|
| Maugham, W. Somerset | "Rain," in *The Maugham Reader* (1921) |
| Cather, Willa | *Death Comes to the Archbishop* (1939) |
| Godden, Rumer (Margaret) | *Black Narcissus* (1941) |
| Hulme, Kathryn C. | *The Nun's Story* (1956) |
| Michener, James A. | *Hawaii* (1959) |
| Achebe, Chinua | *Things Fall Apart* (1959) |
| Achebe, Chinua | *No Longer at Ease* (1960) |
| Matthiessen, Peter | *At Play in the Fields of the Lord* (1965) |
| Elliot, Elisabeth | *No Graven Image* (1966) |
| Johnson, Dorothy M. | *A Man Called Horse* (1968) |
| Endo, Shusaku | *Silence* (1969) |
| Naipaul, V.S. | *In a Free State* (1971) |
| Craven, Margaret | *I Heard the Owl Call My Name* (1973) |
| Morrison, Toni | *Sula* (1973) |
| Morrison, Toni | *Song of Solomon* (1977) |
| Craven, Margaret | *Again I Heard the Owl* (1980) |
| Gordimer, Nadine | *Burgers Daughter* (1979) |
| Naipaul, V.S. | *A Bend in the River* (1979) |
| Michener, James A. | *The Covenant* (1980) |

| Michener, James A. | *Texas* (1985) |
|---|---|
| Gordimer, Nadine | *Selected Stories* (1983) |
| Law-Yone, Wendy | *The Coffin Tree* (1983) |
| Doerr, Harriet | *Stones for Ibarra* (1984) |
| Allende, Isabel | *The House of the Spirits* (1985) |
| Hersey, John | *The Call* (1985) |
| Lapierre, Dominique | *City of Joy* (1985) |
| Moore, Brian | *Black Robe* (1985) |
| Achebe, Chinua | *Anthills of the Savannah* (1987) |
| Coelho, Paulo | *The Alchemist* (1988) |
| Pilkington, D. and Garimara, N. | *Follow the Rabbit-Proof Fence* (1996) |
| Fadiman, Anne | *The Spirit Catches You and You Fall Down* (1997) |
| Gourevitch, Philip | *We Wish to Inform You That Tomorrow We Will Be Killed with Our Families* (1998) |
| Kingsolver, Barbara | *The Poisonwood Bible* (1998) |
| Lamb, Wally | *I Know This Much Is True* (1998) |

## A SELECTION OF FILMS (in chronological order)

*Rain* (1928, 1932, 1953)
*Stanley and Livingston* (1939)
*Keys of the Kingdom* (1944)
*Black Narcissus* (1947)
*The Nun's Story* (1959)
*Inn of the Sixth Happiness* (1958)
*Lilies of the Field* (1963)
*Hawaii* (1966)
*I Heard the Owl Call My Name* (1973)
*A Man Called Horse* (1978)

*Ghandi* (1982)
*The Missionary* (1982)
*El Norte* (1983)
*City of Joy* (1985)
*The Mission* (1986)
*Stones for Ibarra* (1989)
*Romero* (1989)
*Black Robe* (1991)
*At Play in the Fields of the Lord* (1991)
*Hoop Dreams* (1994)
*Rabbit-Proof Fence*(1996)
*First They Killed My Father* (2017)
*Da 5 Bloods* (2020)

## A SELECTION OF ADDITIONAL NON-FICTION RESOURCES NOT IN "WORKS CITED" (alphabetical order by author)

Artress, Lauren. *Walking a Sacred Path – Rediscovering the Labyrinth as a Spiritual Practice* (1995, 2006)

Casie, Aggie and Benson, Herbert. *Mind Your Heart – A Mind/Body Approach to Stress Management, Exercise, and Nutrition for Heart Health* (2004)

Bevans, Stephen and Schroeder, Roger (editors). *Mission for the Twenty-First Century* (2001)

Hanh, Thich Nhat. *The Art of Living – Peace and Freedom in the Here and Now* (2017)

Palmer, Parker. *A Hidden Wholeness - The Journey Toward An Undivided Life* (2004)

Rohr, Richard. *Falling Upward – A Spirituality for the Two Halves of Life* (2011)

Rohr, Richard. *Just This – Prompts and Practices for Contemplation* (2018)

Rolheiser, Ronald. *The Holy Longing – The Search for a Christian Spirituality* (1999)

Sparough, Hipskind, Manning. *What's Your Decision?* (2010)

Stearns, Anne Kaiser. *Living Through Personal Crisis* (1985, 2000, 2010)

Teasdale, Wayne. *A Monk in the World – Cultivating a Spiritual Life* (2002)

Tolle, Eckhart. *A New Earth – Awakening to Your Life's Purpose* (2005)

Weber, Kerry. *Mercy in the City* (2014)

Wicks, Robert. *Bounce - Living a Resilient Life* (2010)

Wicks, Robert. *Riding the Dragon: 10 Lessons for Inner Strength in Challenging Times* (2003, 2012)

**Appendix III**

# Applications of Ritual, Symbols, and Physical Activity: Theory and Suggestions

## Ritual and Transition

Some years ago, close friends and I gathered to celebrate a marker birthday. We shared scripture, letters, poems, and stories of phone calls from family and other good friends who had been a part of the years we were commemorating. Indeed, we broke bread and gave thanks! Into the evening, over shrimp creole and wine, everyone shared a personal, favorite memory or two.

The following day, a long plane ride gave me time to reflect on that celebration, on its significance and the fifty years that it commemorated. With familiar rituals, we had marked a rite of passage, singing the happy-birthday tune. There was I, as often in my youth, making a wish before a decorated cake ablaze with candles–an "ordinary" ritual, one that takes place every year, in many different forms, everywhere in this world.

I was passing over a threshold and into a new stature, and this passage deserved to be celebrated and remembered. In this culture, as in many, it was marked by friends gathering to share food and drink, song and dance, gifts and stories, laughter and tears. It wasn't just *my* celebration. It was *ours*, together. The ritual, enacted within a community of friends, enabled me to walk through the threshold with courage and joy.

While I've made occasional mention of the need for ritualizing the various stages of a transition, this work would not be complete without intentionally naming ritual as an *essential* part of the process. Transition is an opportunity to grow. But as in every rite of passage, the community needs to ritualize the stages to provide the passenger with a sense of safety and intimacy.

## *The Role of Ritual in Transition*

> The primary purpose of ritual is to enable
> individuals to undergo the journey of con-
> version, rendering the experience intelligi-
> ble and less terrifying, and enabling them
> to complete the journey, through encoun-
> ter with the sacred, to newness of life. . . .
> [Ritual] enables an individual and their
> community to face the truth of their exis-
> tence . . . providing a safe locus for encoun-
> tering the Ultimate and Transcendent. . . .
> It assures that the experience has meaning,
> and thus saves the individual from capitu-
> lating to fear of the unknown and . . . from
> being lost in anxiety and confusion (Searle,
> 47, 50).

Many rituals are performed unconsciously, as in routine behavior. Though we might not think of them as such, we carry out rituals everyday: brushing our teeth, taking our morning coffee or tea, religiously observing a time of prayer or an afternoon siesta, walking the dog, reading or watching the evening news, praying with our children, etc. All of these, in some fashion or another, are rituals that have evolved over time and have meaning in our lives.

Other rituals, in the more liturgically correct sense of the term, are *consciously* performed, and the actions, gestures, and objects involved are *symbols*, carrying a deeper, sometimes unconscious, meaning beyond themselves. Some rituals and symbols have been consciously modified throughout history, such as Christian sacrament and liturgical celebration, which are intentionally performed to enable us to "identify the meaning of our experience in terms of the gospel of death and resurrection and to commit ourselves to God in faith" (Searle, 49).

All ritual, if it is real and effective, must be intimately connected with life. In the case of those in transition, or those accompanying them, rituals provide us with the opportunity to *reenact* in some way, through physical action and tangible symbols, what we have been experiencing. At the same time, these simple moments of ritual put us in touch with the Sacred: the inner self, the immanent and the transcendent, the "now and not yet" of God's reign, the ever-present Spirit in all creation.

## *"The Readiness Is All"*

In speaking of ritual and conversion, Searle talks about "four moments of readiness through which a person would have to move if the inner process of conversion and the unfolding ritual process were to mesh together in a single movement of transformation" (52). In effect, we have been talking about moments of readiness throughout this reflective process. They are the familiar:

→ FROM → THROUGH → TO → FROM → THROUGH → TO → FROM → THROUGH→TO→

- Coming to terms with what we have actually gone through
  (*from . . .*)
- Realizing the need to face the truth of our life
  (*from→through . . .*)
- Letting go of illusions and the past, and putting one's trust in the Divine and the future
  (*from→through→to→from→through→to→ . . .*)
- Sharing with others the effects of our new life and vision
  (*to→from→through→to→from→through→to→ . . .*)

First, we need be aware of our "readiness" at each of these four moments, to actually participate in the ritual, but in our transitions, we will have different timing; we all will not be at the stage of being celebrated or ritualized at the same moment. For example, one person told me that she is still not "at home" in her own particular journey.

She believes that part of the reason is because she was so "violently pulled out" of her mission assignment. I asked what had caused that; e.g., the violence in the country at that time? She replied, "I had been asked by my community to come back to administrative work in my province of origin (where I had previously been in administration for fourteen years). I had written a long, detailed letter spelling out all of the very real and valid reasons why I needed to stay where I was for the time being. A few weeks later I received a response telling me to finish up the semester and come home." Then she added, " I realize I didn't do any of the appropriate rituals or ceremonies of departure. In fact I did everything I could to avoid any kind of celebration–my heart wasn't in it." Poor closure, or none at all, is definitely a factor that needs to be addressed in due time–it may happen later rather than sooner, but eventually it will be time.

Second, while we can create an atmosphere with all of the appropriate elements, and we can perform all of the proper actions, the totality of ritual is something that happens both within as well as without an individual or group. It is important for all of us to be creatively involved in ritual that flows from that "Ark" within ourselves, wherein dwells the "Holy of Holies"–our souls, our source of connection with the Divine. What I mean to say is that we cannot *make* ritual happen, neither for ourselves or others. Ultimately, its power to effect change comes from within one's self, not from the ritual itself. If we are the facilitators, as much as possible, we must allow the symbols, words, and gestures to come from the group. Gene Combs and Jill Freedman remind us of another important point: "Although the emphasis in ceremonies is on doing something, preparing for the ceremony, thinking about it, and remembering it afterwards all can contribute significantly to the meaning that ceremonies have" (*Symbol, Story, and Ceremony*, 210).

And, as in all that we do, whatever be our path of transition, ultimately it is this Spirit who gives life. I recall one particular evening during a workshop, each member of the group was invited to create a representation of some gift that was ours by using modeling clay. One of the group didn't consider himself the least bit artistic and was not enthusiastic about molding with clay. In addition, he wasn't feeling too good about himself at this moment, nor what "gift" he had to offer. At the end of the allotted time, each participant presented his or her "sculpture" with a brief explanation about what it meant. We had all sorts of creations: boats and villages and clowns holding daisies. When it was his turn the missioner in question firmly placed on the table in front of him a name plate. You know the type, like the executives have on their desks in gold and wood. His was carved out of clay. The missioner explained to us that the only gift he had to offer at this moment–for better or for worse–was himself.

One of the most poignant moments I've experienced occurred at a From Mission to Mission workshop. We had been using a ritual of placing small candles on a large map of the world laid out before us. In the beginning, we had placed our candles on the spot of the world which represented the place "from" which we had originally been sent on mission. Later in the workshop, we moved the candles to the place "to" which we had been sent; e.g., Guatemala, Zambia, Panama, Peru, Detroit, etc. Then, as the workshop was coming to a close, we were invited to place our candles on that place with which we identified in the present; i.e., the spot on that map where we knew our candle *needed to be at that moment*. After a brief time of reflection, with quiet music in the background, each participant got up, one by one, and moved their candle to its "proper place." After everyone had finished, most of the candles were clustered around the mid-west area of the United States, but one candle remained all by itself. It was still sitting in Peru. A well-intentioned member of the group looked at me and said, "Someone forgot to move their candle." An elderly sister spoke up softly but firmly, "No, I didn't forget. That's where it's supposed to be. I must leave it there for a while."

She had *not* misunderstood the ritual. To the contrary, perhaps she had understood it better than most. The first time that I participated in a similar ritual at my own re-entry workshop, I recall that I reluctantly went to the map and moved my name from Zaire to Chicago, where I was living at the time. I went through the motions of the ritual. But I actually wasn't at "home" in Chicago at that time.

My heart was still in Zaire. In fact, it was at a later workshop that I was intentional about moving my candle from the DRC (Congo) to a spot between Chicago and Milwaukee with a peaceful conviction: "Yes, I am at home here now."

## Suggested Activities, Symbols, and Rituals

Combs and Freedman, in their context of psychotherapy, point out the importance of developing appropriate rituals or ceremonies for the moment, person, or group. They "design ceremonies through strategies based on the purposes for which the ceremonies will be used. . . . Each strategy is based on a therapeutic purpose that lends itself to rituals."(211).

The following simple suggestions have proved useful to me. They can be most meaningful and powerful in different stages of transition. In designing your own rituals, it is important that these suggestions be adapted with sensitivity, discretion, and creativity. For each ritual, a few related scripture texts are offered, but the reader is encouraged to find associations from their own text or perhaps select something from Appendix II.

Finally, take time to review and apply the Process of Naming and Narration, found in Appendix I, to fully explore and integrate any insights that occur.

**1. The Map** (this meaningful practice is used in From Mission to Mission workshops). As described above, locate or situate yourself by placing or transferring candles, flags, pins, names, etc., on the locations from which you've come, where you presently are, and to which you're going–ultimately, where your symbol needs to be at this time.

*Scripture suggestions:*

Gen 12                    Go forth from the land of your family . . . to a
                          land I will show you.(v 1-6)

| Deut 8 | Remember how for forty years now the Lord has directed all your journeying.... (v 1-5) |
| Ruth 1 | Do not ask me to abandon or forsake you.... (v 15-18) |

**2. The Storyteller.** The "storyteller" represents a certain kind of authority, word, history, or tradition within a given community. You may want to use symbols of "authority," such as a rain stick, special stone, hat, scarf, cloth, stole, etc. We can all be storytellers as we tell (dance, sing, mime, etc.) our stories. They may be *marked* as being funny, tragic, difficult, or powerful. They may entail *aspects* of mentors, companions, community moments. They may contain *themes* of vulnerability, discovery, endings, beginnings, etc.

*Scripture suggestions:*

| 2 Samuel 12 | Nathan said to David, "In a certain town there were two men, one rich, the other poor." (v 1) |
| Matthew 13 | And he spoke to them at length in parables. ... (v 3) |
| Luke 7 | "Simon, I have something to say to you...." (v 36-49 ) |

**3. The Walls of Jericho.** For confidence, strength, courage, or a "victory" in some "battle," encircle (figuratively or literally) a person, concern, memory, etc., and dance, walk, or march seven times (or seventy!), symbolically reenacting the Hebrew victory at Jericho.

*Scripture reference:*
(Josh 6: 2-5, 16) I have delivered Jericho and its king into your power.... Circle the city, marching once around it ... for six days.... On the seventh day march around the city seven times, and have the priests blow the horns ... and all the people shout aloud...."

## 4. Natural Elements

**Water**: bowl, pond, lake, fountain, etc. A symbol of birth, life, death, healing, transformation–involving rituals of washing, blessing, or recalling memories of water.

*Scripture suggestions:*

| | |
|---|---|
| John 13 | If I washed your feet ... so you must do.... (v 12-17) |
| 2 Kings 5 | So Naaman went down and plunged into the Jordan seven times at the word of God (v 14) |

**Fire**: candle, fireplace, bonfire, etc. A symbol of warmth, heat, light, purification, death, transformation–involving rituals of burning, offering, incense, or memories of fire.

*Scripture suggestions:*

| | |
|---|---|
| Exodus 3 | As [Moses] looked on, he was surprised to see that the bush, though on fire, was not consumed.... (v 2) |
| Acts 28 | The locals showed us extraordinary kindness by lighting a fire and gathering us.... (v 1-6) |
| Mark 4 | "Is a lamp ... to be placed under a bushel basket?" (v 21-25) |

**Earth**: soil, sand, grass, rock, clay, etc. A symbol of death (burial), life, growth, desert, green–involving rituals of the hard and impenetrable, the soft and malleable, transformation, or memories of earth.

*Scripture suggestions:*

| | |
|---|---|
| Joshua 5 | "Remove your sandals ... the place where you are standing is holy...."(v 13-15) |

| Mark 4 | "And some seed fell on rich soil and pro-duced fruit" (v 1-9, 26-34) |

**Wind**: breath, incense, fan, breeze, storm, etc. A symbol of spirit, movement, change, transformation—involving rituals of storm, loss, blessing, or recalling memories of wind.

*Scripture suggestions:*

| I Kings 19 | And after the fire, there was a tiny whis-pering sound. . . . A voice said to him, "Elijah, why are you here?" (v 9) |
| John 20 | Peace be with you. . . . As the Father has sent me, so I send you. And when he had said this, he breathed on them and said to them, "Receive the Holy Spirit" (v 19-29) |

**5. Food and Drink**: rice, corn, cassava, fish, tortillas, beer, fruit, etc. A symbol of friendship, meals shared, food received/given, lack of food, moments of planting, transformation—involving rituals of food for body and soul, and memories related to food and meals.

*Scripture suggestions:*

| 1 Kings 17 | She left and did as Elijah had said. She was able to eat for a year, and he and her son as well. . . . (v 15) |
| I Cor 11 | Therefore . . . when you come together to eat, wait for one another. . . . (v 17-34) |

**6. Nature**: animals, insects, trees, leaves, plants, sun, moon, stars, etc. Symbols of life, death, and transformation—involving rituals of transformation, such as caterpillars/butterflies, snake/skins, bears/hibernation; eggs/birds, fish, reptiles; clouds, vapor, rain, ice, snow, etc.

*Scripture suggestions:*

| | |
|---|---|
| Jonah 1-4 | God said to Jonah, "Have you reason to be angry over a plant which cost you nothing?" (v 9-10) |
| Matt 6 | Look at the birds of the air ... Learn from the way the wild flowers grow (v 25-34) |

**7. Sounds**: instruments: bells, chimes, drums, flute, guitar, marimbas, rain stick, etc. Also consider other common "noises," like horns, engines, traffic, sirens, rain, thunder, phones, doorbells, etc.

Music and dance often accompany rites of passage. Sounds may evoke memories of transition or of "home." Include music in your rituals, whether instrumental or vocal.

*Scripture suggestions:*

| | |
|---|---|
| Ex 15 | The prophetess, Miriam, Aaron's sister, took a tambourine in her hand, while all the women went out after her with tambourines, dancing, and she led them in the refrain: "Sing to the Lord, gloriously triumphant" (v 20-21) |
| 1 Samuel 16 | David would take the harp and play, and Saul would be relieved and feel better, for the evil spirit would leave him (v 23) |
| Psalm 149 | Sing to the Lord a new song, a hymn in the assembly of the faithful (v 1) |

## Familiar Occasions for Rituals in Most Cultures

- Birthdays, anniversaries, baptisms, initiations, engagements, weddings, wakes, funerals, planting, harvesting, home blessings, exorcisms, clearings, or cleansings, etc.
- Send-offs to battle, mission, new village, new ministry, marriage, new home, death, etc.

- Homecomings from military service, mission, hospital, prison, rehab, the Olympics, etc.
- Welcome parties, parades, showers, banquets, food fests, music

## Other Activities and Body Work

So many important ways recommended for attending to the feelings and stresses of transition happen through the realm of the physical. This would include yoga, qigong, massage, regular exercise, journaling, dream work, creative imagining, prayer, meditation, or EFT (Emotional Freedom Technique. EFT, sometimes simply called "tapping," is a practice still being researched. It has been used to treat people with anxiety and post-traumatic stress disorder .)

*All the above are a sampling of suggestions and ideas. For more on EFT and many other resources, see FMTM website (missiontomission.org.) You are encouraged to find your own way, improvise, and add personal or group touches to any basic ritual. Hopefully, these suggestions may stimulate your creativity!*

*We're all just walking each other home.*
RAM DASS

## APPENDIX IV

# Foreword to the First Edition

Perhaps this book will only have its full impact if you have lived in another nation or culture. It was taken for granted in the past that the *hard* part of cross-cultural living, or of mission and ministry, was *leaving and acculturating.* Coming home was easy—after all it was *home.* Several years ago, one of the general chapters of the Society of the Divine Word (SVD) issued a beautiful and inspiring document about how the essence of being a missionary was "passing over"—really *leaving* the places where we have become comfortable and really *entering into* another land and worldview.

But as many cross-cultural workers and foreign missionaries have discovered, coming home is not an easy adjustment at all, and it might even be the hardest part about crossing cultures. In the SVD document I referred to above, there was no mention at all about the "passing over" involved in returning home—sometimes after years of service, sometimes because our lives were threatened, sometime even because of failure. And when we return "home," things have changed. People have changed, former friends have grown distant, the culture has changed—even the way people *speak* has changed. And it seems like nobody really cares about where you have been, what you have done, and how living in another world has changed *you.* Sure, people will ask "how was the Philippines?" Or "How was it living in El Paso?" But when you try to *tell* them, you soon see signs that they *really* don't want to know. Coming home, you discover, is just as difficult—if not more so—than *leaving* home in the first place. I have always felt that our SVD general chapter should have spoken not only of leaving and entering but also of *returning.*

What JoAnn McCaffrey has succeeded in doing in this marvelous book is to take this process of returning seriously, to recognize the pain of women and men who struggle and suffer after years of service in other lands and other cultures, and to devise a way of working through such pain and disorientation so that they can come to a new place. A person returning from an extended period in another cultural world cannot really come *home*, for they no longer have a home. What Asian theologians Jung Young Lee and Peter Phan (Lee 1995 and Phan 2003, 224-231) say about Asian immigrants applies equally to persons or ministers in transition: they are no longer *in* their home context, and they are both in and outside of their home context, and therefore they are *in-beyond*. If they have a home at all, it is a home on the journey, a sense of wholeness and peacefulness with the fact that they will always be a little foreign, a little different, a little strange. Once a person has determined to cross a culture, my colleague Tony Gittins say, they will always be a stranger, a kind of outsider, both to the guest culture and to their own culture when they return (Gittins 1989).

As I say, this book will only have its full impact if you have lived happily and successfully in another nation or culture. But it can also speak eloquently to *anyone* who is in a major transition in life–after having left a job you loved, or having been let go from it; or in the wake of the collapse of a relationship or the death of a loved one. These moves *from* comfort and security through grief, anger, and loss *to* another place are certainly journeys from a place that has changed us to a place of conversion and faith.

Those who are in any transition from feeling at "home" to not quite at "home" will only find wholeness when they become, as the title of this book indicates, *at home in the journey.* JoAnn McCaffrey shows us how to do this, as we move from the place we have come to love or where we feel safe, recognize our losses, and learn to grieve, *through* the desert where we process all of this in meaning-ful, theological reflection, and then *to* a "new home" on the journey of a constant conversion. This is a book not so much to be read as to be worked through. It is not a book that holds answers as much as it offers a way to wrestle with gnawing but ultimately life-giving questions. It is a book to be read with faith and hope in the one who "emptied himself" (Phil 2:7) to "pitch his tent among us" (Jan 1:14), and revealed to us as he journeyed along the roads of Galilee, that our true home is the "Kindom" of God.

JoAnn McCaffrey does not make the journey easy, she does not promise a smooth ride. But she will give you hope that such a journey is possible, and she proves to be a wise, compassionate, and patient guide.

Stephen B. Bevans, SVD
Louis J. Luzbetak, SVD, Professor of Mission and Culture
Catholic Theological Union, Chicago

# Endnotes

## Introduction

1    Lewis 1983. See also *The Misfit: Haunting the Human-Unveiling the Divine*, 1997

2    Van Gennep, Arnold. *The Rites of Passage*, 1960.

## Chapter One

3    Richard Dooling's "Bush Pigs," is an exaggerated and amusing fictional account of a Peace Corps worker's return from West Africa.

4    Victor Turner's classic essay, "Betwixt and Between: The Liminal Period in Rites of Passage," is generally considered to be the seminal statement on the subject of ritual liminality. First read at the Annual Meeting of the American Ethnological Society in 1964, it became chapter four of one of his major works, *The Forest of Symbols* (1967), and has been reproduced in numerous other journals and edited works. See, for example, *Betwixt and Between: Patterns of Masculine and Feminine Initiation* (LaSalle, IL: Open Court (1987)), in which Turner's essay is the keynote introductory chapter (3-19).

5    In Arnold van Gennep's study of the rituals accompanying the major crises in the life of the individuals within a given tribe, he indicates three distinct phases which he called séparation, marge, agrégation, usually translated by the terms "separation, liminality or transition, and incorporation." (See van Gennep's Foreword, 10-11.) In our process we also want to underline the need and importance of ceremonies or rituals to accompany the "rites of passage" of the missioner as they move through a major life transition.

6    These meditations are primarily drawn from the Center's bi-annual journal, *Oneing*, the first issue of 2020 being devoted to Liminal Space (Vol. 8, No. 1). For more, explore also the "Daily Meditation" archive at cac.org.

7   Turner actually emphasizes the contrast between "state" and
    "transition." It is particularly liminality which is characterized
    as a process more so than the other stages of transition. It is
    precisely its fluidity, its not being a" state" that sets liminality
    apart from other "states of being," even those of "separation"
    and "aggregation," which mark the beginning and end of the
    transition in Van Gennep's "rites de passage." For more on this
    distinction, see *The Forest of Symbols* (1967) Chapter 4, and *The
    Ritual Process* (1969), Chapter 3.

8   See Victor Turner, *The Ritual Process*, 106-107.

9   When quoting actual interviews, pseudo-names will be used.

10  Steve Bevans is a Divine Word Missionary and long-time profes-
    sor of Mission and Theology at Catholic Theological Union in
    Chicago.

11  See Bevans in *New Directions in Mission and Evangelization* 2,
    (Scherer and Bevans) section five, pp. 164-165; see also Gittins'
    *Gifts and Strangers*, particularly Chapter Five, "The Missionary
    as Stranger," 111-138.

12  There is one thing upon which all authors who deal with this topic
    seem to agree. What is really essential to the process of transi-
    tion is that it has a beginning, a middle, and an end. The model
    for this movement, as I see it, was laid out in the seminal classic
    work of Arnold van Gennep, *The Rites of Passage*. See Works
    Cited.

13  It is commonly accepted that the concept of "culture shock" was
    first defined by Oberg as the "anxiety that results from losing
    all of our familiar signs and symbols of social intercourse." See
    Young Yun Kim, "Intercultural Adaptation," especially 276-280,
    in Asante and Gudykunst.

14  For more on this field of cultural psychology see *Thinking Through
    Cultures*, in particular the chapter entitled, "Cultural Psycholo-
    gy: What Is It?" pp. 73-109, in Shweder, 1991.

15  For a detailed discussion of this concept of a context-dependent
    and holistic culture, see Edmund Bourne's essay "Does the
    Concept of Person Vary Cross-Culturally?" in Shweder (1991),
    particularly pp. 146-155.

16  Adapted from Kohls, *Survival Kit for Overseas Living*, 65.

17    Certainly, this could be broadened to include one's entire life, as one's
      ministry is never separate from the person of the minister. It is
      helpful, however, to narrate a specific experience connected to
      one's ministry, and to any emerging feelings, images, and insights.
      For a more detailed outline of this exercise, see Appendix I.

18    According to Stroup, And if it is bound up with one's memory (or in
      some cases the memory of others about one who can no longer
      remember,) it is a hermeneutical act. This is one of the main
      points that Stroup wants to make.

19    For a thorough explanation of "non-judgmental narration" see
      Killen and de Beer, 22-27.

20    See Works Cited.

21    See Appendix III for suggestions of materials, symbols, and rituals
      which may be helpful.

22    See Appendix II for a list of films, novels, and non-fiction resources.
      These and additional resources can also be found on the FMTM
      website: *missiontomission.org*

23    This is a film about the difficulties of missionaries working in the
      cross-culture context of the Amazon. It also highlights, in an
      exaggerated way, the conflict between different missionary en-
      deavors; e.g., the "Protestants" and the "Roman Catholics."

## Chapter Two

24    See Arnold in Works Cited.

25    Elizabeth Bishop in *8 American Poets*. See Works Cited.

26    See also "The Variety and Universality of Loss" (Sullender, 7-24).

27    I am sure that many missioners have similar experiences, and are
      often unable to share them with anyone because of the circum-
      stances of their lives and situations. One often must live in
      remote, isolated areas, cut off from friends or spiritual directors
      because of inadequate means of travel or communication.

28    See for example Carol Ann and Robert Faucett's *Intimacy and Mid-
      life* and the Whitehead's *Christian Life Patterns and Seasons of
      the Heart*. There are also many popular works on this subject,
      such as Angeles Arrien's *The Second Half of Life: Opening the
      Eight Gates of Wisdom*, the pioneering works of Daniel Levinson,
      *The Seasons of a Man's Life*, or Gail Sheehy's *Passages*.

29     *On Death and Dying* (1969), was a pioneering breakthrough in under-
        standing a process that we now almost take for granted. Her five
        stages of dying have been adapted by many writers for many kinds
        of "death." To name a few, Dennis and Matthew Linn use the mod-
        el in their work on forgiveness, *Healing Life's Hurts* (1978); Robert
        and Carol Ann Faucett adapt it for intimacy and mid-life events, in
        their chapter on "Separations and Endings" (1991); Wayne Oates
        refers to these stages as "Rituals of Resistance" (27). I doubt that
        Kübler-Ross ever intended nor suspected that her work would
        be used in such adaptations, and I still recommend Kübler-Ross'
        original work to anyone involved in the grieving process.

30     For more on the re-entry process of missionary families, especially
        "missionary kids," I recommend the work of Clyde Austin and
        Craig Storti (see Works Cited).

31     See Sullender, Chapter 2, "What is Grief?", 25-41. See also Switzer,
        Chapter 4, "Separation Anxiety in Grief," 93-117.

32     See Steve Bevans' article, "Letting Go and Speaking Out: A
        Spirituality of Inculturation" in *The Healing Circle: Essays in
        Cross-Cultural Mission* (133-146).

33     It strikes me that those who abruptly had to leave their mission
        placement, due to Covid-19, didn't even have this leisure of being
        with the people or doing the things they love upon their return.
        For most, they entered a time of lock-down or stay at home,
        which imposed an even stronger psychological and emotional
        shock to their system.

34     Recent research has tended to favor a three- or four-stage pat-
        tern of grief process. John Bowlby suggests that there are three
        stages: "(1) urge to recover lost object (weeping and anger); (2)
        despair (later called disorganization); and (3) reorganization
        towards a new object." Colin Murray Parkes' stages are: (1)
        numbness, (2) yearning, (3) disorganization and despair, and (4)
        reorganization" (see Sullender, 55).

35     An excellent resource is *Praying Our Goodbyes* by Joyce Rupp,
        found in Works Cited.

36     Aden suggests that there are three problems that are pivotal in
        the human struggle: finitude, alienation, and guilt. We find that
        these play a significant role in the struggle of missioners to inte-
        grate change and repatriation into their understanding of their
        missionary vocation. (See Works Cited.)

37    Sullender, Switzer, Mitchell, and Anderson all cite guilt as one of
      the dynamics of grief. Aden names it as one of the three pivotal
      problems that he encounters in pastoral counseling.

38    Robert Grant, a clinical psychologist and psychotherapist, has spe-
      cialized as a formation consultant for religious and international
      relief organizations. He focuses on the area of psychological trau-
      ma. For more on this topic, see Horowitcz (1976), Van der Kolk
      (1986), Figley (1985, 1986) and Herman (1992) in "Works Cited."

39    See Osiek, 24.

40    Many Catholics, not only those directly involved, may have been
      traumatized by the recent sex abuse scandal which has rocked
      the Church in the USA and worldwide. Among many others, see
      for example, nytimes.com, Feb. 6, 2019, "Sexual Abuse of Nuns";
      globalsistersreport.org, April 16, 2019, "Abuse of Sisters."

41    Parts of this chapter are also reproduced in Grant's article, "Trau-
      ma in Missionary Life" (see "Works Cited").

42    For an excellent discussion of these three symptom clusters, see
      Herman, 33-50. See also Wilson (in collaboration with Alice
      Walker), "The Psychobiology of Trauma," 21-37.

43    For a more technical and detailed description of the process of
      healing, see Herman's "Stages of Recovery," in *Trauma and Re-
      covery: the Aftermath of Violence*, 156, in Works Cited.

## Chapter Three

44    See Appendix III for suggestions of materials, symbols, and rituals
      which may be helpful.

45    I interchange image, metaphor, and symbol, even though I am
      aware of the differences and various nuances in such terms. For
      example, McFague points out several clear distinctions between
      metaphor and symbol, symbol belonging to the metaphorically
      religious domain, metaphor lying within the realm of the "ordi-
      nary." (See McFague, 22-29).

46    Building on the cognitive learning theory of Piaget, Robert Kegan
      holds that the human person is always in the process of making
      new meaning out of the ever-changing circumstances of his
      or her life. This evolutionary process enables one to move into
      increasingly complex levels of human maturity. See Kegan, *The
      Evolving Self* (in Works Cited).

47    Quoted in Lewis, *The Misfit*, 16.

48    Robert Johnson is a Jungian analyst and author of several
      best-selling works including *He, She and We, Transformation
      and Owning Your Own Shadow*.

49    In *Inner Work*, Johnson walks us through his "Four-Step Approach,"
      first, to Dreamwork (Chapter Two): 1 - Making associations; 2 -
      Connecting dream images to inner dynamics; 3 – Interpreting;
      and 4 - Doing rituals to make the dream concrete" (51). Next, in
      using Active Imagination (Chapter Three): "1 - Invite the uncon-
      scious; 2 - Dialogue and experience; 3 - Add the ethical element
      of values; and 4 - Make it concrete with physical ritual" (161).

50    Although I encourage that the overall experience of theological
      reflection be done in a group, this particular exercise of exploring
      images must first be done alone. Later one may choose to share
      discoveries with a counselor or group.

51    I have mentioned that rituals play an important role in the process
      of transition, as we'll see in more depth in a later chapter. One
      can create simple and small rituals connected with imagery and
      symbol. In the experience mentioned above, with our objects
      from nature, our sharing them was itself a free-flowing ritual.
      Some placed them in the center of our circle, others passed them
      from one to another, others held them high to be seen, or cradled
      them in the palms of their hands. Some keep them as reminders
      of the insights received. (See also Appendix II.)

52    See Killen and de Beer, 88-89.

53    *Silence* is a novel by the Japanese author Shusaku Endo. It was
      made into a movie in 2019. See Works Cited.

54    See Killen and de Beer, 95-102.

55    Another way of expressing culture is through the missioner's own
      creativity; e.g., design, clay modeling or sculpture, painting,
      dance, photography, etc. See also Appendix II, B.

56    See the FMTM website for some suggested readings and videos
      and for other connections between missionary images and con-
      temporary fiction and cinema.

57    David Bosch called *Silence* "one of the most moving and at the
      same time disturbing novels of our time"(Scherer and Bevans,
      73). *Silence* was the basis of an article by Bosch entitled, "The
      Vulnerability of Mission," originally presented as a talk at the

twenty-fifth anniversary of St. Andrew's College, Selly Oak Colleges, Birmingham, England, in November 1991. "The Vulnerability of Mission" was reprinted from Vidyajyoti: *Journal of Theological Reflection* 56 (November 1992), pp. 577-96.

58    The *fumie* is "a simple copper medal fixed on to a grey plank of dirty wood on which the grains run like little waves . . . the ugly face of Christ, crowned with thorns, and the thin, outstretched arms" (Endo, 270).

59    See Killen and de Beer, 90-95.

60    This passage occurs at the end of Exodus, after Moses and Aaron have completed constructing the desert Tent and Ark, fulfilling all the detailed directions laid out earlier in Chapters 25-31. In this way, the Lord's permanent Dwelling is established in Israel. See CSB: RG 83. (In this work, CSB refers to *The Catholic Study Bible* edition of *The New American Bible*, and RG refers to "Reading Guide.") See also Terrien, "The Tent of Meeting," 175-186.

61    This "cloud" would later overshadow Mary, throwing her life into the mysterious ambiguity of awe and confusion, joy and suffering. Samuel Terrien notes that the same verb "overshadow"(*episkiazein*) used by the Septuagint to translate the "sojourning (shaken) of the cloud" over the tent of meeting, in the Sinai desert, is used in the angelic salutation to Mary (Luke 1:35). "The Lukan story of the annunciation found in Zion—the tabernacle of presence—was a fit symbol for Mary, the maternal bearer of the child" (Terrien, 415).

62    Killen and de Beer offer nine examples of a theological reflection, each example having a different starting point or "source" (87-110). Their schema differs slightly from that of the Whiteheads (*Methods in Ministry*), to whom they are, however, deeply indebted.

63    See in particular Killen and de Beer, 46-53 and 90-94.

64    Those familiar with Ignation spirituality will recognize a similar process in using the imagination to insert oneself into a scene from the life of Jesus.

65    If the Bible can be called the literary classic, which contains the recorded "memories" of the previous generations' experience of faith, then biblical exegesis and hermeneutics help us to understand a people's faith experience. Historical and literary

criticism help us understand their traditions, doctrines, and practices within their context; tradition and formal criticism enlighten us as to how these were orally transmitted; while textual criticism helps us to understand the Bible as it has come to be a written document. For a more complete explanation of the different types of biblical criticism, see "Scientific Study of the Bible," CSB: RG 20-22.

66    It is believed that most of these confessions, where Jeremiah "argues" with God, came from a personal prayer diary, and were never intended to be read or heard by anyone but God. It was probably Baruch who found the diary, and inserted these prayers where he felt they belonged, according to the historical sequence of the prophet's life (Stuhlmueller, 48-49). For the actual text of the confessions, see: Jer 12:1-5; 15:10-21; 17:12-18; 18:18-23, 20:7-18.

67    The actual process of recording and editing Jeremiah's preaching and actions began about thirty-three years later, in 605/604 BC, by his secretary, Baruch (CSB: RG, 309).

68    See CSB: RG, 313. See also Stuhlmueller, 48.

69    CTU Feb. 10, 1993.

70    For a more complete overview of the book of Jeremiah, see the CSB: RG, 307-318.

71    See Killen and de Beer, 103-104.

72    See also Appendix II for resources in fiction, non-fiction, and film.

73    See also Deut 26:5-10 and Ex 13:8.

74    Most contemporary authors interchange the terms "desert" and "wilderness" for this part of the Exodus journey. While "wilderness" seems to indicate both a metaphorical quality as well as a geographical one, "desert" might refer more specifically to the Sinai desert. Nevertheless both terms are powerful metaphors for the kinds of transitional periods experienced by our Israelite ancestors, as well as by missioners today. For a more thorough discussion of this historical/geographical journey, see the CSB: RG, pp. 80-81.

75    For more on the distinction between the historical wilderness period and the priestly narrative of this tradition, see Cohn, "Liminality in the Wilderness" 7-23.

76    Earlier in his essay, Cohn refers to "the words of the folk song, 'freedom is another word for nothing left to lose'" (15).

## Chapter Four

77    See Killen and de Beer, especially 40-43, 61-66, and 80-82.

78    See O'Rourke's article found in Eigo: 13.

79    See also James' essay "The Divided Self and Conversion," in Conn, Conversion 121-136. See also Wayne Oates, "Conversion: sacred and Secular," in Conn, *Conversion* 151-153, where Oates discusses the elements of James' definition as having become somewhat normative for a working definition of conversion.

80    In the Judeo-Christian scriptures, the Hebrew (*shub*) and Greek (*metanoia*) words generally equated with conversion (from the Latin, *converto*), are words that literally mean to turn or return. For more on the Hebrew and Greek origins and the notion of conversion in the Old and New Testament see Michael H. Crosby, "The Biblical Vision of Conversion" in Eigo 31-74. See also Dom Marc-François Lacan, "Conversion and Grace in the Old Testament," "Conversion and Kingdom in the Synoptic Gospels" in Conn, *Conversion*, 75-118.

81    Rambo's stage theory of conversion is decidedly more complex and detailed, but I find Searle's explanation the most helpful and accessible for relating conversion to a missioner's transitional process. For an overview of Rambo's stages see 116-118.

82    See especially pp. 18-23.

83    This title and the "stage" headings which follow are from Searle's article, "Journey of Conversion."

84    Lonergan's *Method in Theology*, according to some analyses of his work, is permeated with the notion of conversion. See *Lonergan on Conversion: The Development of a Notion*, by Michael L. Rende. For a more complete treatment of the three dimensions of conversion, see Lonergan's complete essay, "Theology in Its New Context" in Conn, ed. Conversion: Perspective in Personal and Social Transformation, 3-21. See also Conn's other works, especially *Christian Conversion: A Developmental Interpretation of Autonomy and Surrender*, in particular, Chapters One, Four, Five, and Six. See also Works Cited.

85    Our main resources here are Michael H. Crosby, O.F.M.Cap., "The Biblical Vision of Conversion" in Eigo, 31-74, and Dom Marc-François Lacan's "Conversion and Grace in the Old Testament" in Conn, *Conversion*, 75-96. See Works Cited.

86 Distinguished biblical scholar, Dianne Bergant, CSA, often referred to the Old Testament as "The First Testament" in her teaching.

87 Central to the thinking of Dr. Martin Luther King Jr. was the concept of the "Beloved Community." He believed that a community of love, justice, and solidarity would eventually be actualized. He worked tirelessly for the realization of his dream.

88 See also Michael H. Crosby, "Part One: Individual and Social Conversion in the Old Testament" in Eigo, especially 37-39.

89 Crosby, 37.

90 From "Simple Gifts," a Shaker song written and composed in 1848, generally attributed to Elder Joseph Brackett from Alfred Shaker Village.

91 Some interpretations of this text make this a rich young man, although no gospel account makes this explicit.

## Chapter Five

92 Inspired by Rembrandt's painting, this book, in its entirety, is a prayerful meditation that I recommend for those in transition.

93 For more on this understanding of the "true self," see the writings of Thomas Merton, James Finley, and Thomas Keating, among others.

94 Quoted in the FMTM Newsletter, Vol. 12, No. 1, November 1997.

95 Janet Bennett, educator and author, is co-director (with her husband, Milton Bennett) of the Intercultural Communication Institute located in Portland, Oregon.

96 See Bennett, 116-117.

97 For an excellent study of Dunne's method, see Nilson, 65-86.

98 See Works Cited.

99 Nilson interprets the moments in Dunne's method somewhat differently (see 75-78).

100 Patricia O'Connell Killen confirmed my connection of her work with Dunne's, and also gave me good input for my overall process.

101 An allusion to Robert Frost's poem, "The Road Not Taken."

102 Larry Lewis published several works revolving around the concept of "misfit."

103    See Lonergan, Bernard J. F., 1978, 1972.

104    See "The Identity of a Missioner" in Chapter One.

105    Bishop James E. Walsh, May 22, 1927. See https://maryknollmis-sionarchives.org.

106    From *Markings*, quoted in Dunne, *Church of the Poor Devil*, 173.

107    Dag Hammarskjold, *Markings*. Quoted in Dunne, *The House of Wisdom*, 63. See also Dunne's discussion, "The Heart Speaks," 108-109.

108    For Merton's concept of the false and true selves, I rely heavily upon James Finley's thorough study of Merton's writings and spirituality: Merton's *Palace of Nowhere: A Search for God through Awareness of the True Self*. (See Works Cited.)

109    While I like to apply this analogy here, there is actually very little in the epic traditions about the actual "ark" during this nomad stage of Israel's history. Nevertheless, its "nomadic charac-ter" played a significant role during the establishing of David's kingdom and in the building of the nation. For more on this, see Terrien, "The Ark of Yahweh," 162-175.

110    Edwina Gateley is a poet, theologian, artist, writer, lay minister, single mom, founder of the Volunteer Missionary Movement (VMM) and author of many books, including *Psalms of a Lay-woman* (1986), *There Was No Path So I Trod One* (1996), and *In God's Womb* (2009). She has been described as a modern-day mystic and prophet.

## Moving On: Some Concluding Remarks

111    This prayer is often called "The Romero Prayer," and is attributed to the Archbishop of San Salvador, Saint Oscar Romero (1917 – 1980). It was actually composed in 1979, by the late Bishop Ken Untener of Saginaw, Michigan. It was later delivered by Cardinal Dearden of Detroit, in memory of Romero's death, March 24, 1980.

## Appendix I

112    This process was specifically designed for the "Mission/Ministry Integration Seminar" at Catholic Theological Union in Chicago,

which I helped teach (1996 – 2006), and it is still part of their Intercultural Studies and Ministry curriculum today.

## Appendix II

113   Expanded from an original list of works compiled by Alan Neely of Princeton University. See also the FMTM website missiontomission.org for these and additional resources.

# Works Cited

Aden, Leroy. 1968. "Pastoral Counseling as Christian Perspective." In Homans, Peter. ed. *The Dialogue between Theology and Psychology*. Chicago: University of Chicago Press. 163-182.

Adler, Peter. 1975. "The Transitional Experience: An Alternative View of Culture Shock." *The Journal of Humanistic Psychology*. XV. 4 (Fall). 13-23.

Amaladoss, Michael. 1991. "The Challenges of Mission Today." In Jenkinson and O'Sullivan, eds. *Trends in Mission: Towards the 3rdMillennium*. Maryknoll, NY: Orbis Books. 359-397.

Arasteh, Reza. 1965. *Final Integration in the Adult Personality*. Leiden: E. J. Brill.

Arnold, Magda B., Gasson, John A., and Curran, Charles A., eds. 1954. *The Human Person: An Approach to an Integral Theory of Personality*. New York: Ronald.

Arnold, Magda B. 1960. *Emotion and Personality*. New York: Columbia University Press.

_____. 1970. *Feelings and Emotions: The Loyola Symposium*. New York: Academic.

Asante, Molefi K. and Gudykundst, William B., eds. 1989. *Handbook of International and Intercultural Communication*. Newbury Park, CA: Sage.

Austin, Clyde N. 1988. "Reentry Stress: The Pain of Coming Home." In O'Donnell and O'Donnell, eds. *Helping Missionaries Grow*. Pasadena, CA: William Carey Library. 513-521.

_____. 1983. *Cross-Cultural Reentry: An Annotated Bibliography*. Abilene, TX: Abilene Christian University.

_____. 1986. *Cross-Cultural Reentry: A Book of Readings*. Abilne, TX: Abilene Christian University.

Bennett, Janet M. 1993. "Cultural Marginality: Identity and Issues in Intercultural Training." In Paige, ed. 1 *Education for the Intercultural Experience*. Yarmouth, ME: Intercultural Press. 09-135.

Bevans, Stephen B. 1992. *Models of Contextual Theology*. Maryknoll, NY: Orbis Books. Revised and Expanded edition 2002.

_____. 1994. "Seeing Mission through Images." In Scherer and Bevans, eds. *New Directions in Mission and Evangelization 2: Theological Foundations*. Maryknoll, NY: Orbis Books.158-169.

———. 1999. "Letting Go and Speaking Out: A Spirituality of Inculturation." In Bevans, Doidge, and Schrieter, eds. *The Healing Circle: Essays in Cross-Cultural Mission*. Chicago: CCGM Publications. 133-146.

Bishop, Elizabeth. 1994. "One Art." In Conarroe, Joel, ed. *Eight American Poets*. New York: Vintage. 62-63.

Bosch, David J. 1979. *A Spirituality of the Road*. Scottdale, PA: Herald Press.

———. 1991. *Transforming Mission: Paradigm Shifts in Theology of Mission*. Maryknoll, NY: Orbis Books.

———. 1994. "The Vulnerability of Mission." In Scherer and Bevans, eds. 73-86.

Bourne, Edmund. "Does the Concept of Person Vary Cross-Culturally?" in Shweder, ed. *Thinking through Cultures: Expeditions in Cultural Psychology*. Cambridge, MA: Harvard University Press. 113-155.

Bozarth-Campbell, Alla. 1983. *Life Is Good-bye / Hello: Grieving Well through All Kinds of Loss*. Minneapolis, MN: Campcare.

Bridges, William. 1980. *Transitions: Making Sense of Life's Changes*. Reading, MA: Addison-Wesley.

———. 1991. *Managing Transitions*. New York: Addison-Wesley.

Brown, Raymond, Fizmyer, Joseph and Murphy, Roland, eds. 1990. *The New Jerome Biblical Commentary*. Englewood Cliffs, NJ: Prentice Hall.

Brueggemann, Walter E. 1977. *The Land*. Philadelphia: Fortress Press.

Caird, George B. 1980. *The Language and Imagery of the Bible*. Philadelphia: Westminster.

Carroll, L. Patrick and Dyckman, Katherine M. *Chaos or Creation: Spirituality in Mid-Life*. Mahwah, NJ: Paulist Press.

CSB:RG. 1990. Senior, Donald et al., eds. *The Catholic Study Bible. Reading Guides*. Oxford: Oxford University Press.

Cohn, Robert. 1981. *The Shape of Sacred Space*. Chico, CA: Scholars Press.

Collins, Michael. 1978. *Spirituality for Mission*. Maryknoll, NY: Orbis Books.

Combs, Gene and Freedman, Jill. 1990. *Symbol, Story and Ceremony: Using Metaphor in Individual and Family Therapy*. New York: Norton.

Conn, Joanne Wolski. 1989. *Spirituality and Personal Maturity*. Lanham, MD: University Press of America.

Conn, Walter E., ed. 1978. *Conversion: Perspectives on Personal and Social Transformation*. Staten Island: Alba House.

———. 1981. *Conscience: Development and Self-Transcendence*. Birmingham, AL: Religious Education.

———. 1986. *Christian Conversion: A Developmental Interpretation of Autonomy and Surrender*. Mahwah, NJ.

Crosby, Michael. 1987. "The Human Experience of Conversion." In Eigo, ed. *The Human Experience of Conversion: Person and Structures in Transformation*. Villanova, PA: Villanova University Press. 31-74.

Doehring, Carrie. 1993. *Internal Desecration: Traumatization and Representations of God*. Lanham, MD: University Press of America.

Dooling, Richard. 1994. "Bush Pigs." The New Yorker. October 10: 1-5.

Dunne, John. 1965. *The City of the Gods*. New York: Macmillan.

———. 1977. *A Search for God in Time and Memory*. Notre Dame, IN: University of Notre Dame Press.

———. 1975. *Time and Myth*. Notre Dame, IN: University of Notre Dame Press.

———. 1978. *The Way of All the Earth*. Notre Dame, IN: University of Notre Dame Press.

———. 1978. *Reasons of the Heart*. New York: Macmillan.

———. 1981. "Insight and Waiting on God." In Lamb, Matthew L., ed. *Creativity and Method: Essays in Honor of Bernard Lonergan, S.J.* Milwaukee: Marquette University Press.

———. 1982. *The Church of the Poor Devil*. Notre Dame, IN: University of Notre Dame Press.

———. 1985. *The House of Wisdom*. San Francisco: Harper & Row.

———. 1991. *The Peace of the Present*. Notre Dame, IN: University of Notre Dame Press.

———. 1993. *Love's Mind*. Notre Dame, IN: University of Notre Dame Press.

Eigo, Francis A. 1987. *The Human Experience of Conversion: Person and Structures in Transformation*. Villanova, PA: Villanova University Press.

Eliot, Thomas Stearns. 1971. *Four Quartets*. New York and San Diego: Harcourt, Brace, Javanovich.

Endo, Shusaku. 1969. *Silence*. Tokyo: Sophia University Press.

Faucett, Robert and Carol Ann. 1991. *Intimacy and Midlife: Understanding Your Journey with Yourself, Others and God*. New York: Crossroad.

Finley, James. 1978. *Merton's Palace of Nowhere: A Search for God through Awareness of the True Self*. Notre Dame, IN: Ave Maria Press.

Gittins, Anthony J. 1989. *Gifts and Strangers: Meeting the Challenge of Inculturation*. Mahwah, NJ: Paulist Press.

_____. 1987. "Communities of Concern and Close-up Country: A Parable of Survival." Spirituality Today. 39. 4. Winter. 329-330.

_____. 1994. "Missionary Mythmaking." In Scherer and Bevans, eds., 143-157.

Grant, Robert. 1994. *Healing the Soul of the Church*. Burlingame, CA: R. Grant.

_____. 1995. "Trauma in Missionary Life." *Missiology: An International Review*. XXIII. 1. January. 71-83.

Griffin, Emilie. 1982. *Turning: Reflection on the Experience of Conversion*. New York: Image Books.

Hall, Edward T. 1977. *Beyond Culture*. New York: Anchor Books.

Herman, Judith L. 1992. *Trauma and Recovery*. New York: Basic Books.

Jenkinson, William and O'Sullivan, Helene, eds. 1991. *Trends in Mission: Towards the 3rd Millennium*. Maryknoll, NY: Orbis Books.

John of Taize, Brother. 1985. *The Pilgrim God: A Biblical Journey*. Washington, D.C.: Pastoral Press.

Johnson, Robert. 1986. *Inner Word*. San Francisco: Harper San Francisco.

Kegan, Robert. 1982. *The Evolving Self*. Cambridge, MA: Harvard University Press.

Killen, Patricia O'Connell and de Beer, John. 1994. *The Art of Theological Reflection*. New York: Crossroad.

Kim, Young Yun. 1989. "Intercultural Adaption." In Asante and Gu-
        dykunst, eds. 275-292.

Kohls, Robert L. 1984. *Survival Kit for Overseas Living*. 2nd edition.
        Yarmouth, ME: Intercultural Press.

Kübler-Ross, Elisabeth. 1969. *On Death and Dying*. New York: Macmil-
        lan.

Lee, Jung Young. 1995. *Marginality: The Key to Multicultural Theology*.
        Minneapolis, MN: Fortress Press.

Levinson, Daniel J. 1978. *The Seasons of a Man's Life*. New York: Ballan-
        tine.

Lewis, Larry. 1983. "Waiting." *Maryknoll Formation Journal*. 4. 2. Sum-
        mer. 25- 36.

_____. 1990. "Mirror of the Misfit: Foreign Mission and the Human Mys-
        tery." Unpublished Paper.

_____. 1997. *The Misfit: Haunting the Human–Unveiling the Divine*.
        Maryknoll, NY: Orbis Books.

Loftis, Margaret F. 1992. "Home (Alone) Again: The Re-Insertion of the
        Returned Missionary." CMSM Forum. Spring. 11-16.

Lacan, Dom Marc-Francois. 1978. "Conversion and Grace in the Old
        Testament" and "Conversion and Kingdom in the Synoptic Gos-
        pels." In Conn, ed. 1978. 75-96 and 97-118.

Lonergan, Bernard J. F. 1972. *Method in Theology*. Minneapolis, MN:
        Wionston- Seabury.

_____. 1978. "Theology in Its New Context." In Conn, ed. 1978. 3-21.

Macky, Peter W. 1990. *The Centrality of Metaphors to Biblical Thought*.
        Lewiston, NY: Edwin Mellen.

Mbiti, John S. 1969. *African Religions and Philosophy*. New York:
        Prager.

McFague, Sallie. 1982. *Metaphorical Theology*. Philadelphia: Fortress
        Press.

Merton, Thomas. 1961. *New Seeds of Contemplation*. New York: New
        Directions.

_____. 1961. McDonnell, T. P., ed. *A Thomas Merton Reader*. New York:
        Harcourt, Brace and World.

_____. 1967. *Mystics and Zen Masters*. New York: Delta.

_____. 1971. *Contemplative Prayer*. Second Edition. Garden City, NJ:
        Image Books.

_____. 1971. *Contemplation in a World of Action*. New York: Doubleday.

Mitchell, Kenneth R. and Anderson, Herbert. 1983. *All Our Losses, All Our Griefs*. Philadelphia: Westminster.

Moore, Thomas. 1994. *Care of the Soul*. New York: Harper Perennial.

Nilson, Jon. 1987. "Doing Theology by Heart: John S. Donne's Theological Method." *Theological Studies*. 48. 1. 65-86.

Nouwen, Henri J. M. 1992. *The Return of the Prodigal Son*. New York: Doubleday.

Oates, Wayne E. 1981. *Your Particular Grief*. Philadelphia: Westminster Press.

O'Donnell, Kelly and O'Donnell, Michele L., eds. 1988. *Helping Missionaries Grow*. Pasadena, CA: William Carey Library. 513-521.

O'Rourke, David K. 1978. "The Experience of Conversion." In Eigo, ed. 1-30.

Osiek, Carolyn. 1986. *Beyond Anger*. Mahwah, NJ: Paulist Press.

Paige, R. Michael, ed. 1993. *Education for the Intercultural Experience*. Yarmouth, ME: Intercultural Press.

Patton, Michael. 1990. *Qualitative Evaluation and Research Methods*. Newbury Park, CA: Sage Publications.

Phan, Peter C. 2003. "The Dragon and the Eagle: Toward a Vietnamese American Theology." In *Christianity with an Asian Face: Asian American Theology in the Making*. Maryknoll, N.Y.: Orbis Books.

Polster, Irving. 1987. *Every Person's Life Is Worth a Novel*. New York: W.W. Norton.

Rambo, Lewis R. 1993. *Understanding Religious Conversion*. New Haven, CT: Yale University Press.

Reilly, Michael. 1980. "Developing a Missionary Spirituality." *Missiology: An International Review*. VIII. 4. October. 441-447.

Rende, Michael L. 1991. *Lonergan on Conversion: The Development of a Notion*. Lanham, MD: University Press of America.

Rupp, Joyce. 1988. *Praying Our Goodbyes*. Notre Dame, IN: Ave Maria Press.

Scherer, James A. and Bevans, Stephen B., eds. 1994. *New Directions in Mission and Evangelization* 2: Theological Foundations. Maryknoll, NY: Orbis Books.

Searle, Mark. 1980. "The Journey of Conversion." *Worship*. 54. 35-55.

Senior, Donald and Stuhlmueller, Carroll. 1991. *The Biblical Foundations for Mission*. Maryknoll, NY: Orbis Books.

Sheehy, Gail. 1976. Passages: *Predictable Crises of Adult Life*. New York: Dutton.

Shweder, Richard. 1991. *Thinking Through Cultures: Expeditions in Cultural Psychology*. Cambridge, MA: Harvard University Press.

Solomon, Robert C. 1976. *The Passions*. Garden City, NY: Anchor Books.

Storti, Craig. 1989. *The Art of Crossing Cultures*. Washington, D.C.: Intercultural Press.

_____. 1997. *The Art of Coming Home*. Yarmouth, ME: Intercultural Press.

Stroup, George W. 1981. *The Promise of Narrative Theology*. Atlanta: John Knox Press.

Stuhlmueller, Carroll. 1977. *Thirsting for the Lord*. Staten Island, NY: Alba House.

Sullender, Scott. 1985. *Grief and Growth*. Mahwah, NJ: Paulist Press.

Sullivan, Jack. 1985. "Reentry Revisited." Maryknoll Formation Journal. Spring. 30-38.

Sullivan, Paula F. 1991. *The Mystery of My Story: Autobiographical Writing for Personal and Spiritual Development*. Mahwah, NJ: Paulist Press.

Switzer, David K. 1970. *The Dynamics of Grief*. Nashville: Abingdon Press.

Terrian, Samuel. 1978. *The Elusive God*. San Francisco: Harper & Row.

Ting-Toomey, Stella. 1980. "Identity and Interpersonal Bonding." In Triandis and Lambert, eds. 351-373.

Triandis, H. and Lambert, W., eds. 1980. *Handbook of Cross-Cultural Psychology: Perspectives*. Volume I. Boston: Allyn and Bacon.

Turner, Victor. 1967. "Betwixt and Between: The Liminal Period in Rites of Passage." In *The Forest of Symbols*. Ithaca, NY: Cornell University Press. 1967. 93-1 11.

_____. 1969. *The Ritual Process: Structure and Anti-Structure*. Chicago: Aldin.

_____. "Liminal to Liminoid." In *Play, Flow, and Ritual*. 1974. Rice University Studies. 53-92.

Untener, Kenneth. 1979. "The Romero Prayer." Drafted for a homily given by Cardinal John Dearden in November 1979.

van Gennep, Arnold. 1960. *The Rites of Passage*. Chicago: University of Chicago Press.

Walsh, James E. 1976. "Description of a Missioner." Maryknoll, NY: Development Department.

Westberg, Granger E. 1979. *Good Grief: A Constructive Approach to the Problem of Loss*. Philadelphia: Fortress Press.

Whitehead, Evelyn E. and Whitehead, James D. 1979. *Christian Life Patterns*. New York: Doubleday.

_____. *Method in Ministry: Theological Reflection and Christian Ministry*. Kansas City, MO: Sheed & Ward.

_____. *Seasons of Strength: New Visions of Adult Christian Maturing*. Winona MN: St. Mary's.

Wilson, John P. 1989. *Trauma, Transformation and Healing: An Interpretive Approach to Theory, Research and Post-Traumatic Therapy*. New York: Brunner / Mazel.

Wiseman, Robert L. and Koester, John. 1993. *Intercultural Communication Competence*. Newbury Park, CA: Sage Publications.

# Special Recognition

To the Daughters of Charity of St. Vincent de Paul, from whom I learned the words of Vincent, "It is only because of your love, your love alone, that the Poor will forgive you the bread you give them."

To Catholic Theological Union, for its bold and faithful mission to the universal church; and especially to my friends, Roger Schroeder and Steve Bevans, SVD, without whose support and guidance *At Home in the Journey* would probably never have been written.

To "From Mission to Mission," assisting people for over four decades, in their call to mission, through the preparation and processing of their cross-cultural, ministerial, and life transitions. Without their encouragement and appreciation, this Second Edition of *At Home in the Journey* would never have been conceived (missiontomission.org).

To Marguerite Patricia Gilner, whose cover design was truly a labor of love.

And to Mary Neighbour, whose editing, expertise, and guidance have brought this Second Edition to term (MediaNeighbours.com).

# About the Author

JoAnn McCaffrey's first and most formative mission was the twelve years she lived in the DRC (Democratic Republic of Congo), as a Daughter of Charity of St. Vincent de Paul. Upon her return, she studied, worked, and then taught over fifteen years at CTU (Catholic Theological

Union in Chicago), primarily with people in various stages of transition. During that time, she also worked four years with VMM (Volunteer Missionary Movement), accompanying lay volunteers in Central America and the US. And for the last fifteen years, in Virginia, her primary responsibility in the Mission Division of Bon Secours Health System was developing the Cross-Cultural Services Department, working to build an inclusive and inter-cultural environment for staff and patients, built on self-awareness, humility, and respect. JoAnn still considers herself a "missionary" at heart, and tries to live intentionally and simply, in solidarity with the marginalized of our world, and with all of creation.

Made in the USA
Middletown, DE
20 May 2022

65986453R00166